STECK-VAUGHN

Math Skills for the Workforce

MEASUREMENT, GEOMETRY, AND ALGEBRA

Author
Karen Lassiter
Austin Community College
Austin, Texas

Consultants
Connie Eichhorn
Omaha Public Schools
Omaha, Nebraska

M. Gail Joiner Ward
Swainsboro Technical Institute
Swainsboro, Georgia

STECK-VAUGHN
C O M P A N Y
ELEMENTARY • SECONDARY • ADULT • LIBRARY

About the Author

Dr. Karen Lassiter is currently a mathematics instructor at Austin Community College. She is a former Senior Math Editor for Steck-Vaughn Company, and has done extensive work with standardized test preparation. Dr. Lassiter holds a Ph.D. in Educational Research, Testing, and Instructional Design and a bachelor's degree in mathematics and science education from Florida State University.

About the Consultants

Connie Eichhorn is a supervisor of adult education programs in the Omaha Public Schools. A former mathematics teacher and ABE/GED instructor, she earned an undergraduate degree in math at Iowa State University and is completing a doctoral program in adult education at the University of Nebraska. She conducts workshops on math instruction for teachers of adult basic education.

M. Gail Joiner Ward is presently working at Swainsboro Technical Institute as an adult education instructor. Previously she worked with adult learners in a multimedia lab through the School of Education at Georgia Southern University. She has bachelor's and master's degrees in art and early childhood education from Valdosta State College and Georgia Southern University.

Staff Credits

Executive Editor:	Ellen Northcutt
Assistant Art Director:	Richard Balsam
Design Manager:	Pamela Heaney
Illustration Credits:	Cindy Aarvig, Richard Balsam, David Griffin, Mike Krone
Photo Credits:	Cover: Reagan Bradshaw; p. 9 © Jean Higgins/Unicorn Stock Photos; p. 41 © Rick Browne/Stock Boston; p. 71 © Gale Zucker/Stock Boston; p. 107 © Robert Rathe/Stock Boston; p. 131 © Charles Gupton/Stock Boston; p. 147 © Miro Vintoniv/Stock Boston; p. 165 © Jeff Albertson/Stock Boston.
Cover Design:	Bazzirk Inc.
Photo Editor:	Margie Foster

ISBN 0-8172-6378-0

Copyright © 1997 Steck-Vaughn Company

Contents

Unit 4

ALGEBRA CONCEPTS

Unit 5

ADDITION AND SUBTRACTION EQUATIONS

Unit 6

MULTIPLICATION AND DIVISION EQUATIONS

Unit 7

PUTTING YOUR SKILLS TO WORK

TO THE LEARNER

The four books in the Steck-Vaughn series *Math Skills for the Workforce* are *Whole Numbers; Fractions; Decimals and Percents;* and *Measurement, Geometry, and Algebra.* They are written to help you understand and practice arithmetic skills, real-life applications, and problem-solving techniques.

This book contains features which will make it easier for you to work with measurement, geometry, and algebra and to apply them to your daily life.

A Skills Inventory appears at the beginning and end of the book.
- The first test shows you how much you already know.
- The final test can show you how much you have learned.

Each unit has several Mixed Reviews and a Unit Review.
- The Mixed Reviews give you a chance to practice the skills you have learned.
- The Unit Review helps you decide if you have mastered those skills.

There is also a glossary at the end of the book.
- Turn to the glossary to find the meanings of words that are new to you.
- Use the definitions and examples to help strengthen your understanding of terms used in mathematics.

The book contains answers and explanations for the problems.
- The answers let you check your work.
- The explanations take you through the steps used to solve the problems.

Skills Inventory

Write the equivalent measure.

1. 1 foot = _____ inches

2. _____ sec. = 1 min.

3. 1 qt. = _____ gal.

4. 1 oz. = _____ lb.

5. 30 min. = _____ sec.

6. $3\frac{1}{2}$ years = _____ months

7. 72 in. = _____ ft.

8. 7 pints = _____ quarts

9. $1\frac{1}{2}$ yards = _____ feet

Change each measurement to the units given.

10. 2.5 miles = _____ miles _____ feet

11. 3 cups 4 ounces = _____ cups

12. 2 yards 1 foot = _____ feet

13. 90 min. = _____ hr. _____ min.

Add, subtract, multiply, or divide. Simplify the answer.

14.
$$\begin{array}{r} 7 \text{ weeks 3 days} \\ + 9 \text{ weeks 4 days} \\ \hline \end{array}$$

15.
$$\begin{array}{r} 5 \text{ feet 7 inches} \\ + 1 \text{ yard} \\ \hline \end{array}$$

16.
$$\begin{array}{r} 3 \text{ pounds 4 ounces} \\ - \qquad\qquad 10 \text{ ounces} \\ \hline \end{array}$$

17.
$$\begin{array}{r} 1 \text{ gallon} \\ - \qquad 2 \text{ quarts} \\ \hline \end{array}$$

18.
$$\begin{array}{r} 5 \text{ tons 1,000 pounds} \\ \times \qquad\qquad\qquad 3 \\ \hline \end{array}$$

19.
$$2\overline{)7 \text{ quarts 1 pint}}$$

Change each measurement.

20. 10 meters = _____ centimeters

21. 100 milliliters = _____ liter

Find the measure of each angle.

22. Find ∠ABD.

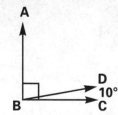

23. Find ∠DBC.

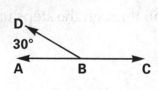

24. Find ∠b.

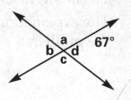

25. Find ∠v.

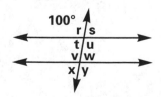

26. Find ∠ABC.

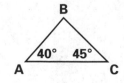

27. Find ∠DEF.

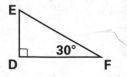

28. Find ∠HIJ.

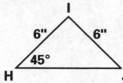

29. △ABC ~ △DEF   Find $\overline{AB}$.

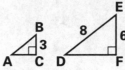

30. Find the perimeter.

31. Find the circumference.

$C = \pi d$ $\pi = \dfrac{22}{7}$

7"

32. Find the area.

$A = lw$

3 cm

2 cm

33. Find the area.

$A = \pi r^2$ $\pi = 3.14$

4 mi.

34. Find the volume.

$V = \pi r^2 h$ $\pi = \dfrac{22}{7}$

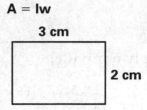

r = 4"
h = 14"

Find each answer.

35.
$6^2 =$

36.
$2^3 =$

37.
$\sqrt{9} =$

38.
$\sqrt{64} =$

Evaluate each expression. Use 5 for x in problems 43-45.

39.
$4 \times 8 - 6$

40.
$13 + 2 \cdot 7$

41.
$3^2 - 9 + 1$

42.
$(7 + 9) \div 2$

43.
$\dfrac{35}{x}$

44.
$x^2 - 10$

45.
$9 - (x - 2)$

Add or subtract.

46.
$7 + (-6)$

47.
$-9 + (-10)$

48.
$-8 - (+2)$

49.
$18 - (-6)$

50.
$-10 + 0$

51.
$0 - 7$

Solve each equation.

52.

$25 + x = 60$

53.

$x + 29 = -53$

54.

$3 + x + 5 = 8$

55.

$x - 10 = 6$

56.

$x - 7 = -15$

57.

$x - 9 = -2$

Multiply or divide.

58.

$(-9)(-6)$

59.

$-5(2)$

60.

$\dfrac{-3}{-1}$

61.

$\dfrac{-12}{4}$

Solve each equation.

62.

$5x = 15$

63.

$-2x = 12$

64.

$\dfrac{x}{2} = 4$

65.

$\dfrac{x}{-5} = -7$

66.

$5x + 4 = 9$

67.

$\dfrac{2}{3}x + 9 = 17$

Below is a list of the problems in this Skills Inventory and the pages on which the skills are taught. If you missed any problems, turn to the pages listed and practice the skills. Then correct the problems you missed in the Skills Inventory.

Problem	Practice Page	Problem	Practice Page	Problem	Practice Page
Unit 1		24	80	43-45	121-124
1-9	24-35	25	81-82	*Unit 5*	
Unit 2		26-28	84-87	46-51	133-139
10-13	43-46	29	88-89	52-57	141-144
14-19	49-54, 57-58	30-34	93-99, 103-104	*Unit 6*	
20-21	60-66	*Unit 4*		58-61	149-152
Unit 3		35-38	113-114	62-65	154-157
22-23	78-79	39-42	115-118	66-67	160-162

Unit 7 — UNDERSTANDING CUSTOMARY MEASUREMENT

You probably see or use customary measures, such as inches, pounds, and cups, every day. Customary, or standard, measures are usually written with fractions to show parts of a whole, such as $3\frac{1}{2}$ feet. Some measurements are shown using abbreviations, such as 7 in. for 7 inches or 3 ft. for 3 feet.

In this unit, you will become familiar with customary measures and their abbreviations, study how to change from one measure to another, and learn how to use measurement tools.

Getting Ready

You should be familiar with the skills on this page and the next before you begin this unit. To check your answers, turn to page 182.

 When working with measurement, you will be working with whole numbers.

Multiply or divide. Write remainders as fractions. Reduce fractions if possible.

1.
$7 \times 30 =$

$$
\begin{array}{r}
30 \\
\times\ 7 \\
\hline
210
\end{array}
$$

2.
$89 \times 5 =$

3.
$149 \times 32 =$

4.
$14 \times 52 =$

5.
$19 \div 2 =$

$$
\begin{array}{r}
9\frac{1}{2} \\
2\overline{)19} \\
-18 \\
\hline
1
\end{array}
$$

6.
$44 \div 6 =$

7.
$251 \div 35 =$

8.
$562 \div 40 =$

Getting Ready

When you change one measurement unit to another unit, the answer may be a fraction.

Change each improper fraction to a whole or mixed number. Reduce fractions.

9.
$$\frac{26}{4} =$$

$$4)\overline{26} \quad \frac{6}{} \quad \frac{2}{4} = 6\frac{1}{2}$$
$$\underline{-24}$$
$$2$$

10.
$$\frac{21}{7} =$$

11.
$$\frac{38}{8} =$$

12.
$$\frac{53}{12} =$$

13.
$$\frac{98}{24} =$$

14.
$$\frac{8}{16} = \frac{1}{2}$$

15.
$$\frac{3}{18} =$$

16.
$$\frac{40}{60} =$$

17.
$$\frac{10}{24} =$$

18.
$$\frac{12}{16} =$$

For review, see pages 15-16 and 33-34 in **Math Skills for the Workforce, Fractions.**

 When working with measurement, you will be working with fractions.

Subtract, multiply, or divide. Cancel and reduce if possible.

19.
$$\frac{5}{6} = \frac{5}{6}$$
$$\underline{-\frac{1}{3} = \frac{2}{6}}$$
$$\frac{3}{6} = \frac{1}{2}$$

20.
$$10$$
$$\underline{-\ \frac{1}{2}}$$

21.
$$3\frac{5}{9}$$
$$\underline{-\ \frac{4}{9}}$$

22.
$$7\frac{2}{3}$$
$$\underline{-\ 5\frac{4}{5}}$$

23.
$$1\frac{3}{5} \times 5 =$$

$$\frac{8}{\cancel{5}} \times \frac{\cancel{5}^{1}}{1} = \frac{8}{1} = 8$$
$$_{1}$$

24.
$$18 \div \frac{1}{3} =$$

25.
$$3 \div \frac{1}{4} =$$

26.
$$4 \times \frac{1}{2} =$$

For review, see Units 3-5 in **Math Skills for the Workforce, Fractions.**

 Units of measurement can be changed by using a proportion.

Find the missing number in each proportion.

27.
$$\frac{1}{2} = \frac{n}{4}$$
$$2 \times n = 4 \times 1$$
$$2n = 4$$
$$n = 4 \div 2 = 2$$

28.
$$\frac{3}{n} = \frac{6}{8}$$

29.
$$\frac{4}{14} = \frac{2}{n}$$

30.
$$\frac{n}{6} = \frac{1}{6}$$

For review, see page 78 in **Math Skills for the Workforce, Decimals and Percents.**

Understanding Units of Length

The common units for measuring length in the customary system are
inches, feet, yards, and *miles.* These units also measure width, depth,
height, and distance. For example, a store room may measure eight feet
wide, ten feet long, and have a ceiling seven feet high.

Office keys are about 2 inches long.
A sheet of paper is about a foot long.
Standard doorways are about a yard wide.
Distances between cities are measured in miles.

Measures of Length	
1 foot (ft. or ') = 12 inches (in. or ")	
1 yard (yd.) = 36 in.	
1 yd. = 3 ft.	
1 mile (mi.) = 5,280 ft.	
1 mi. = 1,760 yd.	

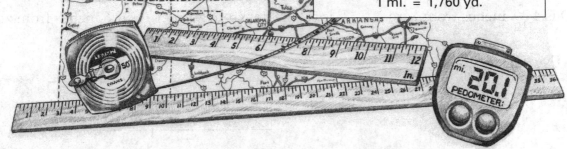

Circle the letter of the measurement you would probably see.

1. the height of a chair seat
   a. 20 feet
   b. 20 inches

2. the distance a car travels between cities
   a. $31\frac{3}{10}$ yards
   b. $31\frac{3}{10}$ miles

3. the depth of a desk drawer
   a. 8 inches
   b. 8 feet

4. the width of a tire
   a. 22 inches
   b. 22 feet

5. the width of a computer screen
   a. 19 feet
   b. 19 inches

6. the amount of rainfall in a day
   a. $\frac{3}{16}$ inch
   b. $\frac{3}{16}$ yard

7. the width of tape for sealing packages
   a. $1\frac{1}{4}$ inches
   b. $1\frac{1}{4}$ feet

8. the thickness of a large dictionary
   a. 4 feet
   b. 4 inches

9. the length of windshield wiper blades
   a. $14\frac{1}{2}$ feet
   b. $14\frac{1}{2}$ inches

10. the length of a notepad
    a. 7 inches
    b. 7 feet

11. the length of a river
    a. 25 inches
    b. 25 miles

12. the length of a screwdriver
    a. 9 inches
    b. 9 feet

Reading a Ruler

Customary rulers are divided into inches and fractions of an inch: halves, fourths, eighths, and sixteenths. When reading a ruler, it is easier to read from left to right.

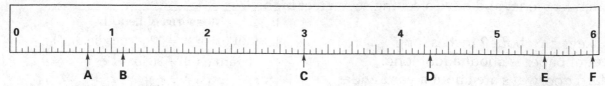

A is $\frac{3}{4}$ inch from zero.

B is $1\frac{1}{8}$ inches from zero.

C is 3 inches from zero.

D is $4\frac{5}{16}$ inches from zero.

E is $5\frac{1}{2}$ inches from zero.

F is 6 inches from zero.

Use These Steps

How far is the arrow from zero?

1. **Find the nearest whole inch before the arrow.**

   1

2. **Find the fraction of an inch the arrow is pointing to.**

   $\frac{3}{16}$

3. **Write the measurement as a mixed number.**

   $1\frac{3}{16}$ inches

Write the measurement shown by each arrow.

1.

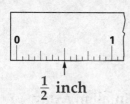

$\frac{1}{2}$ inch

2.

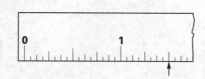

3.

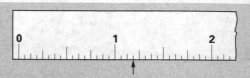

4.

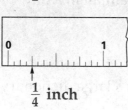

$\frac{1}{4}$ inch

5.

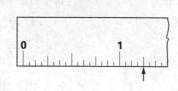

6.

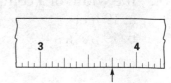

7.

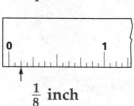

$\frac{1}{8}$ inch

8.

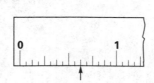

9.

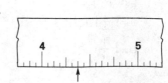

10.

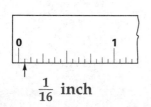

$\frac{1}{16}$ inch

11.

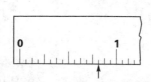

12.

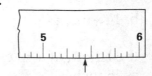

Reading a Ruler

When you need to find the distance between two measurements on a ruler, subtract the smaller number from the larger number. The number farther to the right is larger.

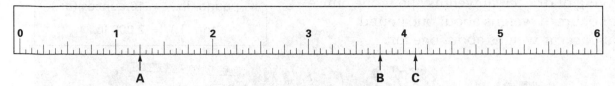

Point B is $3\frac{3}{4}$ inches from zero. $3\frac{3}{4}$ inches

Point A is $1\frac{1}{4}$ inches from zero. $-1\frac{1}{4}$ inches

$2\frac{2}{4} = 2\frac{1}{2}$ inches between points A and B

Use These Steps

Find the distance between B and C on the ruler above.

1. **Find the measurement shown by B.**

   $B = 3\frac{3}{4}$ inches

2. **Find the measurement shown by C.**

   $C = 4\frac{1}{8}$ inches

3. **Subtract the smaller number from the larger number.**

   $4\frac{1}{8} = 4\frac{1}{8} = 3\frac{9}{8}$

   $-3\frac{3}{4} = 3\frac{6}{8} = 3\frac{6}{8}$

   $\phantom{-3\frac{3}{4} = 3\frac{6}{8} = 3}\frac{3}{8}$ inch

Find the distance between each pair of points on the ruler below. Reduce if possible.

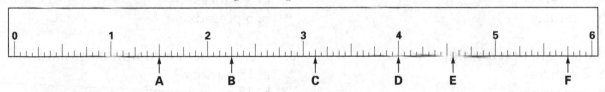

1. A and B

   $2\frac{1}{4} = 2\frac{1}{4} = 1\frac{5}{4}$

   $-1\frac{1}{2} = 1\frac{2}{4} = 1\frac{2}{4}$

   $\phantom{-1\frac{1}{2} = 1\frac{2}{4} = 1}\frac{3}{4}$

2. A and C

3. D and A

4. B and F

5. B and D

6. B and E

7. C and D

8. E and C

9. E and F

Understanding Units of Weight

The common units for measuring weight in the customary system are *ounces*, *pounds*, and *tons*.

A serving of dry cereal weighs about one ounce.
A loaf of bread weighs about one pound.
A compact car weighs about one ton.

Measures of Weight		
1 pound (lb.)	=	16 ounces (oz.)
1 ton (T.)	=	2,000 lb.

Circle the letter of the measurement you would probably see.

1. the weight of a screwdriver
   a. 4 ounces
   b. 4 pounds

2. the weight of an ambulance
   a. 4,000 pounds
   b. 4,000 tons

3. the weight of a full suitcase
   a. 20 ounces
   b. 20 pounds

4. the weight of a delivery van
   a. 3 pounds
   b. 3 tons

5. the weight of a calculator
   a. 6 pounds
   b. 6 ounces

6. the weight of a bag of potatoes
   a. 5 ounces
   b. 5 pounds

7. the weight of a framing hammer
   a. 2 ounces
   b. 2 pounds

8. the weight of a computer monitor
   a. 18 ounces
   b. 18 pounds

9. the weight of a pair of work gloves
   a. 6 ounces
   b. 6 pounds

10. the weight of a stapler
    a. 11 ounces
    b. 11 pounds

11. the weight of a video tape
    a. 15 ounces
    b. 15 pounds

12. the weight of an electric drill
    a. 6 ounces
    b. 6 pounds

13. the weight of a desk phone
    a. 3 ounces
    b. 3 pounds

14. the weight of a truckload of steel
    a. 7 pounds
    b. 7 tons

Reading a Scale

Some scales, especially those found in the produce section of grocery stores, show weight in pounds and fractions of a pound: halves, fourths, eighths, and sixteenths.

Reading a scale marked with pounds and fractions of a pound is similar to reading a ruler. Find the nearest whole pound before the arrow shown on the scale. Then find the fraction of a pound that the arrow is pointing to. The total amount is read as a whole or mixed number, such as 4 pounds or $4\frac{1}{4}$ pounds.

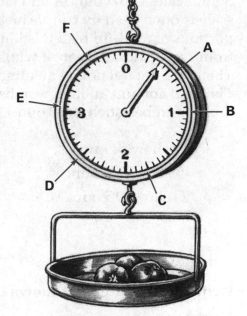

A shows $\frac{9}{16}$ pound.

B shows 1 pound.

C shows $1\frac{3}{4}$ pounds.

D shows $2\frac{1}{2}$ pounds.

E shows $3\frac{1}{16}$ pounds.

F shows $3\frac{5}{8}$ pounds.

Write the measurement shown on each scale.

1.

$\frac{1}{2}$ pound

2.

_____

3.

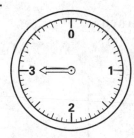

_____

4.

_____

5.

_____

6.

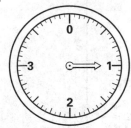

_____

7.

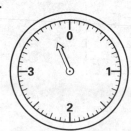

_____

8.

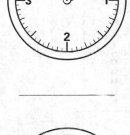

_____

9.

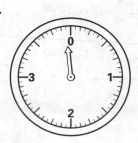

_____

Reading a Scale

Some scales show ounces and half-ounces. This type of scale is often used by people on a special diet to weigh portions of food. To read this kind of scale, read down from zero. Find the nearest whole ounce before the arrow. Then find the fraction of an ounce the arrow is pointing to. The total amount an item weighs is read as a whole or mixed number, such as 10 ounces or $2\frac{1}{2}$ ounces.

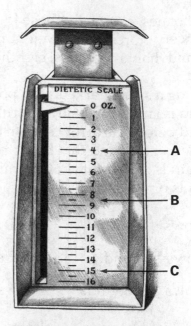

A shows 4 ounces.

B shows $8\frac{1}{2}$ ounces.

C shows 15 ounces.

Write the measurement shown on each scale.

1.

1 ounce

2.

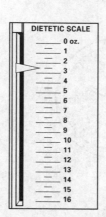

_____

3.

_____

4.

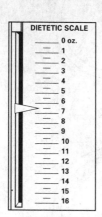

_____

5.

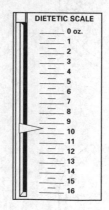

_____

6.

_____

Understanding Units of Capacity

The common units for measuring capacity in the customary system are
fluid ounces, cups, pints, quarts, and *gallons.*

A small bottle of perfume is about one fluid ounce.
A regular cup of coffee is about one cup.
A can of motor oil is about one quart.
A large container of milk is about one gallon.

Measures of Capacity	
1 cup (c.) =	8 fluid ounces (fl. oz.)
1 pint (pt.) =	2 c.
1 quart (qt.) =	4 c.
1 qt. =	2 pt.
1 gallon (gal.) =	4 qt.

Circle the letter of the amount you would probably see.

1. the gas to fill the gas tank of a car
   a. 12 gallons
   b. 12 quarts

2. the water in a full bucket
   a. 3 cups
   b. 3 gallons

3. the paint needed to paint an entire house
   a. 10 quarts
   b. 10 gallons

4. the cough medicine given to a child in several doses
   a. 1 fluid ounce
   b. 1 cup

5. the paint needed to paint a window sill
   a. 4 fluid ounces
   b. 4 quarts

6. the amount of water a veterinarian uses to bathe a large dog
   a. 4 pints
   b. 4 gallons

7. the water you should drink in a day
   a. 64 fluid ounces
   b. 64 gallons

8. the amount of oil to mix with a gallon of gasoline to power a chain saw
   a. 2 fluid ounces
   b. 2 pints

9. the water used to wash a car
   a. 15 cups
   b. 15 gallons

10. the amount of IV solution in a standard dispensing bag
   a. 8 fluid ounces
   b. 8 pints

11. the shampoo in a bottle
   a. 16 fluid ounces
   b. 16 cups

12. the amount of toner used in a small office copier
   a. 6 fluid ounces
   b. 6 quarts

Reading a Measuring Cup

Some measuring cups have two scales of measure. One is marked with cups and fractions of a cup to measure either liquid or dry ingredients. The other is marked with cups and fluid ounces to measure only liquids. Use the table on page 24 to find the equivalent measures.

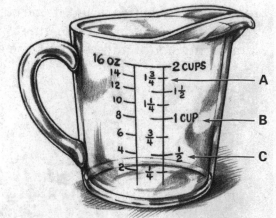

	DRY		LIQUID
A shows	$1\frac{3}{4}$ cups	=	14 ounces
B shows	1 cup	=	8 ounces
C shows	$\frac{1}{2}$ cup	=	4 ounces

Write the amount shown in each measuring cup.

1.

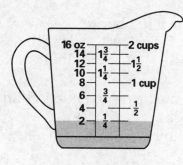

$\frac{1}{4}$ cup = 2 ounces

2.

3.

4.

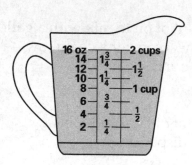

5.

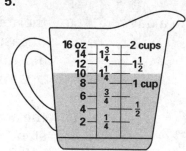

6.

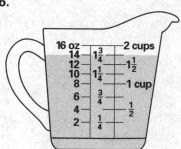

Reading a Medicine Cup

In many medical fields, employees must learn to read the measurements on a medicine cup. This way they can give the correct dosage of liquid medicine to their patients.

Most medicine cups have a scale that shows teaspoons (tsp.) and tablespoons (tbsp.). Sometimes the scale shows fluid ounces (fl. oz.).

> 1 tablespoon (tbsp.) = 3 teaspoons (tsp.)
> 1 tbsp. = $\frac{1}{2}$ fluid ounce (fl. oz.)
> 2 tbsp. = 1 fl. oz.

Write the equivalent measurements using the chart and the medicine cup above.

1. 3 tsp. = _____ tbsp.

2. 3 tsp. = _____ fl. oz.

3. 1 fl. oz. = _____ tbsp.

4. 1 tbsp. = _____ tsp.

Use the chart to write the correct dosage of medicine for each child.

5. an 8-year-old child weighing 54 pounds _____ tsp.

6. an 11-year-old child weighing 90 pounds _____ tsp.

7. a 5-year-old child weighing 42 pounds _____ tsp.

8. a $3\frac{1}{2}$-year-old child weighing 30 pounds _____ tsp.

AGE (YR.)	WEIGHT (LB.)	DOSE (TSP.)
UNDER 2	UNDER 24	CONSULT PHYSICIAN
2–3	24–35	1
4–5	36–47	$1\frac{1}{2}$
6–8	48–59	2
9–10	60–71	$2\frac{1}{2}$
11	72–95	3

Use the measuring cup and the charts above to answer the following questions.

9. What kitchen measuring spoon can be used to give a 7-year-old child the correct dosage?

10. A medicine cup shows only ounces and half-ounces. If a nurse uses it to give an 11-year-old girl the correct dosage of 3 teaspoons, how many ounces of medicine will the girl get?

Answer_____

Answer_____

Understanding Units of Time

The common units for measuring time in the customary system are *seconds*, *minutes*, *hours*, *days*, *weeks*, *months*, and *years*.

It takes about a second to say "one."

It takes about a minute to watch two TV commercials.

A movie at a theatre lasts about two hours.

Measures of Time
1 minute (min.) = 60 seconds (sec.)
1 hour (hr.) = 60 minutes (min.)
1 day = 24 hr.
1 week (wk.) = 7 days
1 year (yr.) = 52 weeks
1 yr. = 12 months (mo.)

Circle the letter of the measurement you would probably see.

1. the time it takes to paint a room
   a. 4 hours
   b. 4 months

2. the time it takes to work one shift
   a. 8 hours
   b. 8 minutes

3. the time it takes to paint a window frame
   a. 30 seconds
   b. 30 minutes

4. the time it takes to drive 200 miles
   a. $3\frac{1}{2}$ hours
   b. $3\frac{1}{2}$ days

5. the time it takes for a doctor to scrub before surgery
   a. 10 minutes
   b. 10 hours

6. the time it takes for a concrete sidewalk to harden
   a. 6 minutes
   b. 6 hours

7. the time it takes to walk 2 miles
   a. 40 seconds
   b. 40 minutes

8. the time it takes to input one page
   a. 5 minutes
   b. 5 hours

9. the time it takes to build an apartment building
   a. 18 months
   b. 18 years

10. the time it takes to read a newspaper headline
    a. 10 seconds
    b. 10 minutes

11. the time it takes to change the oil in a car
    a. 20 minutes
    b. 20 seconds

12. the time it takes to have an interview for a new job
    a. 45 minutes
    b. 45 hours

Reading a 24-Hour Clock

Many foreign countries and all branches of the U.S. military services use a 24-hour clock. Some employers may use a 24-hour time clock to record the hours you work.

The 24-hour clock does not use A.M. or P.M. All hours are counted on a 24-hour basis from midnight to midnight. Times are shown as 4-digit numbers without a colon. Zeros are added, if necessary, to make 4-digit numbers. For example, 1:05 A.M. would be 0105 in 24-hour clock time.

Hours from 1 P.M. to 11:59 P.M. are found by adding the hour to 12. For example, to show 7:00 P.M., add 7 to 12 and add zeros to make a 4-digit number, 1900. 7:00 P.M. is read as 1900, or 1900 hours, on a 24-hour clock.

12-hour clock	24-hour clock
2:00 A.M.	0200
5:30 A.M.	0530
11:45 A.M.	1145
12:00 noon	1200
2:00 P.M.	1400
5:30 P.M.	1730
11:45 P.M.	2345
12:00 midnight	2400

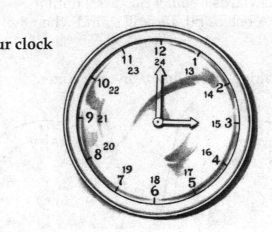

Write the following 12-hour clock times using 24-hour clock time.

1. 8:30 A.M.
   0830

2. 1:00 P.M.

3. 10:25 A.M.

4. 3:25 P.M.

5. 4:00 A.M.

6. 4:30 P.M.

7. 10:15 P.M.

8. 8:30 P.M.

Write the following 24-hour clock times using 12-hour clock time.

9. 1830
   6:30 P.M.

10. 0600

11. 2145

12. 1415

13. Martin punched in on the time clock at work at 0900 and punched out at 1800. According to a 12-hour clock, what time did he leave work?

14. Carla's cash register receipt showed that she bought groceries at 1350. According to a 12-hour clock, what time was Carla in the grocery store?

Answer_____

Answer_____

Reading a Timer

Many commercial washing machines have a timer that you can set for an exact washing time. Each mark on the timer stands for one minute. Marks are also shown for hours and five- or ten-minute intervals. You usually set the timer *clockwise*, to the right from the top.

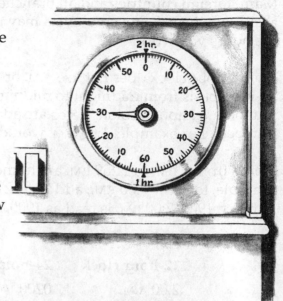

Washing times are often given in hours and minutes. For example, you may need to wash a load of uniforms for 1 hour and 30 minutes. To set the timer to wash for that time, you must move the arrow to the 1 hour and 30 minute mark. The arrow will move backwards (*counter clockwise*) until it reaches zero. A bell or buzzer will sound when the time is up.

Write the washing time shown on each timer.

1.

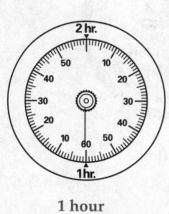

_____1 hour_____

2.

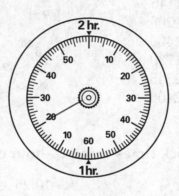

_____

3.

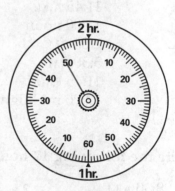

_____

4.

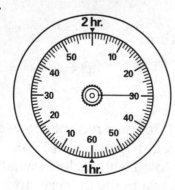

_____

5.

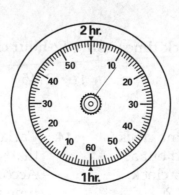

_____

6.

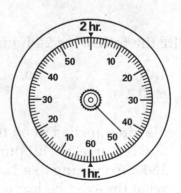

_____

Mixed Review

Write the measurement shown by each arrow.

1.

2.
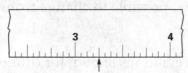

3.
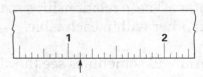

Find the distance between each pair of points on the ruler below. Reduce if possible.

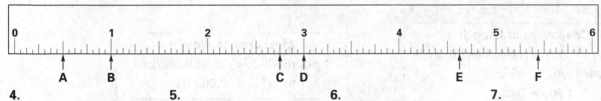

4.

A and B

5.

B and D

6.

E and F

7.

F and C

Write the measurement shown on each scale.

8.

9.

10.

_____   _____   _____

Write the amount in cups and in ounces in each measuring cup.

11.
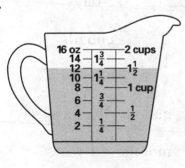

12.
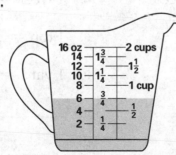

13.
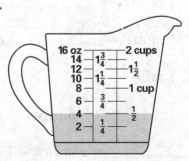

_____   _____   _____

Write the following 12-hour clock times using 24-hour clock time.

14. 7:30 A.M.   15. 7:15 P.M.   16. 11:05 P.M.   17. 5:25 A.M.

Understanding Customary Measurement

The following tables list common units of measurement for length, weight, capacity, and time. They show how these units relate to each other. These relationships make it possible to change from one unit to another within each table.

You will sometimes see the abbreviations shown for different units of measurement in advertisements, on maps, or in recipes.

You can use these tables to help you work the problems in this unit.

Measures of Length

1 foot (ft. or ') = 12 inches (in. or ")
1 yard (yd.) = 36 in.
1 yd. = 3 ft.
1 mile (mi.) = 5,280 ft.
1 mi. = 1,760 yd.

Measures of Weight

1 pound (lb.) = 16 ounces (oz.)
1 ton (T.) = 2,000 lb.

Measures of Capacity

1 cup (c.) = 8 fluid ounces (fl. oz.)
1 pint (pt.) = 2 c.
1 quart (qt.) = 4 c.
1 qt. = 2 pt.
1 gallon (gal.) = 4 qt.

Measures of Time

1 minute (min.) = 60 seconds (sec.)
1 hour (hr.) = 60 minutes (min.)
1 day = 24 hr.
1 week (wk.) = 7 days
1 year (yr.) = 52 weeks
1 yr. = 12 months (mo.)

Write the following equivalent units using the tables.

1. 1 foot = _____12_____ inches

2. 1 hour = _____ minutes

3. 1 pound = _____ ounces

4. 1 week = _____ days

5. 1 quart = _____ cups

6. 1 ton = _____ pounds

7. 1 mile = _____ feet

8. 1 yard = _____ feet

9. _____8_____ ounces = 1 cup

10. _____ quarts = 1 gallon

11. _____ hours = 1 day

12. _____ months = 1 year

13. _____ weeks = 1 year

14. _____ inches = 1 yard

15. _____ seconds = 1 minute

16. _____ cups = 1 pint

Understanding Customary Measurement

When you write the equivalent measure for a small unit, you will have a part or a fraction of the whole larger unit. For example, 1 inch equals $\frac{1}{12}$ foot.

Use These Steps

2 ounces = _____ pound

1. Find the number of ounces in 1 pound in the table on page 24.

    16 ounces = 1 pound

2. Write a fraction with 2 ounces as the numerator and 16 ounces as the denominator.

    $\frac{2}{16}$

3. Reduce the fraction to lowest terms.

    $\frac{2}{16} = \frac{1}{8}$ pound

Use the tables on page 24 to find the following equivalents. Reduce if possible.

1. 1 foot = ___$\frac{1}{3}$___ yard
   3 feet = 1 yard
   $\frac{1}{3}$

2. 1 quart = _____ gallon

3. 1 minute = _____ hour

4. 1 hour = _____ day

5. 1 month = _____ year

6. 1 pint = _____ quart

7. 6 inches = ___$\frac{1}{2}$___ foot
   12 inches = 1 foot
   $\frac{6}{12} = \frac{1}{2}$

8. 30 minutes = _____ hour

9. 2 quarts = _____ gallon

10. 3 days = _____ week

11. 13 weeks = _____ year

12. 24 inches = _____ yard

13. 8 ounces = _____ pound

14. 4 months = _____ year

Comparing Measurements

You use measurement in everyday situations such as shopping, measuring for new curtains, or figuring how many miles you walked. Sometimes you need to compare measurements. For example, if you walked 2,000 yards on a hiking trail and then rode your bike for 1 mile, you may want to know which distance is farther.

> Compare 1 mile and 2,000 yards.
> 1 mile = 1,760 yards
> 1,760 yards < 2,000 yards, so 1 mile < 2,000 yards

To compare measurements, use the tables on page 24 to find the equivalent units of measure. Make sure that the units are the same before you compare.

Compare the units of measure. Write >, <, or =.

1. 9 inches $\boxed{<}$ 1 foot

1 foot = 12 inches
9 inches < 12 inches,
so 9 inches < 1 foot

2. 1 yard $\boxed{>}$ 20 inches

1 yard = 36 inches
36 inches > 20 inches,
so 1 yard > 20 inches

3. 1 mile $\boxed{=}$ 5,280 feet

1 mile = 5,280 feet
5,280 feet = 5,280 feet,
so 1 mile = 5,280 feet

4. 12" ☐ 1'

5. 1 foot ☐ 8 inches

6. 6 inches ☐ 1 foot

7. 5 days ☐ 1 week

8. 1 yd. ☐ 2 ft.

9. 2 qt. ☐ 1 gal.

10. 36 inches ☐ 1 yard

11. 6 months ☐ 1 year

12. 3,000 pounds ☐ 1 ton

13. Susanna needs 3 feet of cord to finish rewiring a lamp. She has a piece 30 inches long. Does she have enough cord to complete the job?

14. Jake needs 6 quarts of oil to change the oil in his delivery van. He has 1 gallon. Does he have enough oil to change the oil in his van?

Answer _____

Answer _____

Mixed Review

Write the following equivalents. Use the tables on page 24 to help you.

1. 1 minute = _____ seconds

2. 1 sec. = _____ min.

3. 1 qt. = _____ pt.

4. 2 pints = _____ quart

5. 12 inches = _____ foot

6. 16 oz. = _____ lb.

7. 1 pint = _____ cups

8. 15 min. = _____ hr.

9. 2,000 pounds = _____ ton

10. 1' = _____ "

11. 8 ounces = _____ pound

12. 7 days = _____ week

13. 1 yd. = _____ in.

14. 4 cups = _____ pints

15. 8 hours = _____ day

16. 60 minutes = _____ hour

Compare the units of measure. Write >, <, or =.

17. 8 cups ☐ 1 quart

18. 1,780 feet ☐ 1 mile

19. 16 ounces ☐ 1 pound

20. 60 sec. ☐ 1 min.

21. 1 yard ☐ 32 inches

22. 4 ounces ☐ 1 cup

23. 1 quart ☐ 4 cups

24. 5,260 feet ☐ 1 mile

25. 16 pints ☐ 1 cup

26. Tameo mailed a package weighing 12 ounces. Did the package weigh more or less than a pound?

27. Quinton took a week-long vacation. Maggie took 5 days. Who took more time off for vacation?

Answer_____

Answer_____

Changing Units of Measurement Using Multiplication

Sometimes you have a measurement in a large unit and you need to find how many smaller units you have. For example, if you have 2 gallons of milk, you may need to know how many quarts you have. To find the answer, you must multiply the number of gallons by the number of quarts in one gallon.

When you change a large unit to a smaller unit, you multiply.

Use the table on page 24 to find the equivalent units and abbreviations.

Use These Steps

2 gallons = _____ quarts

1. Write the number of quarts in 1 gallon.

1 gallon = 4 quarts

2. Multiply 2 gallons by 4 quarts.

$2 \times 4 = 8$ quarts

Change each measurement.

1. 18 pounds = __288__ ounces
   1 pound = 16 ounces
   $18 \times 16 = 288$

2. 9 quarts = _____ pints

3. 2 hr. = _____ min.

4. 7 yd. = _____ ft.

5. 3 tons = _____ pounds

6. 15 min. = _____ sec.

7. 8 yards = _____ inches

8. 4 days = _____ hours

9. 14' = _____ "

10. 10 c. = _____ oz.

11. 3 years = _____ months

12. 17 miles = _____ yards

13. 7 weeks = _____ days

14. 3 years = _____ weeks

15. 18 pints = _____ cups

16. Kim bought 10 gallons of industrial-strength carpet shampoo. How many quarts are in 10 gallons?

    Answer _____

17. Clarise has a 5-foot cord on her telephone. How many inches are in 5 feet?

    Answer _____

Changing Units of Measurement Using Multiplication

Sometimes you have a fractional measurement in a large unit and you need to find how many smaller units you have. For example, if you have $\frac{1}{2}$ ton of hay, you may need to know how many pounds you have. To find the answer, you multiply the number of tons by the number of pounds in one ton.

Use the table on page 24 to find the equivalent units and abbreviations.

Use These Steps

$\frac{1}{2}$ ton = _____ pounds

1. Write the number of pounds in one ton.

2. Multiply $\frac{1}{2}$ ton by 2,000 pounds.

$$1 \text{ ton} = 2,000 \text{ pounds}$$

$$\frac{1}{2} \times 2,000 = \frac{1}{\underset{1}{\cancel{2}}} \times \frac{\overset{1000}{\cancel{2000}}}{1} = 1,000 \text{ pounds}$$

Change each measurement.

1. $2\frac{1}{2}$ pints = ___5___ cups

    1 pint = 2 cups

    $2\frac{1}{2} \times 2 = \frac{5}{\underset{1}{\cancel{2}}} \times \frac{\overset{1}{\cancel{2}}}{1} = 5$

2. $6\frac{1}{4}$ lb. = _____ oz.

3. $1\frac{1}{2}$ hours = _____ minutes

4. $9\frac{1}{3}$ feet = _____ inches

5. $3\frac{1}{2}$ qt. = _____ pt.

6. $10\frac{3}{4}$ cups = _____ ounces

7. $5\frac{2}{3}$ yards = _____ inches

8. $1\frac{1}{2}$ yr. = _____ mo.

9. $\frac{3}{4}$ pound = _____ ounces

10. $12\frac{3}{10}$ mi. = _____ ft.

11. $7\frac{3}{4}$ gal. = _____ qt.

12. $15\frac{1}{3}$ yards = _____ feet

13. Terry spends $3\frac{1}{4}$ hours a day going to and from work. How many minutes are in $3\frac{1}{4}$ hours?

14. Roy's truck can carry a $2\frac{1}{2}$-ton load. How many pounds are in $2\frac{1}{2}$ tons?

Answer_____

Answer_____

Changing Units of Measurement Using Division

Sometimes you have a measurement in a small unit and you need to find out how many larger units you have. For example, if you have a 24-foot roll of tape, you may need to know how many yards you have. To find the answer, you must divide the number of feet (the small unit) you have by the number of feet in one yard (the larger unit).

When you change a small unit to a larger unit, you divide.

Use the table on page 24 to find the equivalents and abbreviations.

Use These Steps

24 feet = ____ yards

1. Write the number of feet in 1 yard.

3 feet = 1 yard

2. Divide 24 feet by 3 feet.

$24 \div 3 = 8$ yards

Change each measurement.

1. 32 ounces = __2__ pounds
16 ounces = 1 pound
$32 \div 16 = 2$

2. 32 oz. = _____ c.

3. 240 min. = _____ hr.

4. 60" = _____ '

5. 96 hours = _____ days

6. 4,000 lb. = _____ T.

7. 16 quarts = _____ gallons

8. 10,560 ft. = _____ mi.

9. 12 cups = _____ pints

10. 48 mo. = _____ yr.

11. 900 sec. = _____ min.

12. 144 inches = _____ yards

13. Alicia spent 21 days in training for her new job. How many weeks are in 21 days?

14. A fork lift can lift 12,000 pounds. How many tons are in 12,000 pounds?

Answer_____

Answer_____

Changing Units of Measurement Using Division

Sometimes you have a measurement in a small unit and you need to find how many larger units you have. For example, if you have 90 minutes to take a test, you may need to know how many hours you have. To find the answer, you must divide the number of minutes you have by the number of minutes in one hour.

Use the table on page 24 to find the equivalents and abbreviations.

Use These Steps

75 minutes = _____ hours

1. Write the number of minutes in 1 hour.

2. Divide 75 minutes by 60 minutes. Show the remainder as a fraction of an hour. Reduce.

$$60 \text{ minutes} = 1 \text{ hour}$$

$$75 \div 60 = 1\frac{15}{60} = 1\frac{1}{4} \text{ hours}$$

Change each measurement. Show remainders as fractions. Reduce if possible.

1. 9 qt. = __$2\frac{1}{4}$__ gal.
   4 quarts = 1 gallon
   $9 \div 4 = 2\frac{1}{4}$

2. 92 ounces = _____ pounds

3. 16 in. = _____ ft.

4. 1,250 lb. = _____ T.

5. 200 sec. = _____ min.

6. 10 feet = _____ yards

7. 136 oz. = _____ lb.

8. 18 ounces = _____ cups

9. 2,000 yards = _____ miles

10. 2,640 ft. = _____ mi.

11. 3,000 pounds = _____ tons

12. 19 pints = _____ quarts

13. 340 min. = _____ hr.

14. 34 days = _____ weeks

15. 9 c. = _____ pt.

16. It will take John another 42 months to complete his training as an EKG technician. How many years are in 42 months?

17. Alex needs a tarp 54 inches long for the back of his truck. How many feet are in 54 inches?

Answer_____

Answer_____

Changing Units of Measurement Using a Proportion

The relationship of one unit to another can be written as a ratio. Then you can write equal ratios, a proportion, to change a large unit to a smaller unit. For example, to change 2 gallons to quarts, write a ratio that shows the relationship of gallons to quarts. Write an equal ratio with the number of quarts as the missing number.

$$\frac{1 \text{ gallon}}{4 \text{ quarts}} = \frac{2 \text{ gallons}}{n \text{ quarts}}$$

It is easier to write the first unit in the problem as the numerator and the second unit as the denominator. When you cross-multiply, it is also easier to multiply by n first so that n is on the left side of the equal sign.

Use These Steps

18 yards = _____ feet

1. Since you are changing yards to feet, write the ratio that shows 1 yard to 3 feet.

    $$\frac{1 \text{ yard}}{3 \text{ feet}}$$

2. Write a proportion with n for the missing number of feet.

    $$\frac{1 \text{ yard}}{3 \text{ feet}} = \frac{18 \text{ yards}}{n \text{ feet}}$$

3. Cross-multiply to find n.

    $$\frac{1}{3} \times \frac{18}{n}$$

    $n \times 1 = 18 \times 3$

    $n = 18 \times 3 = 54 \text{ feet}$

Change each measurement using a proportion.

1. 12 lbs. = __192__ oz.

    $$\frac{1}{16} \times \frac{12}{n}$$

    $n \times 1 = 16 \times 12$

    $n = 16 \times 12 = 192$

2. 15 qt. = _____ pt.

3. 12 min. = _____ sec.

4. 7 yd. = _____ ft.

5. 5 T. = _____ lb.

6. 8 c. = _____ oz.

7. 5 wk. = _____ days

8. 8 mi. = _____ yd.

9. 30 lb. = _____ oz.

10. A tape measure is 6 feet long. How many inches are in 6 feet?

    Answer _____

11. While she is going to school, Janine works 7 hours a week as the front desk clerk in a motel. How many minutes are in 7 hours?

    Answer _____

Changing Units of Measurement Using a Proportion

Sometimes you may have to change a fraction or mixed number measurement to another unit. Write a proportion with the fraction or mixed number in the numerator of the second fraction. For example, to change $\frac{1}{2}$ pound of ground turkey to ounces, write $\frac{1}{2}$ in the numerator.

$$\frac{1 \text{ pound}}{16 \text{ ounces}} = \frac{\frac{1}{2} \text{ pound}}{n \text{ ounces}}$$

Use These Steps

$3\frac{1}{2}$ years = _____ weeks

1. Since you are changing years to weeks, write the ratio that shows 1 year to 52 weeks.

$$\frac{1 \text{ year}}{52 \text{ weeks}}$$

2. Write a proportion with n for the missing number of weeks.

$$\frac{1 \text{ year}}{52 \text{ weeks}} = \frac{3\frac{1}{2} \text{ years}}{n \text{ weeks}}$$

3. Cross-multiply to find n.

$$\frac{1}{52} \times \frac{3\frac{1}{2}}{n}$$

$$n \times 1 = 52 \times 3\frac{1}{2}$$

$$n = \frac{\overset{26}{\cancel{52}}}{1} \times \frac{7}{\underset{1}{\cancel{2}}} = 182 \text{ weeks}$$

Change each measurement using a proportion.

1. $2\frac{1}{2}$ lb. = $\underline{40}$ oz.

$$\frac{1}{16} \times \frac{2\frac{1}{2}}{n}$$

$$n \times 1 = 16 \times 2\frac{1}{2}$$

$$n = \frac{\overset{8}{\cancel{16}}}{1} \times \frac{5}{\underset{1}{\cancel{2}}} = 40$$

2. $6\frac{3}{4}$ gal. = _____ qt.

3. $1\frac{1}{2}$ yr. = _____ wk.

4. $1\frac{1}{4}$ ft. = _____ in.

5. $\frac{3}{4}$ yr. = _____ mo.

6. $3\frac{1}{3}$ hr. = _____ min.

7. The Senior Citizen Center used $6\frac{1}{4}$ pounds of chicken to make chicken salad sandwiches for lunch. How many ounces are in $6\frac{1}{4}$ pounds?

8. The Center served $6\frac{1}{2}$ quarts of lemonade with lunch. How many cups are in $6\frac{1}{2}$ quarts?

Answer_____

Answer_____

Changing Units of Measurement Using a Proportion

You can write a proportion to change small units to larger units. For example, if you are 65 inches tall, you can find how tall you are in feet by writing a proportion. Write a ratio that shows the relationship of inches to feet. Write an equal ratio with the number of feet as the missing number.

$$\frac{12 \text{ inches}}{1 \text{ foot}} = \frac{65 \text{ inches}}{n \text{ feet}}$$

Remember, it is easier to write the first unit in the problem as the numerator in each ratio. Multiply by n first so that n is on the left side.

Use These Steps

48 inches = _____ feet

1. Since you are changing inches to feet, write the ratio that shows 12 inches to 1 foot.

$$\frac{12 \text{ inches}}{1 \text{ foot}}$$

2. Write a proportion with n for the missing number of feet.

$$\frac{12 \text{ inches}}{1 \text{ foot}} = \frac{48 \text{ inches}}{n \text{ feet}}$$

3. Cross-multiply. Divide to find n.

$$\frac{12}{1} \diagdown \frac{48}{n}$$
$$n \times 12 = 1 \times 48$$
$$12n = 48$$
$$n = 48 \div 12 = 4 \text{ feet}$$

Change each measurement using a proportion.

1. 24 oz. = ___3___ c.

$$\frac{8}{1} \diagdown \frac{24}{n}$$
$$n \times 8 = 1 \times 24$$
$$8n = 24$$
$$n = 24 \div 8 = 3$$

2. 12 ft. = _____ yd.

3. 48 oz. = _____ lb.

4. 28 days = _____ wk.

5. 12 pt. = _____ qt.

6. 14,000 lb. = _____ T.

7. 60 mo. = _____ yr.

8. 20 qt. = _____ gal.

9. 15,840 ft. = _____ mi.

10. Eleanor ordered 240 ounces of toner for the fax machines in her office. How many pounds are in 240 ounces?

    Answer_____

11. Terrence mixed 8 quarts of paint. How many gallons are in 8 quarts?

    Answer_____

Changing Units of Measurement Using a Proportion

Remember, when using proportions to change from one unit to another, first write the relationship of one unit to another as a ratio. Then write a proportion to find the missing number.

Use These Steps

34 ounces = _____ pounds

1. Since you are changing ounces to pounds, write the ratio that shows 16 ounces to 1 pound.

$$\frac{16 \text{ ounces}}{1 \text{ pound}}$$

2. Write a proportion with n for the missing number of pounds.

$$\frac{16 \text{ ounces}}{1 \text{ pound}} = \frac{33 \text{ ounces}}{n \text{ pounds}}$$

3. Cross-multiply. Divide to find n. Write the remainder as a fraction.

$$\frac{16}{1} \diagdown \frac{33}{n}$$

$n \times 16 = 1 \times 33$

$16n = 33$

$n = 33 \div 16 = 2\frac{1}{16} \text{ pounds}$

Change each measurement using a proportion. Reduce if possible.

1. 17 ft. = $\underline{\quad 5\frac{2}{3} \quad}$ yd.

$\frac{3}{1} \diagdown \frac{17}{n}$

$n \times 3 = 1 \times 17$

$3n = 17$

$n = 17 \div 3 = 5\frac{2}{3}$

2. 45 sec. = _____ min.

3. 11 c. = _____ pt.

4. $3,500$ lb. = _____ T.

5. 37 ft. = _____ yd.

6. 10 qt. = _____ gal.

7. 40 oz. = _____ lb.

8. 4 mo. = _____ yr.

9. 21 pt. = _____ qt.

10. $1,000$ yd. = _____ mi.

11. 10 in. = _____ ft.

12. 13 wk. = _____ yr.

13. Neil's baby daughter is 19 inches long. Write 19 inches as feet.

14. Neil's baby daughter sleeps 14 hours a day. Write 14 hours as part of a day.

Answer_____

Answer_____

Problem Solving: Using Several Steps

Most problems with measurements require several steps. Sometimes you will be working with different units of measurement. You may need to change from small to larger units or large to smaller units in order to find the answer to a measurement problem.

Example Betty orders supplies for her beauty shop. She buys shampoo by the gallon and pours it into pint containers to use in the shop. How many pints can she fill from 3 gallons of shampoo?

▶ **Step 1.** Find how many pints are in 1 gallon.

2 pints = 1 quart
4 quarts = 1 gallon

$2 \times 4 = 8$ pints in 1 gallon

▶ **Step 2.** Multiply the number of pints in 1 gallon by 3 gallons.

$8 \times 3 = 24$

Betty can fill 24 pint containers from 3 gallons of shampoo.

Solve. Use the tables on page 24 to help you.

1. The employee cafeteria is serving ice cream today. They have $\frac{1}{2}$ gallon of strawberry ice cream. How many 1-cup servings can they get from $\frac{1}{2}$ gallon?

   Answer_____

2. Dot needs 5 yards of trim for a dress she has to alter. She has 30 inches. How much more trim does she need to buy?

   Answer_____

3. Eloise is serving fruit punch at the opening of a bookstore. She made 5 quarts. How many 1-cup servings are in 5 quarts?

   Answer_____

4. Jalissa earns 4 hours vacation for every month she works. She has worked for 14 months. Based on an 8-hour workday, how many days of vacation has she earned?

   Answer_____

Solve. Use the tables on page 24 to help you.

5. Trina puts up holiday lights around the recreation center each year. She needs 60 feet of lights. Each string of lights is 48 inches long. How many strings of lights does she need to cover 60 feet?

Answer_____

6. The faucet in the medical lab leaks $\frac{2}{3}$ cup of water every hour. How many gallons of water does the faucet leak in a 24-hour day?

Answer_____

7. A kitchen helper is making meatballs in barbeque sauce. She used 5 pounds of ground beef to make meatballs weighing about 2 ounces each. How many meatballs did she get?

Answer_____

8. The average letter the post office handles weighs 1 ounce. The city post office handled 642,000 pieces of mail last week. At that rate, how many tons of mail did the post office handle last week?

Answer_____

9. When he works on boat motors, Peter mixes 2 ounces of oil to 1 gallon of gas. He has 1 pint of oil. How many gallons of gas will he need if he uses the whole pint of oil?

Answer_____

10. Walter sold 3 quarts of homemade vegetable soup at his lunch counter. How many $\frac{3}{4}$-cup servings would he get from 3 quarts?

Answer_____

Unit 1 Review

Write the measurement shown by each arrow.

1.

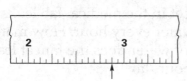

2.

3.

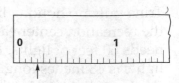

4.

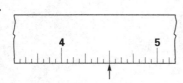

5.

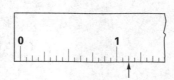

6.

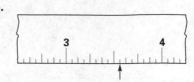

Find the distance between each pair of points on the ruler below. Reduce if possible.

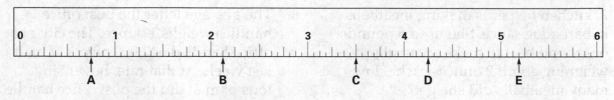

7.   A and D

8.   B and E

9.   C and B

Write the measurement shown on each scale.

10.

11.

12.

13.

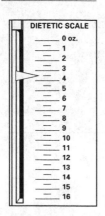

14.

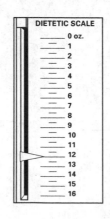

15.

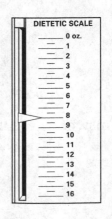

Write the amount in cups and in ounces in each measuring cup.

16.

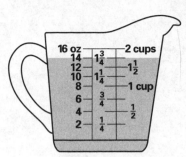

_____

17.

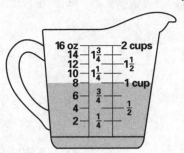

_____

18.

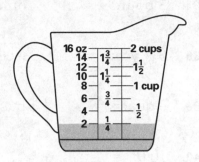

_____

Write the correct time using the 24-hour clock.

19.   6:45 A.M.

20.   1:15 P.M.

21.   6:35 P.M.

Write the washing time shown on each timer.

22.

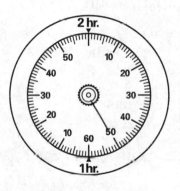

_____

23.

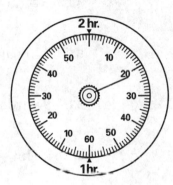

_____

24.

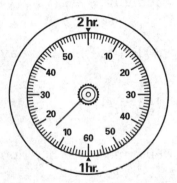

_____

Compare the units of measure. Write >, <, or =.

25.   24 months ☐ 1 year

26.   1 day ☐ 48 hours

27.   1' ☐ 24"

28.   1 lb. ☐ 16 oz.

29.   1,200 lb. ☐ 1 T.

30.   8 qt. ☐ 1 gal.

31.   4 c. ☐ 1 pt.

32.   1 yd. ☐ 36 in.

33.   1 year ☐ 56 weeks

Change each measurement.

34. 3 pounds = _____ ounces

35. 40 oz. = _____ c.

36. $3\frac{1}{2}$ years = _____ weeks

37. 16 inches = _____ feet

38. 7 quarts = _____ pints

39. 90 seconds = _____ minutes

40. 10 pt. = _____ qt.

41. 2,500 pounds = _____ tons

42. $\frac{1}{2}$ ton = _____ pounds

43. 3 days = _____ hours

44. 10 cups = _____ pints

45. 3 feet = _____ inches

46. 10 quarts = _____ gallons

47. 6 minutes = _____ seconds

48. 16 months = _____ years

49. $2\frac{1}{2}$ days = _____ hours

50. 80 hours = _____ days

51. 440 yards = _____ miles

52. 143 weeks = _____ years

53. 9 yards = _____ feet

54. 60 ounces = _____ pounds

55. 20 hr. = _____ min.

56. 4 gal. = _____ qt.

57. 6 weeks = _____ days

Below is a list of the problems in this review and the pages on which the skills are taught. If you missed any problems, turn to the pages listed and practice the skills. Then correct the problems you missed in the Unit Review.

Unit 2 WORKING WITH MEASUREMENT

You work with measurement at home and at work. You may use customary measures in sewing, carpentry, or cooking. You may also use common metric measures such as meters, grams, and liters in working as a lab technician, machinist, or welder. Customary measures are usually written as fractions or as mixed units, such as 3 feet 6 inches. Metric measures are written as decimals, such as 3.5 meters.

In this unit, you will study customary and metric measures, how to compare customary and metric measurements, and how to add, subtract, multiply, and divide using both systems of measurement.

Getting Ready

You should be familiar with the skills on this page and the next before you begin this unit. To check your answers, turn to page 189.

▶ You should be able to change a decimal to a fraction equivalent.

Change each decimal to a fraction or mixed number. Reduce if possible.

1.
$$1.5 = 1\frac{1}{2}$$

2.
$$.2 =$$

3.
$$.01 =$$

4.
$$6.75 =$$

5.
$$3.25 =$$

6.
$$10.8 =$$

7.
$$.35 =$$

8.
$$15.6 =$$

For review, see page 16 in **Math Skills for the Workforce, Decimals and Percents.**

You should be able to change a fraction to a decimal equivalent.

Change each fraction or mixed number to a decimal.

9.
$8\frac{1}{5} = 8.2$

10.
$\frac{1}{4} =$

11.
$\frac{7}{10} =$

12.
$3\frac{3}{8} =$

13.
$4\frac{1}{2} =$

14.
$\frac{7}{8} =$

15.
$12\frac{3}{4} =$

16.
$\frac{3}{100} =$

For review, see pages 12 and 21 in **Math Skills for the Workforce, Decimals and Percents.**

When working with metric measurement, you will be working with decimals.

Add, subtract, multiply, or divide.

17.
$14.07 + 19.3 =$
$$\begin{array}{r} 14.07 \\ + 19.3 \\ \hline 33.37 \end{array}$$

18.
$118 + 3.6 =$

19.
$.6 + .9 =$

20.
$52.5 + 7.59 =$

21.
$18 - 3.6 =$
$$\begin{array}{r} 18.0 \\ - 3.6 \\ \hline 14.4 \end{array}$$

22.
$72.03 - 11.7 =$

23.
$110.83 - 6.09 =$

24.
$25.7 - 12.9 =$

25.
$13.2 \times .7 =$
$$\begin{array}{r} 13.2 \\ \times \quad .7 \\ \hline 9.24 \end{array}$$

26.
$.5 \times .1 =$

27.
$17 \times .3 =$

28.
$2.65 \times .05 =$

29.
$1.7 \div .1 =$
$$\begin{array}{r} 1\,7. \\ .1\,\overline{)\,1.7} \\ -\,1 \\ \hline 7 \\ -\,7 \\ \hline 0 \end{array}$$

30.
$50 \div .5 =$

31.
$1.83 \div .06 =$

32.
$9.3 \div .01 =$

For review, see Units 2 and 3 in **Math Skills for the Workforce, Decimals and Percents.**

Mixed Measurements

Mixed measurements contain more than one unit, such as 2 feet 6 inches. You have already worked with measurements written as fractions or mixed numbers. You can also write a mixed number measurement as an equal decimal measurement. You can write either a fraction or a decimal measurement as a mixed measurement.

$2\frac{1}{2}$ gallons = 2.5 gallons = 2 gallons 2 quarts

$3\frac{1}{10}$ miles = 3.1 miles = 3 miles 528 feet or 3 miles 176 yards

$4\frac{1}{4}$ pounds = 4.25 pounds = 4 pounds 4 ounces

Notice that 4.25 pounds is not equal to 4 pounds 25 ounces and 2.5 gallons is not equal to 2 gallons 5 quarts.

Use These Steps

6.5 pounds = _____ pounds _____ ounces

1. Change .5 pound to ounces.

    1 pound = 16 ounces
    .5 pound = .5 × 16 = 8 ounces

2. Write the number of pounds, 6, and the number of ounces, 8.

    6 pounds 8 ounces

Change each measurement to the units given. Use the tables on page 24 to help you.

1. $2\frac{1}{4}$ feet = __2__ feet __3__ inches

    1 foot = 12 inches
    $\frac{1}{4}$ **foot =** $\frac{1}{4}$ **× 12 = 3 inches**

2. 3.5 ft. = _____ ft. _____ in.

3. $2\frac{1}{3}$ yards = _____ yards _____ feet

4. $1\frac{1}{2}$ miles = _____ mile _____ feet

5. $3\frac{1}{2}$ days = _____ days _____ hours

6. $3\frac{1}{8}$ lb. = _____ lb. __ oz.

7. $1\frac{1}{2}$ years = _____ year _____ weeks

8. 7.75 hr. = _____ hr. _____ min.

9. Adriana volunteered 3.25 hours at the city library. Write 3.25 hours as a mixed measurement.

10. Kerry cut a 16-foot board into pieces $3\frac{1}{2}$ feet long each. Write $3\frac{1}{2}$ feet as a mixed measurement.

Answer_____

Answer_____

Mixed Measurements

Sometimes you need to change a mixed measurement to the larger unit of measure. The larger unit will be a mixed number or decimal. For example, 1 hour 15 minutes is the same as $1\frac{1}{4}$ hours, or 1.25 hours.

Use These Steps

9 feet 4 inches = _____ feet

1. Change 4 inches to feet.

1 foot = 12 inches

4 inches = $\frac{4}{12}$ = $\frac{1}{3}$ foot

2. Add the whole number of feet to the fraction of feet.

$9 + \frac{1}{3} = 9\frac{1}{3}$ feet

Change each measurement to the unit given. Use the tables on page 24 to help you.

1. 5 quarts 1 pint = ___$5\frac{1}{2}$___ quarts

1 quart = 2 pints

1 pint = $\frac{1}{2}$ quart

$5 + \frac{1}{2} = 5\frac{1}{2}$

2. 3 c. 4 oz. = _____ c.

3. 7 pints 1 cup = _____ pints

4. 2 gal. 3 qt. = _____ gal.

5. 3 yd. 2 ft. = _____ yd.

6. 1 mile 1,320 feet = _____ miles

7. 6 ft. 8 in. = _____ ft.

8. 3 days 8 hours = _____ days

9. The newest baby in the maternity ward weighed 7 pounds 8 ounces. Change 7 pounds 8 ounces to pounds.

10. Victor waited tables at Lake Necko Resort for 3 hours and 30 minutes last night. Change 3 hours and 30 minutes to hours.

Answer_____

Answer_____

Mixed Measurements

Sometimes you may need to change a mixed measurement to the smaller unit of measure. The smaller unit will be a whole number. For example, 2 quarts 1 pint is the same as 5 pints.

Use These Steps

2 hours 30 minutes = _____ minutes

1. Change 2 hours to minutes.

1 hour = 60 minutes
2 hours = 2 × 60 = 120 minutes

2. Add the answer, 120, to 30.

120 + 30 = 150 minutes

Change each measurement to the unit given. Use the tables on page 24 to help you.

1. 5 feet 8 inches = __68__ inches
1 foot = 12 inches
5 feet = 5 × 12 = 60
60 + 8 = 68

2. 2 ft. 10 in. = _____ in.

3. 1 yd. 1 ft. = _____ ft.

4. 6 yards 6 inches = _____ inches

5. 5 lb. 6 oz. = _____ oz.

6. 1 T. 500 lb. = _____ lb.

7. 4 hours 15 minutes = _____ minutes

8. 1 year 6 weeks = _____ weeks

9. 1 cup 4 ounces = _____ ounces

10. 1 gallon 2 quarts = _____ quarts

11. In the gift wrapping department, Lucia has 4 yards 2 feet of ribbon to make bows. How many feet of ribbon does she have?

12. Elvin paid off his car loan in 2 years and 8 months. How many months did it take Elvin to pay off his car loan?

Answer_____

Answer_____

Mixed Measurements

Sometimes you may want to change a measurement to a mixed measurement. For example, 63 inches is the same as 5 feet 3 inches.

Use These Steps

15 quarts = _____ gallons _____ quarts

1. Change 15 quarts to gallons.

    1 gallon = 4 quarts
    15 quarts = 15 ÷ 4 = 3 gallons R 3

2. Write the remainder as the number of quarts.

    3 gallons R 3 = 3 gallons 3 quarts

Change to a mixed measurement.

1. 100 min. = __1__ hr. __40__ min.
   1 hr. = 60 min.
   100 min. ÷ 60 = 1 hr. R 40 =
   1 hr. 40 min.

2. 28 oz. = ____ c. ____ oz.

3. 15 c. = ____ pt. ____ c.

4. 11 qt. = ____ gal. ____ qt.

5. 17 feet = ____ yards ____ feet

6. 6,600 ft. = ____ mi. ____ ft.

7. 80 in. = ____ ft. ____ in.

8. 19 days = ____ weeks ____ days

9. 104 hours = ____ days ____ hours

10. 435 min. = ____ hr. ____ min.

11. 65 wk. = ____ yr. ____ wk.

12. 30 months = ____ years ____ months

13. Bonnie shipped a lamp that weighs 70 ounces. Change 70 ounces to pounds and ounces.

14. A copy machine took 750 seconds to make 2,000 copies. Change 750 seconds to minutes and seconds.

Answer_____

Answer_____

Comparing Mixed Measurements

Sometimes you need to compare measurements. If the measurements
are in different units, you must change them to the same unit before you
can compare. For example, you may want to know whether 3' 4" is more
than or less than 40". To compare these two measurements, you will
need to change 3' 4" to inches or 40" to feet and inches.

Use These Steps

Compare 3' 6" and 40".

1. **Change 3' 6" to inches or change 40"
   to feet and inches.**

   $3' = 3 \times 12 = 36$ "
   $36" + 6" = 42"$
       or
   $40" = 40 \div 12 = 3$ feet R $4 = 3'$ 4"

2. **Compare.**

   $42" > 40"$, so 3' 6" > 40"
       or
   3' 6" > 3' 4", so 3' 6" > 40"

Compare. Write >, <, or =.

1. 19 feet $\boxed{=}$ 6 yards 1 foot

   19 feet = 19 ÷ 3 = 6 yards 1 foot
       or
   6 × 3 = 18 feet + 1 foot = 19 feet

2. 18 cups $\square$ 4 quarts 2 cups

3. $6\frac{1}{2}$ gallons $\boxed{>}$ 6 gallons 1 quart

   $6\frac{1}{2}$ **gallons = 6 gallons 2 quarts**
       or
   6 gallons 1 quart = $6\frac{1}{4}$ gallons

4. 8' 9" $\square$ $8\frac{2}{3}$ feet

5. 7 hours 15 minutes $\boxed{<}$ 7.5 hours

   7 hours 15 minutes = $7\frac{1}{4}$ = 7.25
       or
   7.5 hours = $7\frac{1}{2}$ = 7 hours 30 minutes

6. 10.75 pounds $\square$ 10 pounds 7 ounces

7. Bright liquid laundry detergent is
   sold in 12-cup bottles. Dazzle brand is
   sold in 2-quart 3-cup bottles. Which
   brand contains more detergent?

8. An apple tree at Zeke's Nursery is
   5 feet 8 inches tall. A pear tree is
   $5\frac{3}{4}$ feet tall. Which is taller, the apple
   tree or the pear tree?

Answer _____

Answer _____

Application

Katy is doing market research comparing ads in two different newspapers.

Change each measurement as indicated in each problem. Circle the letter beside the correct answer.

1. Katy saw wrapping paper on special at the local discount store. A roll contains 2 feet 10 inches of paper. How many inches are on one roll?
   a. 2.1 inches
   b. 34 inches
   c. 12 inches

2. Katy found an ad for $\frac{3}{4}$-pound boxes of chocolate candy. How much chocolate is there in a box?
   a. .75 ounces
   b. .75 pound
   c. .34 pound

3. Katy spent 85 minutes reading the newspapers. How many hours did she spend reading?
   a. 1.25 hr.
   b. $1\frac{1}{2}$ hr.
   c. 1 hr. 25 min.

4. Katy saw an ad for a 64-ounce bottle of fabric softener. How many cups of fabric softener are in 64 ounces?
   a. 6.4 cups
   b. $6\frac{2}{5}$ cups
   c. 8 cups

5. One store had frozen waffles in the 1.5-pound family box on sale. What is another way to show the weight of a 1.5-pound box of waffles?
   a. $1\frac{1}{2}$ lb.
   b. 1 lb. 5 oz.
   c. $1\frac{5}{16}$ lb.

6. C-Mart advertised powdered laundry detergent in the 42-ounce box on sale. How many pounds are in 42 ounces?
   a. 4.2 lb.
   b. $2\frac{5}{8}$ lb.
   c. 2.1 lb.

7. Katy noticed in the classified pages that most new-car loans are for 60 months. How many years are in 60 months?
   a. 3.75 years
   b. 6 years
   c. 5 years

8. The discount store was selling packages of 54-inch long window insulation. How many feet are in 54 inches?
   a. 4.5 feet
   b. 4.6 feet
   c. $4\frac{5}{12}$ feet

Adding Measurements

When you add measurements, add only like units of measure.

$$
\begin{array}{r}
6 \text{ cups } 2 \text{ ounces} \\
+ 4 \text{ cups } 3 \text{ ounces} \\
\hline
10 \text{ cups } 5 \text{ ounces}
\end{array}
$$

Use These Steps

Add
$$
\begin{array}{r}
9 \text{ hours } 10 \text{ minutes} \\
+ 1 \text{ hour } 35 \text{ minutes} \\
\hline
\end{array}
$$

1. Add the minutes.

$$
\begin{array}{r}
9 \text{ hours } 10 \text{ minutes} \\
+ 1 \text{ hour } 35 \text{ minutes} \\
\hline
45 \text{ minutes}
\end{array}
$$

2. Add the hours.

$$
\begin{array}{r}
9 \text{ hours } 10 \text{ minutes} \\
+ 1 \text{ hour } 35 \text{ minutes} \\
\hline
10 \text{ hours } 45 \text{ minutes}
\end{array}
$$

Add.

1.
$$
\begin{array}{r}
5 \text{ feet } 6 \text{ inches} \\
+ 4 \text{ feet} \\
\hline
9 \text{ feet } 6 \text{ inches}
\end{array}
$$

2.
$$
\begin{array}{r}
7 \text{ inches} \\
+ 3 \text{ feet } 2 \text{ inches} \\
\hline
\end{array}
$$

3.
$$
\begin{array}{r}
3 \text{ ft. } 4 \text{ in.} \\
+ 7 \text{ ft. } 5 \text{ in.} \\
\hline
\end{array}
$$

4.
$$
\begin{array}{r}
6 \text{ wk. } 4 \text{ days} \\
+ 1 \text{ wk. } 2 \text{ days} \\
\hline
\end{array}
$$

5.
$$
\begin{array}{r}
20 \text{ min. } 10 \text{ sec.} \\
+ 12 \text{ min. } 15 \text{ sec.} \\
\hline
\end{array}
$$

6.
$$
\begin{array}{r}
9 \text{ lb. } 7 \text{ oz.} \\
+ 4 \text{ lb. } 5 \text{ oz.} \\
\hline
\end{array}
$$

7.
$$
\begin{array}{r}
8 \text{ hr. } 30 \text{ min.} \\
+ 2 \text{ hr. } 15 \text{ min.} \\
\hline
\end{array}
$$

8.
$$
\begin{array}{r}
14 \text{ gal. } 3 \text{ qt.} \\
+ 3 \text{ gal.} \\
\hline
\end{array}
$$

9.
$$
\begin{array}{r}
2 \text{ c. } 1 \text{ oz.} \\
+ 5 \text{ c. } 4 \text{ oz.} \\
\hline
\end{array}
$$

10.
$$
\begin{array}{r}
52 \text{ yd.} \\
+ 13 \text{ yd. } 2 \text{ ft.} \\
\hline
\end{array}
$$

11.
$$
\begin{array}{r}
12 \text{ hr. } 25 \text{ min.} \\
+ 6 \text{ hr. } 25 \text{ min.} \\
\hline
\end{array}
$$

12.
$$
\begin{array}{r}
8 \text{ T. } 700 \text{ lb.} \\
+ 12 \text{ T. } 800 \text{ lb.} \\
\hline
\end{array}
$$

13. Kirk needs to replace the counter tops in a dental clinic. He needs one piece 2 ft. 8 in. long and a second piece 3 ft. 2 in. long. How much material does he need in all?

Answer _____

14. To paint the countertops, Kirk bought 2 gallons and 2 quarts of white paint. He mixed them with 1 gallon and 1 quart of blue paint. How much paint does he have in all?

Answer _____

Simplifying Mixed Measurements

Sometimes you may have a mixed measurement that can be simplified. For example, 1 foot 12 inches is the same as 2 feet. The simplified measurement is 2 feet.

You should simplify any mixed measurements by changing smaller units to larger units. Use the tables on page 24 to find equivalent units.

Use These Steps

Simplify 2 feet 16 inches

1. Change 16 inches to feet.

   16 inches = 16 ÷ 12 = 1 foot 4 inches

2. Add the answer to 2 feet.

   2 feet
   + 1 foot 4 inches
   3 feet 4 inches

Simplify each measurement.

1. 3 feet 36 inches = 6 feet
   36 ÷ 12 = 3 feet
   3 feet + 3 feet = 6 feet

2. 7 yards 13 feet =

3. 5 pounds 32 ounces =

4. 3 tons 4,000 pounds =

5. 3 cups 16 ounces =

6. 4 quarts 9 pints =

7. 2 gallons 18 quarts =

8. 3 pints 3 cups =

9. 2 hours 90 minutes =

10. 3 days 42 hours =

11. 3 miles 7,920 feet =

12. 1 pound 16 ounces =

13. 10 minutes 240 seconds =

14. 4 years 36 months =

Adding Measurements

When you add measurements, set up the problem vertically. Add like units. Simplify the answer if possible.

$$
\begin{array}{r}
6 \text{ yd. } 2 \text{ ft.} \\
+ 3 \text{ yd. } 2 \text{ ft.} \\
\hline
9 \text{ yd. } 4 \text{ ft.} = 10 \text{ yd. } 1 \text{ ft.}
\end{array}
$$

Use These Steps

Add 5 lb. 12 oz. + 7 lb. 10 oz.

1. Add the ounces.

$$
\begin{array}{r}
5 \text{ lb. } 12 \text{ oz.} \\
+ 7 \text{ lb. } 10 \text{ oz.} \\
\hline
22 \text{ oz.}
\end{array}
$$

2. Add the pounds.

$$
\begin{array}{r}
5 \text{ lb. } 12 \text{ oz.} \\
+ 7 \text{ lb. } 10 \text{ oz.} \\
\hline
12 \text{ lb. } 22 \text{ oz.}
\end{array}
$$

3. Simplify the answer.

22 oz. = 22 ÷ 16 =
1 lb. 6 oz.

$$
\begin{array}{r}
12 \text{ lb.} \\
+ 1 \text{ lb. } 6 \text{ oz.} \\
\hline
13 \text{ lb. } 6 \text{ oz.}
\end{array}
$$

Add. Simplify if possible.

1.
$$
\begin{array}{r}
1 \text{ c. } 3 \text{ oz.} \\
+ 2 \text{ c. } 6 \text{ oz.} \\
\hline
3 \text{ c. } 9 \text{ oz.} = 4 \text{ c. } 1 \text{ oz.}
\end{array}
$$

2.
$$
\begin{array}{r}
4 \text{ wk. } 2 \text{ days} \\
+ 3 \text{ wk. } 6 \text{ days} \\
\hline
\end{array}
$$

3.
$$
\begin{array}{r}
1 \text{ ft. } 6 \text{ in.} \\
+ 1 \text{ ft. } 10 \text{ in.} \\
\hline
\end{array}
$$

4.
$$
\begin{array}{r}
3 \text{ hr. } 20 \text{ min.} \\
+ 4 \text{ hr. } 45 \text{ min.} \\
\hline
\end{array}
$$

5.
$$
\begin{array}{r}
8 \text{ lb. } 8 \text{ oz.} \\
+ 4 \text{ lb. } 6 \text{ oz.} \\
\hline
\end{array}
$$

6.
$$
\begin{array}{r}
4 \text{ yd. } 2 \text{ ft.} \\
+ 8 \text{ yd. } 1 \text{ ft.} \\
\hline
\end{array}
$$

7.
$$
\begin{array}{r}
7 \text{ gal. } 2 \text{ qt.} \\
+ 2 \text{ gal. } 2 \text{ qt.} \\
\hline
\end{array}
$$

8.
$$
\begin{array}{r}
2 \text{ T. } 800 \text{ lb.} \\
+ 3 \text{ T. } 1{,}400 \text{ lb.} \\
\hline
\end{array}
$$

9.
$$
\begin{array}{r}
5 \text{ min. } 30 \text{ sec.} \\
+ 8 \text{ min. } 35 \text{ sec.} \\
\hline
\end{array}
$$

10. Gilbert mailed a package weighing 14 pounds 4 ounces and another package weighing 7 pounds 12 ounces. What was the total weight of the two packages?

Answer _____

11. Emma connected two extension cords. One was 3 feet 6 inches long and the other was 4 feet 10 inches long. How long were the two extension cords together?

Answer _____

Adding Measurements

Sometimes you have to add units that are not the same. To add unlike units, you need to change one of the units. For example, to add 3 feet 6 inches and 2 yards 18 inches, change feet to yards or yards to feet.

$$
\begin{array}{l}
\text{1 yd.} \quad \text{6 in.} \\
+\ \text{2 yd. 18 in.} \\
\hline
\text{3 yd. 24 in.} \ = \text{3 yd. 2 ft.}
\end{array}
\qquad \text{or} \qquad
\begin{array}{l}
\text{3 ft.} \quad \text{6 in.} \\
+\ \text{6 ft. 18 in.} \\
\hline
\text{9 ft. 24 in.} \ = \text{11 ft.} = \text{3 yd. 2 ft.}
\end{array}
$$

You should simplify any mixed measurements by changing smaller units to larger units.

Use These Steps

Add   1 pint 1 cup + 2 quarts 3 cups

1. Set up the problem.

$$
\begin{array}{l}
\text{1 pt. 1 c.} \\
+\ \text{2 qt.} \quad \text{3 c.} \\
\hline
\end{array}
$$

2. Change 2 quarts to pints.

$$
\begin{array}{l}
\text{1 pt. 1 c.} = \text{1 pt. 1 c.} \\
+\ \text{2 qt.} \quad \text{3 c.} = \text{4 pt. 3 c.} \\
\hline
\end{array}
$$

3. Add and simplify if possible.

$$
\begin{array}{l}
\text{1 pt. 1 c.} \\
+\ \text{4 pt. 3 c.} \\
\hline
\text{5 pt. 4 c.} \ = \text{7 pt.} = \text{3 qt. 1 pt.}
\end{array}
$$

Add. Simplify if possible.

1. 7 ft. 8 in. + 3 yd. 13 in. =

$$
\begin{array}{l}
\text{7 ft.} \quad \text{8 in.} = \text{7 ft.} \quad \text{8 in.} \\
+\ \text{3 yd.} \quad \text{13 in.} = \text{9 ft. 13 in.} \\
\hline
\text{16 ft. 21 in.} \ = \\
\text{17 ft. 9 in.} = \text{5 yd. 2 ft. 9 in.}
\end{array}
$$

2. 5 gal. 2 pt. + 6 qt. 3 pt. =

3. 9 pt. 4 oz. + 2 c. 6 oz. =

4. 48 hr. 15 min. + 2 days 30 min. =

5. 8 qt. 5 pt. + 2 gal. 3 pt. =

6. 5,000 lb. 14 oz. + 1 T. 4 oz. =

7. 4 yd. 6 in. + 3 ft. 10 in. =

8. 2 yr. 2 days + 26 wk. 5 days =

Subtracting Measurements

When you subtract measurements, set up the problem vertically.
Subtract like units. Sometimes you will need to borrow. Be sure to
change the borrowed number to the correct unit before you subtract.

$$
\begin{array}{l}
\overset{5}{\cancel{6}}\text{ yards}\,\overset{4}{\cancel{1}}\text{ foot} \\
-\ 2\text{ yards } 2\text{ feet} \\
\hline
\ \ 3\text{ yards } 2\text{ feet}
\end{array}
$$

Use These Steps

Subtract   1 pound 8 ounces − 10 ounces

1. Borrow 1 pound. Change 1 pound to 16 ounces.
   Add 16 ounces and 8 ounces. Write 24 above the 8.

$$
\begin{array}{r}
24 \\
\cancel{1}\text{ pound }\ \cancel{8}\text{ ounces} \\
-\qquad 10\text{ ounces} \\
\end{array}
$$

2. Subtract.

$$
\begin{array}{r}
24 \\
1\text{ pound }\ \cancel{8}\text{ ounces} \\
-\qquad 10\text{ ounces} \\
\hline
14\text{ ounces}
\end{array}
$$

Subtract.

1.
$$
\begin{array}{r}
\overset{2}{\cancel{3}}\text{ hr.}\ \overset{75}{\cancel{15}}\text{ min.} \\
-\ 1\text{ hr. } 45\text{ min.} \\
\hline
1\text{ hr. } 30\text{ min.}
\end{array}
$$

2.
$$
\begin{array}{r}
8\text{ ft. } 6\text{ in.} \\
-\qquad 10\text{ in.} \\
\end{array}
$$

3.
$$
\begin{array}{r}
12\text{ pt. } 2\text{ c.} \\
-\ 8\text{ pt. } 3\text{ c.} \\
\end{array}
$$

4.
$$
\begin{array}{r}
10\text{ hr. } 35\text{ min.} \\
-\qquad 50\text{ min.} \\
\end{array}
$$

5.
$$
\begin{array}{r}
8\text{ c. } 3\text{ oz.} \\
-\ 7\text{ c. } 6\text{ oz.} \\
\end{array}
$$

6.
$$
\begin{array}{r}
6\text{ min. } 25\text{ sec.} \\
-\ 4\text{ min. } 45\text{ sec.} \\
\end{array}
$$

7.
$$
\begin{array}{r}
\overset{2}{\cancel{3}}\text{ hr.}\quad\overset{60}{} \\
-\ 1\text{ hr. } 53\text{ sec.} \\
\hline
1\text{ hr. }\ \ 7\text{ sec.}
\end{array}
$$

8.
$$
\begin{array}{r}
7\text{ qt.} \\
-\ 1\text{ qt. } 1\text{ pt.} \\
\end{array}
$$

9.
$$
\begin{array}{r}
12\text{ yd.} \\
-\ 9\text{ yd. } 2\text{ ft.} \\
\end{array}
$$

10. The total shipping weight for a
computer is 57 pounds. The shipping
materials weigh 4 pounds 6 ounces.
How much does the computer weigh?

11. Martin bought a 50-foot roll of wire
to connect the speakers in the
dispatcher's office. He used 16 feet
4 inches. How much wire was left on
the roll?

Answer _____

Answer _____

Subtracting Measurements

When you subtract measurements, subtract only like units. For example, to subtract 8 feet 10 inches from 4 yards 16 inches, you change yards to feet. It is easier to subtract if you always change to the smaller unit.

$$
\begin{array}{r}
4 \text{ yd.} \quad 16 \text{ in.} = 12 \text{ ft. } 16 \text{ in.} \\
- \qquad 8 \text{ ft. } 10 \text{ in.} = \underline{8 \text{ ft. } 10 \text{ in.}} \\
4 \text{ ft. } 6 \text{ in.}
\end{array}
$$

Use These Steps

Subtract   3 quarts 1 cup − 2 pints 3 cups

1. Set up the problem.

$$
\begin{array}{r}
3 \text{ qt.} \quad 1 \text{ c.} \\
- \qquad 2 \text{ pt. } 3 \text{ c.} \\
\hline
\end{array}
$$

2. Change 3 quarts to pints.

$$
\begin{array}{r}
3 \text{ qt.} \quad 1 \text{ c.} = 6 \text{ pt. } 1 \text{ c.} \\
- \qquad 2 \text{ pt. } 3 \text{ c.} = 2 \text{ pt. } 3 \text{ c.} \\
\hline
\end{array}
$$

3. Borrow. Subtract.

$$
\begin{array}{r}
\overset{5}{\cancel{6}} \text{ pt. } \overset{3}{\cancel{1}} \text{ c.} \\
- \quad 2 \text{ pt. } 3 \text{ c.} \\
\hline
3 \text{ pt.}
\end{array}
$$

Subtract.

1.

6 yd. 8 in. − 9 ft. 4 in. =

$$
\begin{array}{r}
6 \text{ yd.} \qquad 8 \text{ in.} = 18 \text{ ft. } 8 \text{ in.} \\
- \qquad 9 \text{ ft. } 4 \text{ in.} = \underline{9 \text{ ft. } 4 \text{ in.}} \\
9 \text{ ft. } 4 \text{ in.}
\end{array}
$$

2.

3 T. − 500 lb. =

3.

4 qt. 3 c. − 5 pt. 1 c. =

4.

2 gal. − 3 qt. 1 pt. =

5.

4 pt. 12 oz. − 7 c. 6 oz. =

6.

5 hr. 48 sec. − 45 min. 28 sec. =

7. A custodian had 2 gallons of disinfectant. He used 5 quarts 1 pint to clean the hallways and bathrooms in the high school. How much disinfectant was left?

Answer_____

8. Rochelle bought 3 yards of hose to install a washing machine. She used 1 foot 10 inches. How much hose was left?

Answer_____

Problem Solving: Using Elapsed Time

Elapsed time is the amount of time that has passed since a given time. To find the elapsed time, subtract the earlier time from the later time. The elapsed time from 8:00 A.M. to 11:00 A.M. is 3 hours. Sometimes in figuring elapsed time the later time has fewer minutes than the earlier time. In that case you will need to borrow first.

Example Sue arrived at work at 8:30 A.M. and left for lunch at 12:05 P.M. How many hours did she work in the morning?

▶ **Step 1.** Subtract 8:30 from 12:05. Borrow 1 hour. Change to 60 minutes. Add to the 5 minutes.

$$\begin{array}{r} {\scriptstyle 11\ \ 65} \\ \cancel{12}\!:\!\cancel{05} \\ -\ \ 8\!:\!30 \\ \hline \end{array}$$

▶ **Step 2.** Subtract the minutes. Subtract the hours.

$$\begin{array}{r} {\scriptstyle 11\ \ 65} \\ \cancel{12}\!:\!\cancel{05} \\ -\ \ 8\!:\!30 \\ \hline 3\!:\!35 \end{array}$$

Sue worked 3 hours and 35 minutes in the morning.

Solve.

1. Louis was an usher at the movie theatre. The evening movie started at 5:35 P.M. and ended at 8:15 P.M. How long was the movie?

   Answer_____

2. Jake missed the train that left at 6:49 P.M. He had to wait for the train that left at 9:17 P.M. How long did Jake have to wait for the later train?

   Answer_____

3. Terrence hurt his eye at work and went to the emergency room at 10:40 P.M. He left at 12:10 A.M. How long was he in the emergency room?

   Answer_____

4. Inez left work to go to a dentist's appointment at 9:30 A.M. She got back from the dentist's office at 10:25 A.M. How long was she away from work?

   Answer_____

When you figure elapsed time, sometimes you are not able to subtract the earlier time from the later time because one time is a morning hour and the other time is an afternoon or evening hour. Since the same 12 hours are used two times in a 24-hour day, you can add 12 hours to the later time to include morning or afternoon hours.

Example Sarah arrived at work at 8:30 A.M. and left at 3:45 P.M. How many hours was she at work?

▶ **Step 1.** Set up the problem.

$$\begin{array}{r} 3:45 \\ - \ 8:30 \end{array}$$

▶ **Step 2.** Since 8:30 is in the morning and the later time is in the afternoon, add 12 hours to 3.

$$\begin{array}{r} 15 \\ \cancel{3}:45 \\ - \ 8:30 \end{array}$$

▶ **Step 3.** Subtract the minutes. Subtract the hours.

$$\begin{array}{r} 15 \\ \cancel{3}:45 \\ - \ 8:30 \\ \hline 7:15 \end{array}$$

Sarah was at work 7 hours and 15 minutes.

Solve.

5. Beatrice substituted as a food service worker in the school lunchroom. She worked from 7:15 A.M. until 1:30 P.M. How many hours did she work?

Answer_____

6. Lucille flew from Miami, Florida, to Toronto, Canada. She left Miami at 10:30 A.M. and arrived in Toronto at 2:55 P.M. How long was the flight?

Answer_____

7. Tammy dropped her son off at the day care center at 11:45 A.M. She picked him up at 5:25 P.M. How many hours was he at the center?

Answer_____

8. Oliver went to bed at 11:30 P.M. and got up at 6:15 A.M. How long did Oliver sleep?

Answer_____

Multiplying Measurements by Whole Numbers

When you multiply measurements by whole numbers, set up the problem vertically. Multiply each unit separately. Simplify the answer if possible.

$$
\begin{array}{r}
2 \text{ tons} \quad 400 \text{ pounds} \\
\times \qquad\qquad\qquad 5 \\
\hline
10 \text{ tons } 2{,}000 \text{ pounds} \ = 11 \text{ tons}
\end{array}
$$

Use These Steps

Multiply
$$
\begin{array}{r}
5 \text{ hours } 15 \text{ minutes} \\
\times \qquad\qquad\qquad 8
\end{array}
$$

1. Multiply the minutes.

$$
\begin{array}{r}
5 \text{ hours } \; 15 \text{ minutes} \\
\times \qquad\qquad 8 \\
\hline
120 \text{ minutes}
\end{array}
$$

2. Multiply the hours.

$$
\begin{array}{r}
5 \text{ hours } \; 15 \text{ minutes} \\
\times \qquad\qquad 8 \\
\hline
40 \text{ hours } 120 \text{ minutes}
\end{array}
$$

3. Simplify the answer.

40 hours 120 minutes = 42 hours

Multiply. Simplify if possible.

1.
$$
\begin{array}{r}
3 \text{ lb. } 4 \text{ oz.} \\
\times \qquad\quad 6 \\
\hline
18 \text{ lb. } 24 \text{ oz.} \ = 19 \text{ lb. } 8 \text{ oz.}
\end{array}
$$

2.
$$
\begin{array}{r}
8 \text{ gal. } 1 \text{ qt.} \\
\times \qquad\quad 5 \\
\hline
\end{array}
$$

3.
$$
\begin{array}{r}
9 \text{ ft. } 8 \text{ in.} \\
\times \qquad\quad 3 \\
\hline
\end{array}
$$

4.
$$
\begin{array}{r}
5 \text{ yd. } 2 \text{ ft.} \\
\times \qquad\quad 5 \\
\hline
\end{array}
$$

5.
$$
\begin{array}{r}
2 \text{ qt. } 3 \text{ c.} \\
\times \qquad\quad 4 \\
\hline
\end{array}
$$

6.
$$
\begin{array}{r}
1 \text{ hr. } 25 \text{ min.} \\
\times \qquad\qquad 3 \\
\hline
\end{array}
$$

7.
$$
\begin{array}{r}
10 \text{ lb. } 8 \text{ oz.} \\
\times \qquad\quad 5 \\
\hline
\end{array}
$$

8.
$$
\begin{array}{r}
2 \text{ days } 8 \text{ hr.} \\
\times \qquad\qquad 3 \\
\hline
\end{array}
$$

9.
$$
\begin{array}{r}
3 \text{ pt. } 11 \text{ oz.} \\
\times \qquad\qquad 3 \\
\hline
\end{array}
$$

10. Russell is building wooden storage shelves in the office supply room. He needs 6 shelves each 4 feet 3 inches long. How much wood does Russell need in all to make the shelves?

11. Gloria works part-time at a convenience store. She worked 3 nights last week for 4 hours and 20 minutes each night. How many total hours did she work last week?

Answer_____

Answer_____

Dividing Measurements by Whole Numbers

When you divide measurements by whole numbers, set up the problem like a whole numbers division problem. Divide into the larger unit first. Change any remainder to the smaller unit. Add. Then divide again.

Use These Steps

Divide $6\overline{)15\text{ pounds }6\text{ ounces}}$

1. Divide 6 into 15 pounds.

$$\begin{array}{r} 2\text{ lb.} \\ 6\overline{)15\text{ lb. }6\text{ oz.}} \\ -12 \\ \hline 3\text{ lb.} \end{array}$$

2. Since 6 doesn't divide into 3, change 3 pounds to 48 ounces. Add 48 ounces to 6 ounces.

$3 \times 16 = 48$ ounces
$48 + 6 = 54$ ounces

3. Divide 6 into 54 ounces.

$$\begin{array}{r} 2\text{ lb.} \quad\quad 9\text{ oz.} \\ 6\overline{)15\text{ lb.}\quad\quad 6\text{ oz.}} \\ -12 \\ \hline 3\text{ lb.} = +48\text{ oz.} \\ 54\text{ oz.} \\ -54 \\ \hline 0 \end{array}$$

Divide.

1.
$$\begin{array}{r} 2\text{ qt.}\quad\quad 1\tfrac{1}{2}\text{ pt.} \\ 2\overline{)5\text{ qt.}\quad\quad 1\text{ pt.}} \\ -4 \\ \hline 1\text{ qt.} = +2\text{ pt.} \\ 3\text{ pt.} \\ -2 \\ \hline 1 \end{array}$$

2. $3\overline{)3\text{ hr. }45\text{ min.}}$

3. $4\overline{)15\text{ ft. }8\text{ in.}}$

4. $5\overline{)19\text{ lb. }6\text{ oz.}}$

5. $2\overline{)3\text{ T. }600\text{ lb.}}$

6. $4\overline{)9\text{ yd. }1\text{ ft.}}$

7. $3\overline{)14\text{ min. }30\text{ sec.}}$

8. $5\overline{)17\text{ gal. }2\text{ qt.}}$

9. $5\overline{)7\text{ ft. }6\text{ in.}}$

Mixed Review

Change each measurement.

1. 4.75 gallons = _____ gallons _____ quarts

2. 9 yd. 8 in. = _____ in.

3. 340 sec. = _____ min. _____ sec.

4. 18 cups = _____ quarts _____ cups

5. 4 lb. 10 oz. = _____ oz.

6. 2 T. 200 lb. = _____ lb.

7. 9 pt. 1 c. = _____ pt.

8. 5 years 8 months = _____ years

9. $3\frac{1}{2}$ ft. = _____ ft. _____ in.

10. 6.25 lb. = _____ lb. _____ oz.

11. 15 in. = _____ ft. _____ in.

12. 90 min. = _____ hr. _____ min.

Compare. Write >, <, or =.

13. 1 gallon 1 quart ☐ 6 quarts

14. $3\frac{1}{2}$ pounds ☐ 3 pounds 2 ounces

Simplify.

15. 3 cups 25 ounces =

16. 8 feet 92 inches =

Add, subtract, multiply, or divide. Simplify if possible.

17.
```
   2 pt. 1 c.
+ 6 pt. 5 c.
```

18.
```
            3 ft. 7 in.
+ 1 yd.          9 in.
```

19.
```
  6 hr. 20 min.
− 3 hr. 30 min.
```

20.
```
  15 tons
−        700 pounds
```

21.
```
  5 gal. 3 qt.
×           4
```

22.
```
5) 21 hours 30 minutes
```

Solve.

23. Norma is putting together baskets of fresh fruit for residents of a nursing home. She has 24 pounds 12 ounces of oranges to divide evenly into 18 baskets. How many pounds of oranges will Norma put in each basket?

24. Lorenzo attends class 3 nights a week at the community college. Each class is 1 hour 10 minutes long. How much time does Lorenzo spend each week in class?

Answer_____

Answer_____

Understanding the Metric System

The metric system is the most widely used system of measurement in the world. It is based on the decimal system so all metric measurements can be multiplied or divided by 10, 100, 1,000, and so on. The three basic units of the metric system are the meter, the gram, and the liter.

1 gram

The meter is used to measure length. A meter is about 3 inches longer than a yard.

The gram is used to measure weight. A gram is about the weight of an aspirin.

The liter is used to measure capacity. A liter is a little more than a quart.

1 liter
33.8 oz.

1 quart
32 oz.

1 meter
about 39"

1 yard
36"

Circle the letter of the correct basic unit: meter, gram, or liter.

1. A paper clip weighs about 1
   a. meter.
   b. gram.
   c. liter.

2. The length of a checkout counter is about 3
   a. meters.
   b. grams.
   c. liters.

3. A large can of paint remover is about 1
   a. meter.
   b. gram.
   c. liter.

4. A quarter weighs about 5
   a. meters.
   b. grams.
   c. liters.

5. A gallon of liquid floor stripper is about 4
   a. meters.
   b. grams.
   c. liters.

6. An office building is about 400 _____ high.
   a. meters
   b. grams
   c. liters

7. A 5-gallon container holds about 19 _____ of gasoline.
   a. meters
   b. grams
   c. liters

8. One aisle of the local hardware store is about 20 _____ long.
   a. meters
   b. grams
   c. liters

9. A gallon of industrial cleaner is about 4
   a. meters.
   b. grams.
   c. liters.

10. The amount of amalgam in a tooth filling is about 2
   a. meters.
   b. grams.
   c. liters.

Understanding the Metric System

The metric system combines prefixes and the basic units to form other units. For example, kilogram has the prefix, *kilo-*, in front of the basic unit, gram. Kilo- means 1,000, so a kilogram is 1,000 grams.

The table below lists the commonly used prefixes and their meanings.

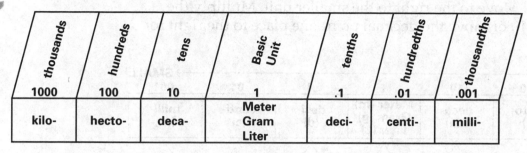

thousands	hundreds	tens	Basic Unit	tenths	hundredths	thousandths
1000	100	10	1	.1	.01	.001
kilo-	hecto-	deca-	Meter Gram Liter	deci-	centi-	milli-

You write small metric measurements using milli-, centi-, and deci- with a basic unit.

> A milligram is .001 gram.
> A centimeter is .01 meter.
> A deciliter is .1 liter.

You write large metric measurements using deca-, hecto-, and kilo- with a basic unit.

> A decagram is 10 grams.
> A hectoliter is 100 liters.
> A kilometer is 1,000 meters.

Circle the letter of the measurement you would probably see.

1. A delivery route is about 200
   a. centimeters.
   b. meters.
   c. kilometers. *(circled)*

2. An eyedropper full of medicine is about 1
   a. milliliter.
   b. liter.
   c. hectoliter.

3. A postage stamp weighs about 15
   a. milligrams.
   b. grams.
   c. kilograms.

4. A screwdriver weighs about 50
   a. milligrams.
   b. grams.
   c. kilograms.

5. A half-gallon of liquid hand soap is about 2
   a. milliliters.
   b. liters.
   c. hectoliters.

6. The length of a pencil is about 12
   a. centimeters.
   b. meters.
   c. kilometers.

Changing from a Large Unit to a Smaller Unit

When working with metric measurements, you may want to change a large unit to a smaller unit. For example, a decimal number such as .001 liter can be changed to a whole number by changing liters to milliliters.

To change from a large unit to a smaller unit, use the chart below. Find the original unit. Move to the right to the smaller unit. Multiply the original unit by 10 or move the decimal point one place to the right for each step.

LARGE ← ———————————————————————————————— → SMALL

1000	100	10	1	.1	.01	.001
kilo- (k)	hecto- (h)	deca- (da)	Meter (m) Gram (g) Liter (L)	deci- (d)	centi- (c)	milli- (m)

You can write abbreviations for metric units by combining the first letters of the prefix with the letter for the basic unit. For example, the abbreviation for kilometer is *km*, *k* for kilo- and *m* for meter.

Use These Steps

.02 kilometers = _____ meters

1. **Find *kilo-* in the table.**

2. **Find *meter* in the table.**

3. **Count the number of steps, 3, from kilo- to meter. Move the decimal point 3 places to the right. Add a zero.**

Kilo- is in the far left box.

Meter is in the center box.

.020

.02 kilometers = 20 meters

Change each measurement.

1. .05 km = __50__ m
   .05 km = .050 m

2. .9 m = _____ cm

3. .14 cm = _____ mm

4. .006 L = _____ mL

5. 8.3 L = _____ dL

6. 1.2 g = _____ mg

7. 13 kg = _____ g

8. 53 hL = _____ L

9. 50 dg = _____ mg

10. An average cab ride is 5 km. How many meters are in 5 km?

11. A fully-packed box of truck parts weighs 45.25 kg. How many grams are in 45.25 kg?

Answer_____

Answer_____

Changing from a Small Unit to a Larger Unit

When working with metric measurements, you may want to change from a small unit to a larger unit. For example, a large metric measurement such as 250,000 cm can be changed to a smaller metric measurement by changing cm to km.

To change from a small unit to a larger unit, use the chart below. Find the original unit. Move to the left to the larger unit. Divide the original measurement by 10 or move the decimal point one place to the left for each step.

LARGE ←——————————————————————————→ SMALL

1000	100	10	1	.1	.01	.001
kilo- (k)	hecto- (h)	deca- (da)	Meter (m) Gram (g) Liter (L)	deci- (d)	centi- (c)	milli- (m)

Use These Steps

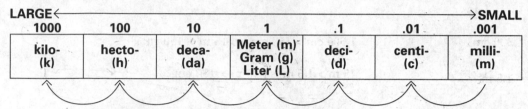

120 centimeters = _____ meters

1. **Find *centi-* in the table.**

   Centi- is on the right.

2. **Find *meter* in the table.**

   Meter is in the center box.

3. **Count the number of steps, 2, from centi- to meter. Move the decimal point 2 places to the left.**

   120.

   120 centimeters = 1.2 meters

Change each measurement.

1. 1,700 mm = __170__ cm
    1,700 mm = 1700. cm

2. 8,200 liters = _____ kiloliters

3. 9 milligrams = _____ grams

4. 5,000 centimeters = _____ meters

5. 650 deciliters = _____ liters

6. 20,000 g = _____ kg

7. 32,000 m = _____ km

8. 100,000 mL = _____ L

9. Jason walks 800 meters to work. How many kilometers is 800 meters?

    Answer_____

10. A large serving of juice in the employee cafeteria contains 340 mL. What part of a liter is 340 mL?

    Answer_____

Comparing Metric Measurements

To compare metric measurements, you must compare like units. For example, which is larger, 15 m or 150 cm? You can change 15 meters to centimeters or change 150 centimeters to meters.

Use These Steps

Compare 15 m to 150 cm.

1. Change 15 m to centimeters or change 150 cm to meters.

   15 m = 1500 = 1,500 cm
   or
   150 cm = 150 = 1.5 m

2. Compare.

   1,500 cm > 150 cm, so 15 m > 150 cm
   or
   15 m > 1.5 m, so 15 m > 150 cm

Compare the units of measure. Write >, <, or =.

1. 2 L $\boxed{>}$ 20 mL
   2 L = 2000 = 2,000 mL
   or
   20 mL = 020 = .02 L
   2,000 mL > 20 mL or 2 L > .02 L

2. 35 cm $\boxed{}$ 35 km

3. 750 mg $\boxed{}$ 7.5 hg

4. 3.6 kL $\boxed{}$ 36,000 L

5. 39 cg $\boxed{}$ 390 mg

6. 4 km $\boxed{}$ 400 m

7. 8 L $\boxed{}$ 8 daL

8. 9.5 dam $\boxed{}$ 95 m

9. 11 mL $\boxed{}$ .00011 kL

10. 3 kg $\boxed{}$ 30 g

11. .7 g $\boxed{}$ 700 mg

12. 10 cm $\boxed{}$ 10 mm

13. 14 g $\boxed{}$ 14 kg

14. 1,800 mm $\boxed{}$ 18 m

15. .2 dg $\boxed{}$ .02 g

Working with Metric Measurements

When you add or subtract metric units, add or subtract only like units. Change the smaller unit to the larger unit. Then add or subtract.

Use These Steps

Add   18 m + 500 cm = ____ m

1. Change 500 centimeters to meters, the larger unit.

   500 cm = 500 = 5 m

2. Add the meters.

   18
   + 5
   ___
   23

Change to the larger unit. Then add.

1. $45 g + 3 cg = \underline{45.03} g$
   3 cg = .03 = .03 g
      45
   +   .03
   _____
      45.03

2. $190 L + 2 kL = \underline{\quad} kL$

3. $800 mm + 3 cm = \underline{\quad} cm$

4. $15 L + 190 mL = \underline{\quad} L$

5. $89 dag + 6 g = \underline{\quad} dag$

6. $2 km + 500 m = \underline{\quad} km$

Change to the larger unit. Then subtract.

7. $25 L - 160 mL = \underline{24.84} L$
   160 mL = 160 = .16 L
      25.00
   -    .16
   _____
      24.84

8. $95 cm - 10 mm = \underline{\quad} cm$

9. $17 hL - 5 L = \underline{\quad} hL$

10. $10 kg - 10,000 mg = \underline{\quad} kg$

11. $3.5 km - 100 m = \underline{\quad} km$

12. $6.7 g - 12 dg = \underline{\quad} g$

13. Sami rode 3 km on her bicycle on Saturday making deliveries. On Sunday she rode 3,000 m. How far did she ride all together?

    Answer_____

14. Carl installed an air conditioning unit that weighed 90.5 kg. When he removed the box and packing material, it weighed 9,000 g less. How much did the air conditioning unit actually weigh?

    Answer_____

Working with Metric Measurements

When you multiply or divide metric measurements, follow the same steps you use in multiplying and dividing decimals. Be sure to put the decimal point in the correct place in your answer.

If your answer in a multiplication problem is a large number, change to a smaller number by changing to a larger unit. If your answer in a division problem is a small decimal number, change to a larger number by changing to a smaller unit.

Use These Steps

Multiply 30×350 m = _____ km

1. Set up the problem.

$$\begin{array}{r} 350 \\ \times\ 30 \\ \hline \end{array}$$

2. Multiply.

$$\begin{array}{r} 350 \\ \times\ 30 \\ \hline 10{,}500 \end{array}$$

3. Change to kilometers, the largest meter unit.

10,500 m = 10500 = 10.5 km

Multiply. Change each answer to the larger unit given.

1. 900 L $\times$ 15 = __13.5__ kL

$$\begin{array}{r} 900 \\ \times\ 15 \\ \hline 13{,}500\ \text{L} \end{array}$$

13,500 L = 13500 = 13.5 kL

2. 625 mg $\times$ 10 = ____ g

3. 1,460 cm $\times$ 40 = ____ km

4. 200 mL $\times$ 6 = ____ L

5. 25 mg $\times$ 7 = ____ cg

6. 350 dm $\times$ 50 = ____ dam

Divide. Change each answer to the smaller unit given.

7. 2.4 kL $\div$ 4 = __600__ L

$$\begin{array}{r} .6\ \text{kL} \\ 4\overline{)2.4} \\ -2\,4 \\ \hline \end{array}$$

.6 kL = 600 = 600 L

8. 60 m $\div$ 100 = ____ cm

9. .03 g $\div$ 2 = ____ mg

Problem Solving: Comparing Measurements Between Systems

In the United States, we use the metric system for science, medicine, and photography. The customary system is used in the building trades. Auto part and food product information may be given in metric as well as customary measurements.

Sometimes it is necessary to compare the units in one system to units in the other system. There are five important changes or approximate equivalents in the tables below. Only the change from the inch to the centimeter is exact. The others are approximations. The symbol ≈ means *approximately equal to.*

> 1 inch = 2.54 centimeters

> 1 meter ≈ 39.37 inches
> 1 kilometer ≈ 0.62 miles
> 1 kilogram ≈ 2.2 pounds
> 1 liter ≈ 1.06 quarts

Example While stocking shelves at the market, Jake noticed that 1 quart of orange juice and 1 liter of orange juice were the same price. Which is the better value, the quart or the liter?

▶ **Step 1.** Find the relationship of liters and quarts in the table.

1 liter ≈ 1.06 quarts

▶ **Step 2.** Compare the two measures. Since 1 liter holds more than 1 quart, 1 liter is larger.

The liter of orange juice is the better value.

Compare each measurement.

1. Dwayne noticed a road sign showing the distance to Tarrytown as 1 kilometer. Does Dwayne have to drive more than a mile or less than a mile to get to Tarrytown?

2. Isaiah has entered the 1,000 meter charity walkathon at work. Pete says 1,000 meters is about $\frac{6}{10}$ of a mile. Is Pete right?

Answer_____

Answer_____

Compare each measurement.

3. Scott drove to Canada to attend a training seminar. The gas tank of his car holds 22 gallons. Will he be able to fill the gas tank when it is empty if he puts in 22 liters of gas?

Answer_____

4. Mariana found 1 kilogram of hamburger in the freezer at the diner. She needs 2 pounds to make a meat loaf. Does she have enough hamburger?

Answer_____

5. Gwen needs 10 yards of wire fence to put around a garden. She has 10 meters. Will she have enough wire fence?

Answer_____

6. Penny told one of her patients she should gain about 3 pounds a month while she is pregnant. Should Penny's patient gain more or less than a kilogram a month?

Answer_____

7. The speedometer on Ken's delivery van shows kilometers per hour instead of miles per hour. Will he be speeding if he goes 40 kilometers per hour in a 40 mile-per-hour speed zone?

Answer_____

8. Bart needed a 2-inch screw to fix a broken chair leg. He found one 2 centimeters long. Will the screw he found be too short or too long to fix the chair?

Answer_____

9. Casey has to mail a package to a client overseas. The package weighs 5 kilograms. The postal service has a 15-pound limit on the weight of packages sent to that location. Will Casey be able to mail the package?

Answer_____

10. Sherry bought a gallon of ice cream for a party at the warehouse. Did she buy more or less than a liter of ice cream?

Answer_____

Unit 2 Review

Change each measurement.

1. $2\frac{1}{2}$ days = _____ days _____ hours

2. 3.75 miles = _____ miles _____ feet

3. 9 yards 2 feet = _____ yards

4. 6 hours 45 minutes = _____ hours

5. 3 feet 4 inches = _____ inches

6. 2 tons 1,000 pounds = _____ pounds

7. 5,000 lb. = _____ T. _____ lb.

8. 45 ounces = _____ cups _____ ounces

Compare the units of measure. Write >, <, or =.

9. 5' 5" ☐ $5\frac{1}{2}$ feet

10. 3.6 hours ☐ 3 hours 10 minutes

Simplify.

11. 3 gallons 9 quarts =

12. 9 yards 15 feet =

Add, subtract, multiply, or divide. Simplify if possible.

13.
$$\begin{array}{r} 5 \text{ pints } 2 \text{ cups} \\ + \ 7 \text{ pints } 8 \text{ cups} \\ \hline \end{array}$$

14.
$$\begin{array}{r} 3 \text{ gal.} \quad\ \ 3 \text{ pt.} \\ + \qquad 7 \text{ qt. } 3 \text{ pt.} \\ \hline \end{array}$$

15.
$$\begin{array}{r} 6 \text{ miles } 100 \text{ feet} \\ - \ 2 \text{ miles } 900 \text{ feet} \\ \hline \end{array}$$

16.
$$\begin{array}{r} 10 \text{ hr.} \qquad\ \ 70 \text{ sec.} \\ - \qquad 40 \text{ min. } 30 \text{ sec.} \\ \hline \end{array}$$

17.
$$\begin{array}{r} 12 \text{ feet } 11 \text{ inches} \\ \times \qquad\qquad\quad 7 \\ \hline \end{array}$$

18.
$$4\overline{)17 \text{ pounds } 4 \text{ ounces}}$$

Circle the correct metric measurement.

19. A box of sugar weighs about 453
    a. meters.
    b. grams.
    c. liters.

20. The height of a tree is about 16
    a. meters.
    b. grams.
    c. liters.

21. It takes about 20 minutes to walk 2
    a. centimeters.
    b. meters.
    c. kilometers.

22. A serving of salt is about 80
    a. milligrams.
    b. grams.
    c. kilograms.

Change each measurement.

23. 2 kilometers = _____ meters

24. 17 meters = _____ centimeters

25. 40 grams = _____ milligrams

26. 5 liters = _____ dekaliters

27. 15 liters = _____ kiloliters

28. 200 grams = _____ kilograms

29. 30 mm = _____ cm

30. 300 cg = _____ grams

Compare. Write >, <, or =.

31. 97 L ☐ 2 kL

32. 3.6 m ☐ 3,600 mm

33. 470 g ☐ 5 dag

34. 2 km ☐ 5,000 m

Add, subtract, multiply, or divide.

35. 35 grams + 150 milligrams =

36. 57 kL − 200 L =

37. 14.6 m × 9 =

38. 1,600 cm ÷ 40 =

Below is a list of the problems in this review and the pages on which the skills are taught. If you missed any problems, turn to the pages listed and practice the skills. Then correct the problems you missed in the Unit Review.

Problems	Pages		Problems	Pages
1-2	43		17-18	57-58
3-4	44		19-20	60
5-6	45		21-22	61
7-8	46		23-30	62-63
9-10	47		31-34	64
11-12	50		35-38	65-66
13-16	51-54			

Unit **3** GEOMETRY

Geometric shapes are all around us: windows and doors are rectangles, many roofs form triangles, and most pots, pans, plates, cups, and cans are circular. Street signs and road intersections are based on geometric shapes and ideas.

In this unit you will learn about angles and geometric shapes. You will become familiar with the formulas to find perimeter, area, and volume. You will also learn how to solve problems using perimeter, area, and volume.

Getting Ready

You should be familiar with the skills on this page and the next before you begin this unit. To check your answers, turn to page 196.

 When working with geometry, you will be working with whole numbers.

Add, subtract, multiply, or divide.

1.
$$\begin{array}{r} 7 \\ 8 \\ 12 \\ +\ 3 \\ \hline 30 \end{array}$$

2.
$$\begin{array}{r} 14 \\ \times\ 14 \\ \hline \end{array}$$

3. $3\overline{)180}$

4.
$$\begin{array}{r} 20 \\ 19 \\ +\ 7 \\ \hline \end{array}$$

5. $4\overline{)360}$

6.
$$\begin{array}{r} 12 \\ \times\ 8 \\ \hline \end{array}$$

7.
$$\begin{array}{r} 90 \\ -\ 35 \\ \hline \end{array}$$

8.
$$\begin{array}{r} 56 \\ +124 \\ \hline \end{array}$$

9.
$$\begin{array}{r} 100 \\ -\ 45 \\ \hline \end{array}$$

10.
$$\begin{array}{r} 12 \\ \times\ 10 \\ \hline \end{array}$$

For review, see **Math Skills for the Workforce, Whole Numbers.**   71

Getting Ready

 When working with geometry, you will also be working with fractions.

Add, subtract, multiply, or divide. Reduce if possible.

11.

$1\frac{1}{4} - \frac{3}{4} =$

$1\frac{1}{4} = \frac{5}{4}$

$-\frac{3}{4} = \frac{3}{4}$

$\frac{2}{4} = \frac{1}{2}$

12.

$17\frac{3}{4} + 6 =$

13.

$90 - 15\frac{1}{2} =$

14.

$27 \div 4\frac{1}{2} =$

15.

$15 \div \frac{1}{3} =$

16.

$3\frac{1}{2} \times 6 =$

17.

$7\frac{1}{10} + 2\frac{3}{5} =$

18.

$\frac{5}{7} - \frac{1}{3} =$

19.

$15\frac{1}{4} \times 4 =$

For review, see **Math Skills for the Workforce, Fractions.**

 You should also be familiar with decimal operations.

Add, subtract, multiply, or divide. Round division answers to the nearest hundredth.

20.

$19 - 3.7 =$

19.0

$- \ \ 3.7$

15.3

21.

$8.5 \times 7 =$

22.

$10 - 3.5 =$

23.

$4.1 + 2.9 =$

24.

$3.2 - 2.7 =$

25.

$.9 \times .2 =$

26.

$2.6 \div 1.3 =$

27.

$45 \div 5.5 =$

28.

$8.2 \times 19 =$

For review, see **Math Skills for the Workforce, Decimals and Percents.**

Lines and Angles

When two lines come together at a common point, they form an angle. The point where they come together is called the vertex of the angle. The symbol for an angle is ∠. The angle shown can be written as ∠B or ∠ABC. When three letters are used to name an angle, the middle letter is the vertex.

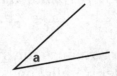

Sometimes a small letter or number is used to name an angle. The letter or number is usually placed inside the angle.

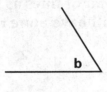

Write the name of each angle.

1.

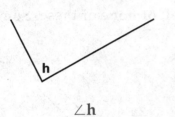

∠h

2.

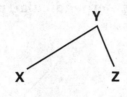

_____

3.

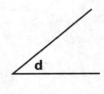

_____

4.

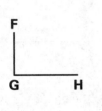

_____

5.

_____

6.

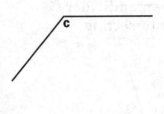

_____

Label this angle ∠LMN.

7.

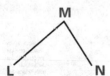

Label this angle ∠s.

8.

Draw two different angles. Label the first one ∠k and label the second one ∠MNO.

9.

10.

Lines and Angles

When two lines cross, the lines intersect. Intersecting lines form four angles with a point in common.

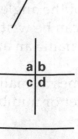

When two lines cross forming two or four equal angles, the lines are perpendicular. The equal angles may be written as ∠a = ∠b = ∠c = ∠d. The symbol for perpendicular lines is ⊥.

When two lines run side-by-side and never cross, the lines are parallel. Parallel lines are always the same distance apart. The symbol for parallel lines is ||.

Label each pair of lines as intersecting, perpendicular, parallel, or none of these. Some questions will have more than one answer.

1.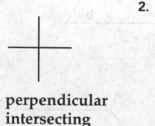

perpendicular
intersecting

2.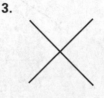

_____

3.

_____

4.

_____

5.

_____

6.

_____

7.

_____

8.

_____

Label the pairs below as parallel, perpendicular, or intersecting.

9. Pacific Avenue and the railroad

_____

10. Atlantic Avenue and Ocean Blvd.

_____

11. Ocean Blvd. and Pacific Avenue

_____

12. Pacific Avenue and Atlantic Avenue

_____

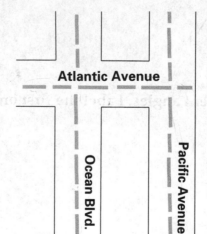

Measuring Angles

The size of the opening of an angle is measured in degrees. The symbol for degrees is °. An angle of 30 degrees is written 30°. A large angle has a larger opening and will have a greater number of degrees than a smaller angle.

A measuring device called a protractor is used to measure angles. A protractor has marks showing degrees from 0° to 180°.

Most protractors have two scales. The bottom line of the angle will cross 0° either on the outside scale or the inside scale. Use the correct scale to measure each angle.

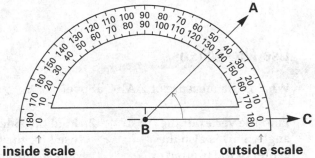

↑
inside scale   ↑
                          outside scale

Use These Steps

What is the measure of ∠ABC above?

1. Find the vertex of the angle. This is also the center of the protractor.

2. Find the side of the angle used for the bottom or base line. This side of the angle crosses at 0° on the outside scale.

3. Find the mark on the outside scale where the other side of the angle crosses the protractor. Write the measure of this angle with the degree symbol.

∠ABC = 45°

Find the measure of each angle.

1.

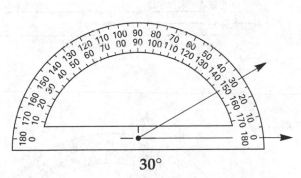

30°

2.

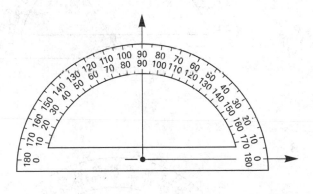

3.

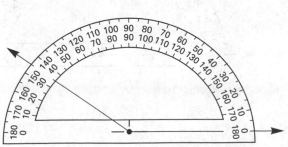

4.

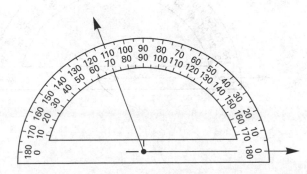

75

Measuring Angles

Protractors have two scales to make measuring angles easier. Find the scale where the base line of the angle crosses 0°. Use that scale to measure the angle.

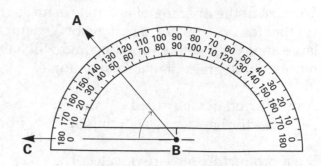

Use These Steps

What is the measure of ∠ABC above?

1. Find the vertex of the angle. This is also the center of the protractor.

2. Find the side of the angle used for the base line. This side of the angle crosses at 0° on the inside scale.

3. Find the mark on the inside scale where the other side of the angle crosses the protractor. Write the measure of this angle with the degree symbol.

∠ABC = 50°

Find the measure of each angle.

1.

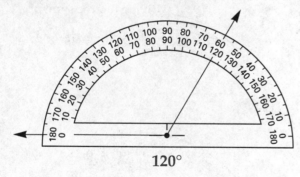

120°

2.

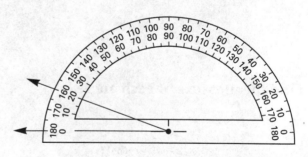

3.

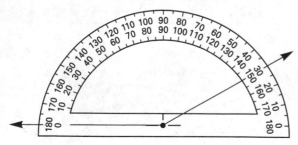

4.

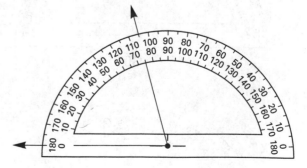

Measuring Angles

Types of angles are named according to their measures. Right angles are marked with a box at the vertex of the 90° angle.

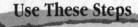

| 90° right angle | between 0° and 90° acute angle | between 90° and 180° obtuse angle | 180° straight angle |

Use These Steps

Find the measure of the angle.
Write the name of the angle.

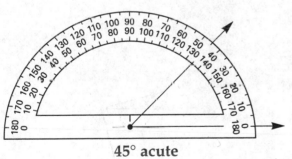

1. Find the vertex of the angle.

2. Find the side of the angle used for the base line. Use either the outside or inside scale to find the measure of the angle.

90°

3. Write the type of angle.

right angle

Find the measure of each angle. Write the type of angle.

1.

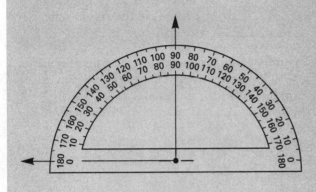

45° acute

2.

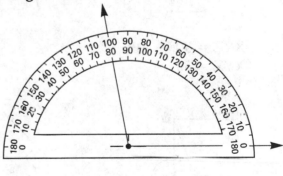

3.

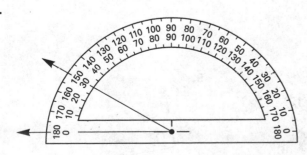

4.

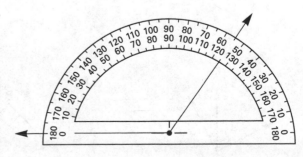

Complementary Angles

Two angles are called complementary angles if the sum of both angles is 90°. For example, ∠ABC is the complement of ∠CBD, and ∠CBD is the complement of ∠ABC. The small box in the vertex of the angle means 90°.

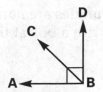

When you are given an angle and asked to find its complement, subtract the given angle from 90°.

Use These Steps

Find the measure of ∠ABD.

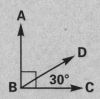

1. Set up the problem.

   ∠ABD = 90° − ∠DBC

2. Subtract 30°, the given angle, from 90°, the total degrees in the right angle, ∠ABC.

   ∠ABD = 90° − 30°
   ∠ABD = 60°

Find the measure of the complementary angle.

1.

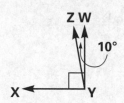

∠XYZ = 90° − 10°
∠XYZ = 80°

2.

3.

4.

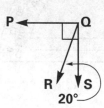

5.

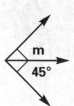

6.

7.

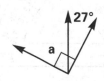

8.

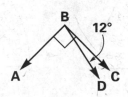

9.

78

Supplementary Angles

Two angles are called supplementary angles if the sum of both angles is 180°, the number of degrees in a straight line. For example, ∠XYZ is the supplement of ∠ZYW, and ∠ZYW is the supplement of ∠XYZ.

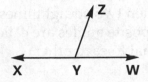

When you are given an angle and asked to find its supplement, subtract the given angle from 180°.

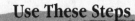

Use These Steps

Find the measure of ∠CBD.

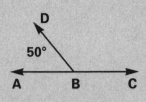

1. Set up the problem.

∠CBD = 180° − ∠ABD

2. Subtract 50°, the given angle, from 180°, the total degrees in the straight angle, ∠ABC.

∠CBD = 180° − 50°
∠CBD = 130°

Find the measure of the supplementary angle.

1.

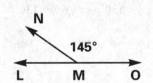

∠LMN = 180° − 145°
∠LMN = 35°

2.

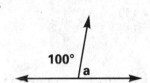

3.

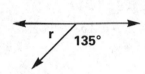

4.

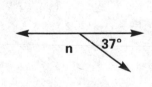

5.

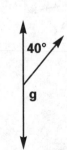

6.

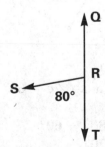

Vertical Angles

When two straight lines cross, they form four angles. The opposite angles are called vertical angles. Vertical angles are equal to each other.

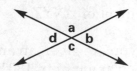

∠a and ∠c are vertical angles, so ∠a = ∠c.
∠b and ∠d are vertical angles, so ∠b = ∠d.

Notice that ∠a + ∠b = 180° and ∠c + ∠d = 180°. These angles are two examples of supplementary angles. You can also see that ∠a + ∠d = 180° and ∠c + ∠d = 180°.

Use These Steps

If ∠a = 50°, what are the measures of ∠b, ∠c, and ∠d?

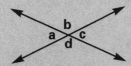

1. ∠a and ∠c are vertical angles, so ∠c = ∠a.

   ∠a = 50°
   ∠a = ∠c, so ∠c = 50°

2. ∠a and ∠b are supplementary angles and equal 180°. Subtract to find ∠b.

   ∠b = 180° − 50°
   ∠b = 130°

3. ∠b and ∠d are vertical angles, so ∠d = ∠b.

   ∠b = 130°, so ∠d = 130°

Find the measure of the three remaining angles in each figure.

1.

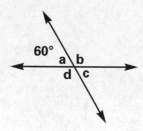

∠a = 60°
∠c = ∠a, so ∠c = 60°

∠b = 180° − 60°
∠b = 120°

∠d = ∠b
∠b = 120°, so ∠d = 120°

2.

100°

3.

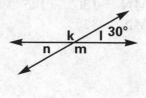

Transversals

When two parallel lines are cut by a third line, a transversal, eight angles are formed. Certain pairs of angles are equal and each pair has a name.

Corresponding angles are equal.

$$\angle 1 = \angle 5$$
$$\angle 2 = \angle 6$$
$$\angle 3 = \angle 7$$
$$\angle 4 = \angle 8$$

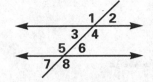

Alternate interior (inside) angles are equal.

$$\angle 3 = \angle 6$$
$$\angle 4 = \angle 5$$

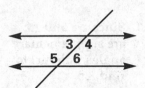

Alternate exterior (outside) angles are equal.

$$\angle 1 = \angle 8$$
$$\angle 2 = \angle 7$$

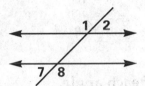

Use These Steps

If $\angle 1 = 115°$, what is the measure of $\angle 8$?

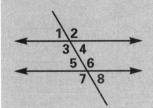

1. Find $\angle 1$ and $\angle 8$.

2. Since these angles are alternate exterior angles, they are equal.

$$\angle 1 = 115°$$
$$\angle 8 = \angle 1, \text{ so } \angle 8 = 115°$$

Find the measure of the angles given using the figure below.

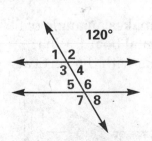

120°

1. $\angle 1 =$
$\angle 1 + \angle 2 = 180°$
$\angle 1 = 180° - \angle 2$
$\angle 1 = 180° - 120°$
$\angle 1 = 60°$

2. $\angle 4 =$

3. $\angle 3 =$

4. $\angle 7 =$

5. $\angle 6 =$

6. $\angle 5 =$

Transversals

When two parallel lines are crossed by a transversal, certain angles are equal. You can find unknown angles if you know one of the angles. The four acute angles that are formed are equal. The four obtuse angles that are formed are equal.

You can also use complements and supplements to find the measure of an unknown angle.

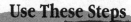

Use These Steps

Find the measure of each unknown angle.

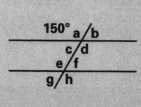

1. Since ∠a and ∠b are supplementary angles, subtract to find ∠b.

   ∠b = 180° − ∠a
   ∠b = 180° − 150°
   ∠b = 30°

2. The four acute angles are equal.

   ∠b = ∠c = ∠f = ∠g = 30°

3. The four obtuse angles are equal.

   ∠a = ∠d = ∠e = ∠h = 150°

Find the measure of each angle.

1.

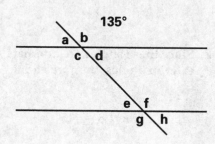

2.

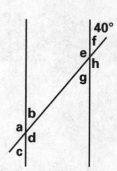

3. Airport Road crosses Eighth and Ninth Streets at a 45° angle. What is the measure of ∠a?

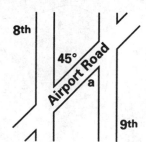

4. This cross brace makes an angle of 30° with each horizontal board. What angle does it make with the vertical boards?

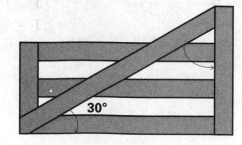

Mixed Review

Write acute, obtuse, or right for the type of each angle.

1.

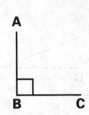

2.

3.

4.

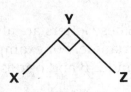

Find each angle measure.

5.

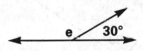

6.

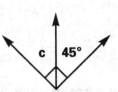

Find the measure of each angle. All right angles are marked.

7.

8.

9.

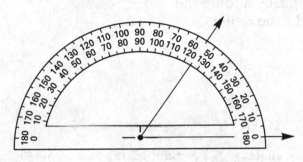

10.

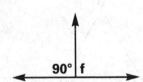

11.

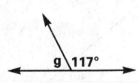

12.

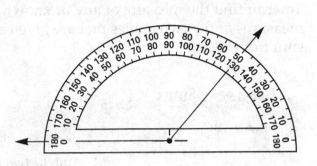

13.

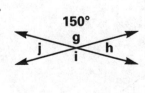

14.

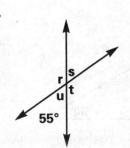

15.

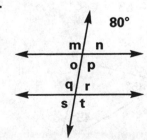

Triangles

A triangle has three sides and three angles. Triangles are usually shown with a letter at the vertex of each angle to name the angles.

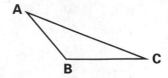

These letters are also used to represent each side of the triangle. For example, line AB or $\overline{AB}$, is the line between $\angle A$ and $\angle B$ and opposite $\angle C$.

The sum of the three angles in a triangle is 180°.
$\angle A + \angle B + \angle C = 180°$.

You can find the measure of any unknown angle by adding the measures of the two angles that are given and subtracting the sum from 180°.

Use These Steps

Find $\angle ABC$.

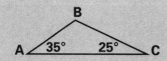

1. Add the two given angles.

$$35° + 25° = 60°$$

2. Subtract the sum from 180°.

$$180° - 60° = 120°$$
$$\angle ABC = 120°$$

Find the measure of each unknown angle.

1.

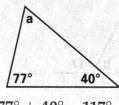

$$77° + 40° = 117°$$
$$180° - 117° = 63°$$
$$\angle a = 63°$$

2.

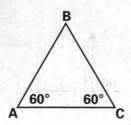

3.

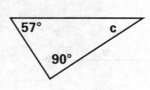

4.

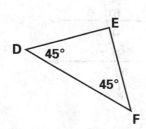

5.

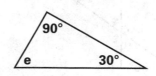

6.

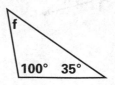

84

Triangles

A scalene triangle has no equal sides and no equal angles.

A scalene triangle may sometimes be a right triangle. A triangle with a 90° angle, or a right angle, is called a right triangle.

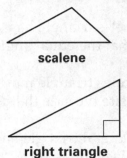

scalene

right triangle

Use These Steps

Find ∠E.

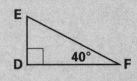

1. **Find the measure of ∠D.**

   ∠D = 90° since △EDF is a right triangle.

2. **Add ∠D + ∠F.**

   90° + 40° = 130°

3. **Subtract the sum from 180°.**

   180° − 130° = 50°
   ∠E = 50°

Find the measure of the unknown angle in each triangle.

1.

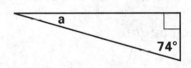

74° + 90° = 164°
180° − 164° = 16°
∠a = 16°

2.

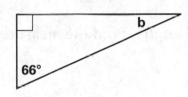

3.

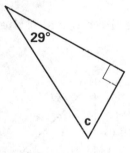

4.

5.

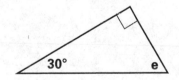

6.

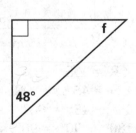

Triangles

An isosceles triangle has two equal sides and two equal angles. Notice that the equal angles are opposite the equal sides.

An isosceles triangle may be a right triangle. The 90° angle will be opposite the side that is not equal to the other two sides.

An equilateral triangle has three equal sides and three equal angles. Each angle is 60°.

Use These Steps

Find the measure of each angle.

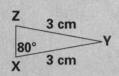

1. Since $\overline{XY} = \overline{ZY}$, this is an isosceles triangle. Find ∠XZY.

∠XZY = ∠ZXY
∠ZXY = 80°, so
∠XZY = 80°

2. Add the measures of the two angles.

80° + 80° = 160°

3. Subtract 160° to find ∠ZYX.

180° − 160° = 20°, so ∠ZYX = 20°

Write the names of the equal angles. Find the measure of each angle.

1.

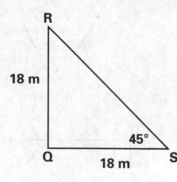

∠R = ∠S
∠S = 45°, so ∠R = 45°
45° + 45° = 90°
180° − 90° = 90°, so ∠Q = 90°

2.

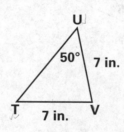

3.

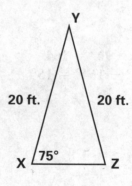

4.

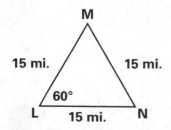

5.

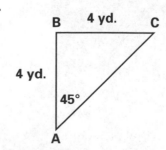

6.

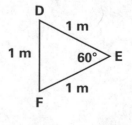

Triangles

If you know the measure of the unequal angle in an isosceles triangle, you can find the two equal angles.

Use These Steps

Find the measure of the two equal angles.

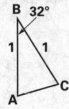

1. Subtract the given angle, B, from 180°.

   $180° - 70° = 110°$

2. Divide 110°, the sum of the two equal angles, A and C, by 2.

   $110° \div 2 = 55°$
   ∠A and ∠ C each measure 55°.

3. Check by adding the three angles.

   $70° + 55° + 55° = 180°$

Find the measure of the equal angles in each triangle. Check. All right angles are marked.

1.
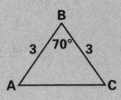

$180° - 32° = 148°$
$148° \div 2 = 74°$
$32° + 74° + 74° = 180°$

2.
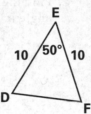

3.
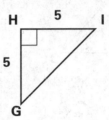

4.
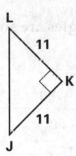

5.

6.
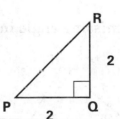

7.
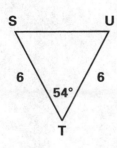

8.
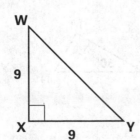

9.
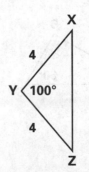

Similar Triangles

When two triangles are the same shape and have equal corresponding angle measures, they are called similar triangles. The sides of the two triangles may have different lengths, but the triangles are similar because they are the same shape and their corresponding angles are the same. For example, ∠A = ∠a and ∠C = ∠c.

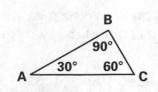

The names of the similar triangles must be listed in the order of their corresponding angles. The symbol △ means *triangle*. The symbol ~ means *similar to*.

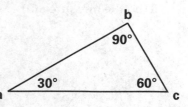

△ABC ~ △abc means that triangle ABC is similar to triangle abc.

Use These Steps

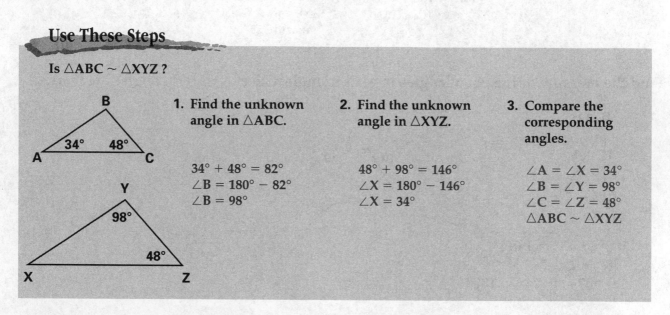

Is △ABC ~ △XYZ ?

1. Find the unknown angle in △ABC.

   34° + 48° = 82°
   ∠B = 180° − 82°
   ∠B = 98°

2. Find the unknown angle in △XYZ.

   48° + 98° = 146°
   ∠X = 180° − 146°
   ∠X = 34°

3. Compare the corresponding angles.

   ∠A = ∠X = 34°
   ∠B = ∠Y = 98°
   ∠C = ∠Z = 48°
   △ABC ~ △XYZ

Find the missing angle in each set of triangles below. Decide if the triangles are similar.

1.

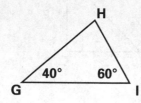

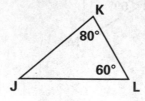

60° + 40° = 100°
180° − 100° = 80°

80° + 60° = 140°
180° − 140° = 40°

∠G = ∠J = 40°

∠H = ∠K = 80°

∠I = ∠L = 60°

△GHI ~ △JKL

2.

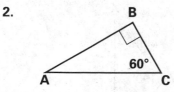

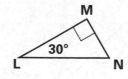

Similar Triangles

Corresponding sides of similar triangles form a fraction, or ratio. The ratios can be written as equivalent fractions, or a proportion.

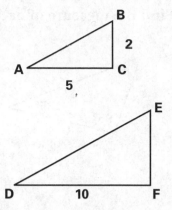

$$\triangle ABC \sim \triangle DEF, \text{ so } \frac{\overline{AB}}{\overline{DE}} = \frac{\overline{BC}}{\overline{EF}} = \frac{\overline{AC}}{\overline{DF}}$$

You can use a proportion to find the length of a side in a triangle if you know the length of its corresponding side in a similar triangle. You must also know the lengths of one more pair of corresponding sides.

Use These Steps

Find the length of $\overline{EF}$ in the triangle above.

1. Write a proportion using the pairs of corresponding sides.

$$\frac{\overline{EF}}{\overline{BC}} = \frac{\overline{DF}}{\overline{AC}}$$

2. Substitute the length of the sides in the proportion. Use n for the length of $\overline{EF}$.

$$\frac{n}{2} = \frac{10}{5}$$

3. Cross multiply to find the unknown side.

$$\frac{n}{2} \diagtimes \frac{10}{5}$$
$$5 \times n = 2 \times 10$$
$$5n = 20$$
$$n = 20 \div 5 = 4$$
$$\overline{EF} = 4$$

Find the length of the unknown side in each set of similar triangles.

1.

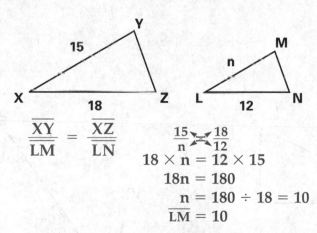

$$\frac{\overline{XY}}{\overline{LM}} = \frac{\overline{XZ}}{\overline{LN}}$$

$$\frac{15}{n} \diagtimes \frac{18}{12}$$
$$18 \times n = 12 \times 15$$
$$18n = 180$$
$$n = 180 \div 18 = 10$$
$$\overline{LM} = 10$$

2.

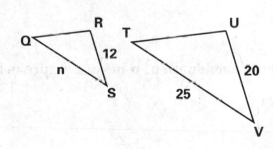

3.

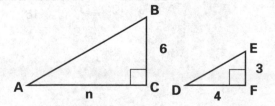

4.

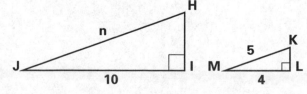

Mixed Review

Find the measure of each unknown angle.

1.

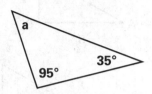

a
35°
95°

2.

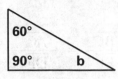

60°
90° b

3.

37°
c 55°

4.

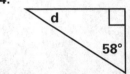

d
58°

5.

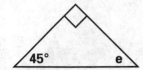

45° e

6.

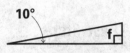

10°
f

7.

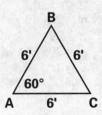

B
6' 6'
60°
A 6' C

8.

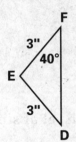

F
3"
40°
E
3"
D

9.

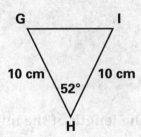

G I
10 cm 10 cm
52°
H

Find the length of n in each figure below.

10.

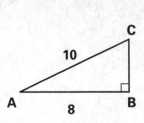

C
10
A B
8

Z
n
X Y
24

11.

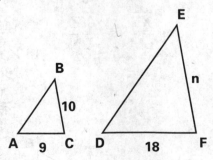

E
B
10 n
A 9 C D 18 F

Polygons

Flat figures with many sides and angles are called polygons.

A triangle is a polygon with three sides and three angles.

A rectangle is a polygon with four sides and four right angles. Each angle is 90°. The opposite sides are parallel and equal.

A square is a rectangle with four equal sides and four 90° angles.

A parallelogram is a polygon with four sides and four angles. The opposite sides are equal and parallel. The opposite angles are equal.

A trapezoid is a polygon with four sides and four angles. Only one pair of sides is parallel. All four sides and all four angles may be different.

triangle

rectangle

square

parallelogram

trapezoid

Write the name of each polygon.

1.

rectangle

2.

_____

3.

_____

4.

_____

5.

_____

6.

_____

7.

_____

8.

_____

9.

_____

Polygons

Regular polygons have equal sides and equal angles. An equilateral triangle and a square are regular polygons.

Equilateral triangle
3 equal sides
3 equal angles

Square
4 equal sides
4 right angles

Pentagon
5 equal sides
5 equal angles

Hexagon
6 equal sides
6 equal angles

Heptagon
7 equal sides
7 equal angles

Octagon
8 equal sides
8 equal angles

Write the name of each polygon.

1.

pentagon

2.

3.

4.

5.

6.

7.

8.

9.

Perimeter

Perimeter is the measure of the distance around the outside of a figure. To find the perimeter, add the lengths of the sides. The lengths of the sides may be written in a customary unit of length, such as inches or feet. The length of the sides may also be written in a metric unit of length, such as centimeters.

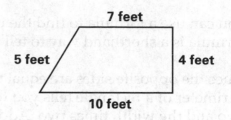

Use These Steps

Find the perimeter of the figure above.

1. Add the lengths of all the sides.

$$7 + 4 + 5 + 10 = 26$$

2. Since the units are in feet, write ft. after the total.

$$\text{perimeter} = 26 \text{ ft.}$$

Find the perimeter of each figure.

1.

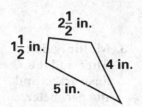

$$1\frac{1}{2} + 2\frac{1}{2} + 4 + 5 = 12\frac{2}{2} = 13 \text{ in.}$$

2.

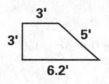

3.

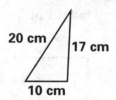

4.

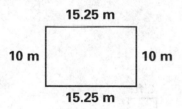

5.

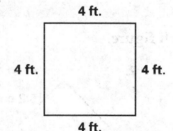

6.

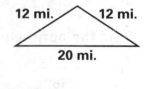

7. Bobbie is making shawls to sell. Each shawl is in the shape of a triangle with two sides each $5\frac{1}{2}$ feet long and one side 4 feet long. How many feet of fringe does Bobbie need to trim all three sides of the shawl?

8. Matt is building a fence around the public garden. The four sides are 20 feet, 15 feet, 18 feet, and 22 feet long. How many feet of fencing will Matt use in all?

Answer _____

Answer _____

Perimeter

You can use a formula to find the perimeter of a rectangle. A formula is a shorthand way to tell you how to solve a problem.

Since the opposite sides are equal in length, the formula for the perimeter of a rectangle tells you to multiply the length times two and the width times two. Add the two answers to find the perimeter.

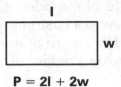

P = 2l + 2w

When a number and a letter are written together, like 2w, this means to multiply 2 times the width.

To find the perimeter of any figure with all equal sides, multiply the length of one side by the number of sides. For example, the formula for the perimeter of a square is P = 4s.

P = 4s

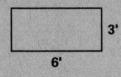

Find the perimeter.

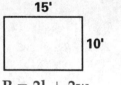

1. Write the formula.

2. Substitute 6' for the length and 3' for the width.

3. Multiply first. Then add the answers to find the perimeter.

P = 2l + 2w

P = 2 × 6 + 2 × 3

P = 2 × 6 + 2 × 3
P = 12 + 6
P = 18'

Find the perimeter of each figure.

1.

15'

10'

P = 2l + 2w
P = 2 × 15 + 2 × 10
P = 30 + 20
P = 50'

2.

5.2 cm

5.2 cm

3.

2 ft.

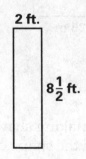

$8\frac{1}{2}$ ft.

4.

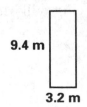

9.4 m

3.2 m

5.

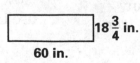

$18\frac{3}{4}$ in.

60 in.

6.

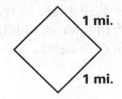

1 mi.

1 mi.

Circles and Circumference

A circle is also a flat figure. The distance from the center of a circle to any point on the edge is called the radius. The distance from one side of a circle to the other through the center is the diameter. The diameter is 2 times the length of the radius.

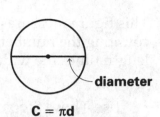

C = 2πr

The distance around a circle is called the circumference. The ratio of the circumference to the diameter is the same for all circles. This ratio, $\frac{c}{d}$, is *approximately equal to* ($\approx$) $\frac{22}{7}$ or 3.14. The Greek letter π (pi) is used to show this ratio.

You can use either formula to find the circumference.

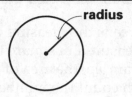

C = πd

Use These Steps

Find the circumference. Use $\frac{22}{7}$ for π.

7 in.

1. Since you have the radius, use this formula.

   $C = 2\pi r$

2. Substitute 7 for r and $\frac{22}{7}$ for π.

   $C = 2 \times \frac{22}{7} \times 7$

3. Cancel and multiply.

   $C = \frac{2}{1} \times \frac{22}{\cancel{7}} \times \frac{\cancel{7}^1}{1} = \frac{44}{1}$

   C = 44 inches

Find the circumference. Use $\frac{22}{7}$ for π.

1.

63"

2.

•70cm

3.

14 m

$C = 2\pi r$
$C = 2 \times \frac{22}{7} \times 63$

$C = \frac{2}{1} \times \frac{22}{\cancel{7}_1} \times \frac{\cancel{63}^9}{1} = \frac{396}{1}$

$C = 396"$

Find the circumference. Use 3.14 for π.

4.

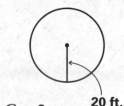

20 ft.

5.

4 mi.

6.

10'

$C = 2\pi r$
$C = 2 \times 3.14 \times 20$
$C = 125.6$ ft.

Area

Area is the measure of the space inside a flat figure. Area is measured in square units, even if the shape is not a square. For example, the area of the figure shown is 5 square units. You can count the number of whole squares and half squares to get 5 square units.

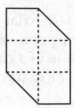

This figure measures 2 units on a side. You can find the area by counting the number of square units, 4, or by multiplying the length times the width, 2 × 2. The area is 4 square units.

Use These Steps

Find the area of the rectangle two ways.

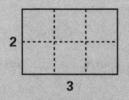

2

3

1. Count the number of square units.

   6 square units

   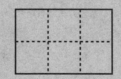

2. Multiply the length times the width. It does not matter which side is the length or width.

   2 × 3 = 6 square units

Find the area. Use both methods.

1.

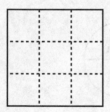

9 square units
3 × 3 = 9 square units

2.

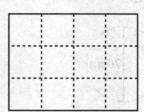

3.

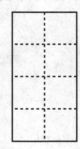

4.

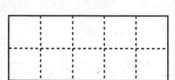

5.

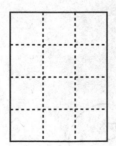

6.

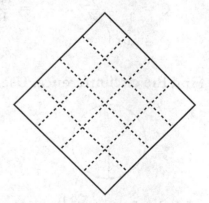

Area

You can find the area of a rectangle or square by using a formula. For example, you can find the area of a rectangle by multiplying its length times its width.

$A = lw$

Since all the sides of a square are equal, you can find the area of a square by multiplying side by side, or squaring the sides.

$A = s^2$

Use These Steps

Find the area.

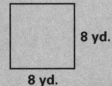

8 yd.

8 yd.

1. Write the formula for the area of a square.

   $A = s^2$

2. Substitute 8 for the length of any side.

   $A = 8^2$

3. Multiply. Write the answer in square units.

   $A = 8 \times 8$
   $A = 64$ sq. yd.

Find the area of each figure.

1.
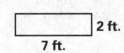
2 ft.
7 ft.

$A = lw$
$A = 7 \text{ ft.} \times 2 \text{ ft.}$
$A = 14$ sq. ft.

2.

3.1 m
3.1 m

3.

12 yd.
6 yd.

4.
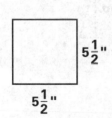
$5\frac{1}{2}$"
$5\frac{1}{2}$"

5.
7.25 cm
10.5 cm

6.
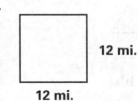
12 mi.
12 mi.

7. A contractor is painting a concrete driveway. The driveway is 30 feet long and 18 feet wide. What is the area of the driveway?

8. Stan needs to buy a sheet of plywood to cover the sandbox in front of the elementary school. The square sandbox is $7\frac{1}{2}$ feet long on each side. How many square feet of plywood does Stan need?

Answer _____

Answer _____

Area

The formula for finding the area of a triangle is $\frac{1}{2}$ the base (b) times the height (h). Any side can be used for the base. The height is a line drawn from the top and perpendicular to the base or to an extension of the base.

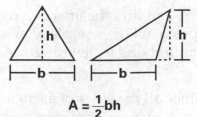

$$A = \frac{1}{2}bh$$

The area of a parallelogram equals the base (b) times the height (h). Any side can be used for the base. The height is a line perpendicular to the base or to an extension of the base.

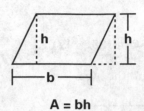

$$A = bh$$

Use These Steps

Find the area.

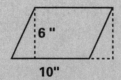

6 "

10"

1. Write the formula for the area of a parallelogram.

    $$A = bh$$

2. Substitute 10 for the base, b, and 6 for the height, h.

    $$A = 10 \times 6$$

3. Multiply. Write the answer in square units.

    $$A = 10 \times 6$$
    $$A = 60 \text{ sq. in.}$$

Find the area of each figure.

1.

9'

17'

$$A = \frac{1}{2}bh$$
$$A = \frac{1}{2} \times 17 \times 9$$
$$A = \frac{1}{2} \times \frac{17}{1} \times \frac{9}{1}$$
$$A = 76\frac{1}{2} \text{ sq. ft.}$$

2.

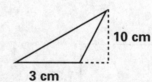

10 cm

3 cm

3.

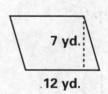

7 yd.

12 yd.

4.

20"

9"

5.

9'

8'

6.

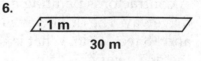

1 m

30 m

Area

The formula for finding the area of a circle is π, either 3.14 or $\frac{22}{7}$, times r^2, the radius squared. To square the radius, multiply $r \times r$.

Remember, the diameter is 2 times the radius. If you have the diameter, divide it by 2 to find the radius.

$$r = d \div 2$$

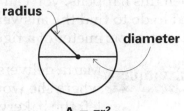

$$A = \pi r^2$$

Use These Steps

Find the area. Use 3.14 for π.

20 ft.

1. Write the formula for the area of a circle.

$$A = \pi r^2$$

2. Find r.

$$r = d \div 2$$
$$r = 20 \div 2$$
$$r = 10 \text{ ft.}$$

3. Substitute 10 for r and 3.14 for π. Multiply.

$$A = 3.14 \times 10 \times 10$$
$$A = 3.14 \times 100$$
$$A = 314 \text{ sq. ft.}$$

Find the area. Use $\frac{22}{7}$ for π.

1.

28 m

2.

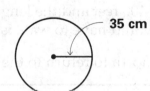

35 cm

3.

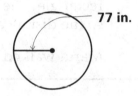

77 in.

$A = \pi r^2$

$r = 28 \div 2 = 14$ m

$A = \frac{22}{7} \times 14 \times 14$

$A = \frac{22}{\overset{1}{\cancel{7}}} \times \frac{\overset{2}{\cancel{14}}}{1} \times \frac{14}{1} = \frac{616}{1}$

$A = 616$ sq. m

Find the area. Use 3.14 for π.

4.

2 mi.

5.

5'

6.

6 "

$A = \pi r^2$

$r = 2 \div 2 = 1$ mi.

$A = 3.14 \times 1 \times 1$

$A = 3.14$ sq. mi.

Problem Solving: Drawing a Picture

Sometimes it is not clear what you need to do to solve a math problem. When this happens, you can draw a picture in order to see what you need to do to find the answer. You may need to use a formula to find the area or perimeter of a figure that you have drawn.

Example Marta delivers baked goods door to door in the block where she works for the Old World Bakery. One day she left the bakery and walked 400 feet east, stopping at stores along the block. She turned right and continued 200 feet south. She then turned right again and continued 400 feet west. She made a final turn right in order to return to work. How many feet did she have to walk to the north to return to the bakery?

▶ **Step 1.** Make a drawing of the route that Marta took.

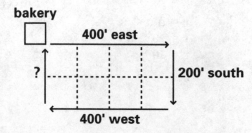

▶ **Step 2.** You should see that the area covered by Marta is a rectangle. The width is 400 feet and the length is 200 feet, so the distance Marta would have to walk is 200 feet.

Marta walked 200 feet north to return to the bakery.

Draw a picture based on the information given. Solve. Use a formula if necessary.

1. Bart drove 13 miles west from Centerville to Smithville. He then drove 9 miles south from Smithville to the interstate highway. If there is a road from the interstate back to Centerville, what is the size of the area between these three points?

2. $\triangle ABC \sim \triangle XYZ$
   $\overline{AB} = 24"$
   $\overline{BC} = 12"$
   $\overline{XY} = 36"$

   Find $\overline{YZ}$.

Answer_____   Answer_____

Draw a picture based on the information given. Solve. Use a formula if necessary.

3. Joe is putting a new roof on the post office. He knows that half of the roof is 36' by 15' and that the roof is divided into equal parts. What is the total area of the roof?

Answer _____

4. The diameter of a circular garden is 25'. If a landscaper adds a 3-foot border around the entire garden, what will the diameter of the garden be including the border?

Answer _____

5. Al is building a storage shed at the golf course. Each side of the shed is 18' wide and 10' high. How many square feet of aluminum siding does Al need for each side of the shed?

Answer _____

6. Barry installed a water sprinkler that sprays water in a circular pattern. The water reaches out from the sprinkler 7 feet. How much area does the sprinkler cover at a time? (Hint: Use $\frac{22}{7}$ for π.)

Answer _____

7. Mac is a dog walker. Yesterday he walked four dogs around the neighborhood. They walked $\frac{1}{2}$ mile south from Mac's house, turned, and walked $1\frac{1}{4}$ miles east. They turned and walked $\frac{3}{4}$ mile north. They turned again and walked $\frac{1}{2}$ mile west to the park before returning home. What was the total distance they walked from the house to the park?

Answer _____

8. Arnold wants to have a sign made in the shape of a round clock face to advertise his clock repair shop. The sign will have to fit on the side of his shop that has an area of 150 square feet. If the sign he has made is 12 feet across, how much of the area of the side of the store will not be covered by the sign? (Hint: Use 3.14 for π.)

Answer _____

Solids

Solids are three-dimensional figures. They take up space. For example, a stick of margarine, a cardboard box, a block of wood, and an aluminum soda can are solids.

If the opposite faces of a solid are equal, you have a rectangular solid. There are six faces on a rectangular solid.

If each side, or face, of the solid is equal, you have a cube. There are six faces on a cube. Each face is a square.

If the top and bottom or ends of a solid are circles, then you have a cylinder. The distance between the top and bottom is the height.

Label each figure as rectangular solid, cube, or cylinder.

1.

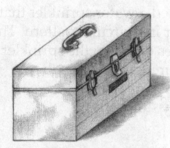

rectangular solid

2.

3.

4.

5.

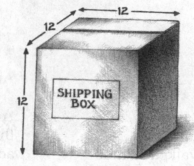

SHIPPING BOX

6.

7.

8.

GLUE

9.

OFFICE PRODUCTS CATALOG

Volume

Volume is the measure of the space inside a three-dimensional or solid figure. Volume is measured in cubic units, even if the shape is not a cube. For example, the volume of the first figure shown is four cubic units.

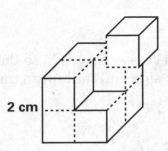

The second figure measures 2 centimeters on a side. You can find the volume by counting the number of cubic centimeter units, 8. You can also find the volume by multiplying the length times the width times the height, $2 \times 2 \times 2$. The volume is 8 cubic centimeters.

2 cm

Use These Steps

Find the volume in two ways.

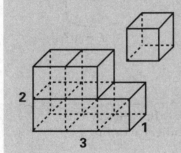

2

3

1. Count the number of cubic units.

   6 cubic units

2. Multiply the length times the width times the height. Write the answer in cubic units.

   $3 \times 1 \times 2 = 6$ cubic units

Find the volume of each cube. Use both methods.

1.

2.

3.

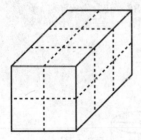

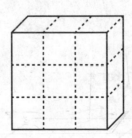

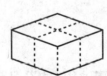

12 cubic units
$2 \times 3 \times 2 = 12$ cubic units

4.

5.

6.

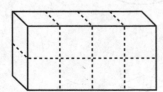

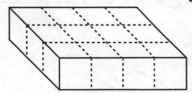

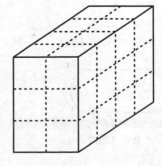

Volume

You can use formulas to find the volume of a rectangular solid, a cube, and a cylinder.

To find the volume of a rectangular solid, multiply the length times the width times the height.

$$V = lwh$$

In a cube, l = w = h, so the formula is shorter. Use s for the length of one side and multiply s times s times s, or s^3.

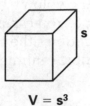

$$V = s^3$$

To find the volume of a cylinder, notice that you can first find the area of the circular top or end, πr^2. Then multiply times the height.

$$V = \pi r^2 h$$

Use These Steps

Find the volume. Use $\frac{22}{7}$ for π.

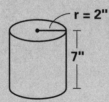

1. Write the formula.

$$V = \pi r^2 h$$

2. Substitute the correct numbers. Multiply.

$$V = \frac{22}{7} \times 2^2 \times 7$$

$$V = \frac{22}{\cancel{7}} \times \frac{4}{1} \times \frac{\cancel{7}}{1} = \frac{88}{1}$$

$$V = 88 \text{ cubic inches}$$

Find the volume of each figure. Use $\frac{22}{7}$ for π.

1.

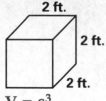

2 ft.

2 ft.

2 ft.

$V = s^3$
$V = 2 \times 2 \times 2$
$V = 8$ cubic feet

2.

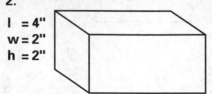

l = 4"
w = 2"
h = 2"

3.

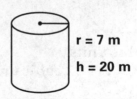

r = 7 m
h = 20 m

4.

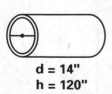

d = 14"
h = 120"

5.

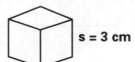

s = 3 cm

6.

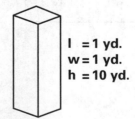

l = 1 yd.
w = 1 yd.
h = 10 yd.

Unit 3 Review

Find the measure of each unknown angle.

1.

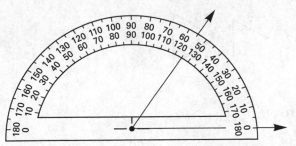

2.

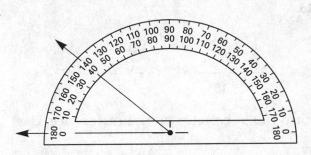

3.

70°
c

4.

35° d

5.

120°
a

6.

e

7.

100°
h   f
g

8.

60° i
k j
o l
n m

9.

x
39°   50°

10.

y
30°

11.

z   45°

12.

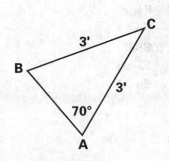
C
3'
B
3'
70°
A

13.

Z
10"
X 30°
10"
Y

14.

L
7 m   7 m
M   N

Find the length of the unknown side of the similar triangles below.

15.

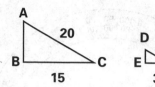

16.

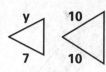

Find the perimeter or circumference. Use $\frac{22}{7}$ for π.

17.

s = 6 cm

18.

12' 12'

9'

19.

7"

8" 6"

5"

20.

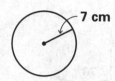

7 cm

Find the area. Use 3.14 for π.

21.

7'

11'

22.

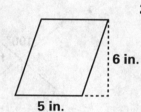

6 m

12 m

23.

6 in.

5 in.

24.

14 mi.

Find the volume. Use $\frac{22}{7}$ for π.

25.

8'

8'

8'

26.

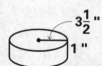

$3\frac{1}{2}$"

1"

27.

1 m 1 m

5 m

Below is a list of the problems in this review and the pages on which the skills are taught. If you missed any problems, turn to the pages listed and practice the skills. Then correct the problems you missed in the Unit Review.

Problems	Pages	Problems	Pages
1-2	75-77	12-14	86-87
3-4	78	15-16	88-89
5-6	79	17-20	93-95
7	80	21-24	96-99
8	81-82	25-27	103-104
9-11	84-85		

Unit 4 ALGEBRA CONCEPTS

You can solve certain problems in math by using the information you have and applying the concepts of algebra to find the unknown information. You use the four basic operations of math—addition, subtraction, multiplication, and division. You also use whole numbers, fractions, or decimals.

In this unit you will become familiar with both positive and negative numbers. You will also learn how to write and evaluate expressions and how to recognize and solve some simple equations.

Getting Ready

You should be familiar with the skills on this page and the next before you begin this unit. To check your answers, turn to page 202.

▶ You should know basic addition facts when working with algebra.

Complete the following addition facts.

1. $9 + 3 = \boxed{12}$ 2. $15 = 8 + \square$ 3. $6 + 7 = \square$ 4. $11 = 5 + \square$

5. $4 + \square = 9$ 6. $8 = 5 + \square$ 7. $7 + 4 = \square$ 8. $6 + \square = 12$

9. $16 = 8 + \square$ 10. $6 + \square = 14$ 11. $\square + 3 = 10$ 12. $13 = 9 + \square$

Getting Ready

 You should know basic subtraction facts when working with algebra.

Complete the following subtraction facts.

13. $14 - 7 = \boxed{7}$ **14.** $4 = 6 - \square$ **15.** $12 - 4 = \square$ **16.** $8 = 13 - \square$

17. $9 - 3 = \square$ **18.** $11 - 4 = \square$ **19.** $18 - 9 = \square$ **20.** $5 + \square = 17$

21. $7 = \square - 8$ **22.** $9 - \square = 0$ **23.** $\square - 3 = 4$ **24.** $15 - 11 = \square$

For review, see **Unit 3, Math Skills for the Workforce, Whole Numbers.**

 You should know basic multiplication facts when working with algebra.

Complete the following multiplication facts.

25. $7 \times 7 = \boxed{49}$ **26.** $48 = 6 \times \square$ **27.** $4 \times 9 = \square$ **28.** $32 = 8 \times \square$

29. $5 \times 6 = \square$ **30.** $7 \times 0 = \square$ **31.** $\square \times 3 = 27$ **32.** $2 \times \square = 10$

33. $40 = \square \times 5$ **34.** $6 \times \square = 54$ **35.** $\square \times 9 = 81$ **36.** $9 \times 5 = \square$

For review, see **Unit 4, Math Skills for the Workforce, Whole Numbers.**

 You should know basic division facts when working with algebra.

Complete the following division facts.

37. $18 \div 2 = \boxed{9}$ **38.** $21 \div 3 = \square$ **39.** $63 \div \square = 7$ **40.** $5 = 25 \div \square$

41. $0 \div 6 = \square$ **42.** $\square \div 6 = 7$ **43.** $72 \div 8 = \square$ **44.** $15 \div \square = 3$

45. $7 = \square \div 7$ **46.** $35 \div \square = 5$ **47.** $\square \div 4 = 5$ **48.** $24 \div 8 = \square$

For review, see **Unit 5, Math Skills for the Workforce, Whole Numbers.**

The Meaning of Algebra

Algebra is a math tool used for solving problems. Algebra uses numbers that are greater than zero, or positive numbers. Algebra uses numbers that are less than zero, or negative numbers. Negative numbers are written with a minus sign in front of the number. Positive numbers can be written with or without the plus sign in front of the number.

Positive numbers: 1 or +1   7 or +7   26 or +26   100 or +100
Negative numbers: −1   −7   −26   −100

Algebra uses a letter to stand for an unknown number. You can use any letter to stand for an unknown number.

$x + 4 = 6$ means "some unknown number plus four equals six"

This kind of number sentence is called an equation. An equation always has an equal sign.

$3x - 12 = 20$ means "three times some unknown number minus twelve equals twenty"

To solve an equation means to find the value of the unknown number. You can probably solve the first equation, $x + 4 = 6$, in your head. You know that two plus four equals six, so $x = 2$.

You will find that the second equation, $3x - 12 = 20$, is not as simple. The rules of algebra will help you solve this equation easily.

Write the correct word or phrase from the list. You may use some answers more than once.

positive number   equation
negative number   four times a number equals seven
solving an equation   unknown number

1. −7 _____ negative number _____   2. $3 + x = 4$ _____

3. +13 _____   4. $x - 4 = 1$ _____
                                              $x = 5$

5. $4y = 7$ _____   6. $-1\frac{1}{2}$ _____

7. n _____   8. 25 _____

9. z _____   10. $\frac{1}{4}a + 9 = 10$ _____

11. $5 + y = 10$ _____   12. $4b = 7$ _____
       $y = 5$

Positive and Negative Numbers

A weather thermometer is an example of a vertical number line that has both positive and negative numbers. The numbers above zero are positive numbers. For example, 10 degrees above zero is a positive number and can be written with a plus sign, +10. If the + is not shown, the number is understood to be positive.

The numbers below zero are negative numbers. For example, 10 degrees below zero is a negative number and is written with a minus sign, −10. A negative number must be written with a minus sign.

Zero is neither positive nor negative.

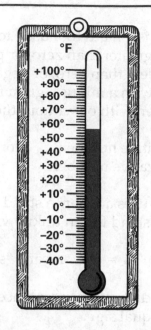

Use These Steps

Write 1 degree below zero.

1. Write the number of degrees with the degree sign.

2. Because the word *below* is used, put a minus sign in front of the number.

$1°$

$-1°$

Write each expression as either a positive or negative number.

1. 20 degrees below zero

    $-20°$

2. 98 degrees above zero

3. 5 degrees above zero

4. 5 degrees below zero

5. 16 degrees below zero

6. 65 degrees above zero

Write the temperature shown by each arrow. Use the + or − sign with each number.

7. A $+30°$

8. B _____

9. C _____

10. D _____

11. E _____

12. F _____

13. G _____

14. H _____

15. I _____

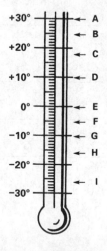

Positive and Negative Numbers

If you turn a thermometer sideways, you will have a horizontal number line with positive and negative numbers. The positive numbers are on the right of zero. The negative numbers are on the left of zero.

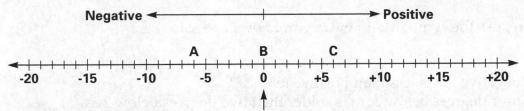

Use These Steps

Use the number line above to find the letter that corresponds to −6.

1. Find zero on the number line above.

   The arrow is pointing to zero.

2. Since negative numbers are to the left of zero, move to the left by counting 6 marks. Write the letter that corresponds to −6.

   A

Use the number line below to find the letter that corresponds to the number in each problem.

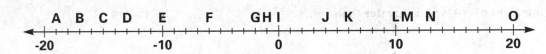

1. 0 __I__   2. 6 _____   3. −6 _____   4. −10 _____   5. −15 _____

6. 20 _____   7. 13 _____   8. −13 _____   9. −1 _____   10. 4 _____

11. −2 _____   12. −17 _____   13. 11 _____   14. −19 _____   15. 10 _____

Use the number line below to find the number that corresponds to the letter in each problem.

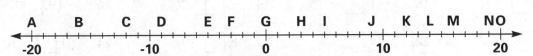

16. A __−20__   17. C _____   18. F _____   19. G _____   20. I _____

21. D _____   22. B _____   23. H _____   24. K _____   25. O _____

26. N _____   27. L _____   28. E _____   29. J _____   30. M _____

Comparing Positive and Negative Numbers

You can use a number line to compare positive and negative numbers. The numbers on a number line get larger as you move to the right and smaller as you move to the left. Notice that -10 is larger than -11 since -11 is farther to the left than -10.

When you compare, use the symbols > to mean *greater than* and < to mean *less than*.

$-10 < 10$ negative ten is less than positive ten
$-4° < -2°$ four degrees below zero is colder than two degrees below zero
$6' > 5'$ six feet is higher than five feet

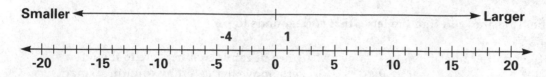

Use These Steps

Compare 1 and -4.

1. **Find each number on the number line above.**

   1 is to the right of -4, so 1 is greater than -4.

2. **Write > between the numbers to show that 1 is greater than -4.**

   $1 > -4$

Use the number line above to compare each set of numbers. Write < or >.

1. $-6 \boxed{<} -5$
2. $-12 \boxed{} -15$
3. $-7 \boxed{} -1$
4. $-20 \boxed{} -10$

5. $-2 \boxed{} 2$
6. $7 \boxed{} -3$
7. $-9 \boxed{} 10$
8. $15 \boxed{} -18$

9. $-3 \boxed{} 0$
10. $-15 \boxed{} 6$
11. $-13 \boxed{} -8$
12. $-1 \boxed{} 5$

13. $4 \boxed{} -4$
14. $1 \boxed{} -2$
15. $5 \boxed{} -8$
16. $20 \boxed{} -20$

17. $-9 \boxed{} -10$
18. $-11 \boxed{} -15$
19. $9 \boxed{} -17$
20. $-19 \boxed{} 0$

21. $13 \boxed{} -6$
22. $-1 \boxed{} 1$
23. $8 \boxed{} -18$
24. $10 \boxed{} -10$

25. Which is colder: $-15°$ or $5°$?

26. Which is higher: 2,500 ft. or $-3,000$ ft.?

27. Which is warmer: $1°$ or $-10°$?

28. Which is lower: -130 ft. or -200 ft.?

Exponents and Powers

Often in mathematics, there is a shorthand way to write numbers. For example, you know that $10 \times 10 = 100$. We can write 10^2 to mean 10×10, or 100. We read this as 10 to the second power or 10 squared. The number 10 is called the base. The number 2 is called the exponent. The exponent tells the number of times the base is multiplied by itself.

Every whole number is that number to the first power. For example, 10 is 10^1 and 2 is 2^1.

The most common powers used are the second and the third. 10^3 means $10 \times 10 \times 10$ or 10 to the third power or 10 cubed.

10^1 = 10 to the first power   = 10

4^2 = 4 to the second power or four squared = 4×4 = 16

5^3 = 5 to the third power or five cubed   = $5 \times 5 \times 5$ = 125

Use These Steps

Find 9^3

1. Write the problem as a multiplication problem. The exponent, 3, tells you to multiply three nines.

$$9 \times 9 \times 9$$

2. Multiply 9×9. Multiply the answer, 81, times 9.

$$9 \times 9 = 81$$
$$81 \times 9 = 729$$

Find each answer.

1. $1^7 = 1$
2. $2^2 -$
3. $3^2 =$
4. $0^2 =$
5. $5^2 =$

6. $6^2 =$
7. $7^2 =$
8. $8^2 =$
9. $9^2 =$
10. $10^2 =$

11. $1^3 =$
12. $2^3 =$
13. $3^3 =$
14. $4^3 =$
15. $5^3 =$

16. $11^2 =$
17. $10^3 =$
18. $15^2 =$
19. $0^3 =$
20. $12^2 =$

21. Lucas bought square tiles to retile the lobby of Town Travel Agency. Each side of a tile is 11 inches long. If Lucas uses the formula for the area of a square, $A = s^2$, how many square inches will each tile cover?

22. To build a circular wading pool, Claudia has to find its area. The distance from the center of the pool to the outside edge, or the radius, is 4 feet. If she uses the formula for the area of a circle, $A = \pi r^2$, what number will she get when she squares the radius?

Answer_____

Answer_____

Square Roots

Finding the root of a number is the opposite of finding the power of a number. If a number is raised to a power, you can find the base by finding the root. The most commonly used root is the square root shown by the symbol $\sqrt{}$.

When you find 3 squared, or 3^2, you multiply 3 times 3 to get 9. When you find the square root of 9, or $\sqrt{9}$, ask yourself *what number multiplied times itself equals 9?* The answer is 3.

$$\sqrt{9} = 3 \text{ because } 3 \times 3 = 9$$

Use These Steps

Find $\sqrt{25}$

1. What number times itself equals 25?

$$5 \times 5 = 25$$

2. The square root of 25 is 5.

$$\sqrt{25} = 5$$

Find each square root. You can refer to the problems on page 113 to help you.

1. $\sqrt{16} = 4$ **2.** $\sqrt{4}$ **3.** $\sqrt{9}$ **4.** $\sqrt{36}$

5. $\sqrt{49}$ **6.** $\sqrt{64}$ **7.** $\sqrt{81}$ **8.** $\sqrt{100}$

9. $\sqrt{144}$ **10.** $\sqrt{25}$ **11.** $\sqrt{121}$ **12.** $\sqrt{225}$

13. $\sqrt{169}$ **14.** $\sqrt{1}$ **15.** $\sqrt{196}$ **16.** $\sqrt{0}$

17. Petersons' Auto Body Shop is built in the shape of a square. The total area of the shop is 225 square feet. What is the length of one side of the shop? (Hint: Find the square root of 225. The answer will be the length of one side.)

18. Alejandro used 144 square yards of carpet to recarpet one of the rooms in a restaurant. The room is in the shape of a square. How long is each side of the room he recarpeted? (Hint: Find the square root of 144.)

Answer_____

Answer_____

Writing Numerical Expressions

A numerical expression is a group of numbers and math operations. For example, $2 + 7 - 9$ is an expression. The word expression for the same idea is *two plus seven minus nine*. As you can see, the expression is shorter and easier to read if you use numbers instead of words.

Word Expression	Numerical Expression
three plus two	$3 + 2$
one times five	1×5 or $1 \cdot 5$
seven and three tenths minus one and three tenths	$7.3 - 1.3$
three and one half plus one and one half	$3\frac{1}{2} + 1\frac{1}{2}$
forty divided by eight	$40 \div 8$ or $\frac{40}{8}$

You can show multiplication using the expression $2 \cdot 5$. The expression $\frac{40}{8}$ is the most common way to show division in algebra.

To evaluate a numerical expression means to find the answer. For example, $\frac{40}{8} = 5$.

Use These Steps

Write a numerical expression for *three plus four*. Then evaluate.

1. Write a numerical expression.

$3 + 4$

2. Evaluate by adding.

$3 + 4 = 7$

Write a numerical expression for each word expression. Then evaluate.

1. six plus ninety
   $6 + 90 = 96$

2. twelve minus seven

3. nineteen times three

4. four divided by ten

5. eight plus six plus two

6. one hundred times seven times two

7. two thousand divided by four

8. twenty-five minus zero

9. three times four times three

10. fifty-five divided by eleven

Order of Operations

When you write numerical expressions, the order in which you write the numbers for subtraction or division expressions is important. For example, sixteen divided by four must be written as $16 \div 4$, not $4 \div 16$.

$$16 \div 4 = 4 \qquad\qquad 4 \div 16 = \frac{1}{4}$$

In addition and multiplication, however, the order is not important. For example, 23×5 is the same as 5×23.

$$23 \times 5 = 115 \qquad\qquad 5 \times 23 = 115$$

When expressions have more than one operation, you must do the operations in a specific order. The chart below shows the rules for the order in which math operations should be done.

Order of Operations

1. Do operations within parentheses.

2. Do operations with powers and roots.

3. Do all multiplication and division operations from left to right.

4. Do all addition and subtraction operations from left to right.

Note: If expressions do not have parentheses or powers and roots, start with Rule 3.

Use These Steps

PEMDAS

Evaluate $3 \times 6 - 4 \times 2$ $18 - 8 = 10$

1. Do both multiplication operations first.

$$\underbrace{3 \times 6}_{18} - \underbrace{4 \times 2}_{8}$$

2. Subtract the two answers.

$$18 - 8 = 10$$

Evaluate using the correct order of operations.

1.
$3 + \underbrace{7 \cdot 4}$
$3 + 28 = 31$

2. $5 \div 1 + 4$

3. $8 - 6 \div 2$

4. $10 \cdot 9 + 10$

5. $30 \div 5 + 6$

6. $27 - 10 \cdot 2$

7. $8 - 6 \div 3$

8. $9 \cdot 4 - 5$

9.
$\underbrace{4 \div 2} + \underbrace{6 \div 3}$
$\ \ 2 \ \ + \ \ 2 = 4$

10. $12 + 11 \cdot 2 - 14$

11. $29 - 6 \cdot 4 - 5$

12. $8 + 42 \div 7 + 1$

Evaluating Numerical Expressions with Exponents

Some numerical expressions may contain exponents. Remember to evaluate all numbers with exponents first. Refer to the rules for the correct order of operations on page 116. Follow the steps in order.

Use These Steps

Evaluate $3^2 + 4^2 \div 2$

1. Evaluate the numbers with exponents.

$3^2 + 4^2 \div 2$
$9 + 16 \div 2$

2. Divide.

$9 + \underbrace{16 \div 2}$
$9 + \quad 8$

3. Add.

$9 + 8 = 17$

Evaluate.

1.
$5 - 16 \div 2^3$
$5 - \underbrace{16 \div 8}$
$5 - \quad 2 = 3$

2.
$1 + 6^2 \cdot 4$

3.
$10 \cdot 3^2 - 9$

4.
$3^3 + 2 \div 2$

5.
$12 \cdot 4^2 - 9$

6.
$1 + 6^2 \div 4$

7.
$9^2 + 2^3$

8.
$10^3 \div 20$

9.
$8^2 - 4^2$

10.
$3^2 \cdot 2^3$

11.
$12^2 \div 2^2$

12.
$2^3 + 5^2$

13.
$4 + 4^2 \cdot 6$

14.
$7^2 - 9 \div 3$

15.
$10^3 \div 4 + 89$

16.
$1 + 9^2 - 2^3$

17.
$10^2 \cdot 3^3 + 14$

18.
$6^3 \div 3 - 2^2$

19. four squared minus three plus seven

20. twenty-five plus six cubed

21. eight squared plus four squared

22. four cubed minus forty

117

Evaluating Numerical Expressions Using Parentheses

The correct order of operations is to multiply or divide first and then add or subtract. In some cases, you may want to add first and then divide the result. To show this, put parentheses around the addition part of the expression. Operations within parentheses are always done first.

$$(8 + 24) \div 4$$
$$32 \div 4 = 8$$

Refer to the rules for the correct order of operations on page 116.

Use These Steps

Evaluate $(10 - 3) \cdot 5$

1. Do the operation within the parentheses first.

$$(10 - 3) \cdot 5$$
$$7 \cdot 5$$

2. Multiply the result, 7, by 5.

$$7 \cdot 5 = 35$$

Evaluate.

1. $(4 + 7) \cdot 2$
$11 \cdot 2 = 22$

2. $(36 + 4) \cdot 4$

3. $(9 - 7) \div 2$

4. $10 - (2 + 3)$

5. $15 + (8 - 6)$

6. $18 - (6 + 2)$

7. $2 \cdot (3 + 4)$

8. $20 \div (1 + 4)$

9. $(5 - 3) \cdot (6 + 2)$

10. $(14 + 7) \div (2 + 1)$

11. $(10 - 6) \cdot (4 + 4)$

12. $42 \div (3 \cdot 2)$

13. $100 \cdot (6 \div 3)$

14. $25 \div (2 + 3)$

15. $4 \cdot (7 + 3)$

16. $20 \div (3 + 7)$

17. $49 \div (3 + 4)$

18. There were 10 mechanical pencils in one box and 8 in another. Three architects took an equal number of the pencils. How many pencils did each architect take?

19. Super Save Pharmacy ordered four cases of rubbing alcohol. There are 24 bottles in each case. Six bottles in each case were damaged in shipment and could not be sold. How many total bottles are left that can be sold?

Answer _____

Answer _____

Application

When figuring out how much paint you need to paint a house, you first need to figure out the surface area of the exterior walls. You can use the formula $A = lw$ to find the area of a rectangle. Multiply the length times the width to find the area.

You may need to add, subtract, multiply, or divide several numbers. Use parentheses to help make expressions easier to evaluate.

Example Price Construction is building a house. One side of the house measures 30 feet long by 9 feet high. There is a window that measures 3 by 6 feet. What is the surface area of this side of the house?

total area − window area = area of side
$$(30 \cdot 9) - (3 \cdot 6)$$
$$270 - 18 = 252$$

The surface area of this side of the house is 252 square feet.

Solve using the correct order of operations.

1. Another part of the house measures 20 feet by 9 feet. There is one patio door measuring 6 feet by 8 feet. What is the surface area of this side?

   Answer_____

2. The ends of the house measure 20 feet by 9 feet. The area for each end of the house must also include 80 square feet for the area of the triangular part of the roof. What is the total area of one end of the house?

   Answer_____

3. The house also needs a new roof. One section measures 30 feet by 14 feet. Another section measures 30 feet by 20 feet because it covers a porch. What is the total area of the roof?

   Answer_____

4. A storage shed measures 8 feet by 8 feet on each side. There are no windows. The door also needs to be painted so its area is included. What is the surface area of the shed? (Hint: You can use 8^2 for each side.)

   Answer_____

Mixed Review

Write a positive or a negative number for each expression.

1. 2 degrees below zero

2. 50 degrees above zero

3. 32 degrees above zero

4. 14 degrees below zero

Use the number line to find the corresponding number or letter for each problem.

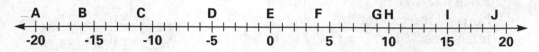

5. -11 _____

6. 4 _____

7. -20 _____

8. 9 _____

9. 15 _____

10. B _____

11. E _____

12. H _____

13. D _____

14. J _____

Compare. Write < or >.

15. $-3 \;\square\; 3$

16. $-9 \;\square\; -11$

17. $7 \;\square\; -2$

18. $0 \;\square\; -1$

19. $-15 \;\square\; 14$

20. $-5 \;\square\; 5$

21. $1 \;\square\; -12$

22. $10 \;\square\; -3$

Find each answer.

23. $9^2 =$

24. $4^3 =$

25. $13^2 =$

26. $5^3 =$

27. $10^2 =$

Find each square root.

28. $\sqrt{16}$

29. $\sqrt{49}$

30. $\sqrt{121}$

31. $\sqrt{4}$

Write an expression. Evaluate.

32. twelve minus nine

33. eight plus ten

34. three times seven times two

Evaluate.

35. $2 + 9 \cdot 2$

36. $7 - 6 \div 3$

37. $5 \cdot 2 + 8 \div 4$

38. $3^2 \div 9 + 1$

39. $4^2 + 6^3$

40. $10^2 \div 5$

41. $(3 + 6) \cdot 7$

42. $2 + (8 - 4)$

43. $(3 + 7) \div (2 + 3)$

Algebraic Expressions

An algebraic expression may contain a variable as well as numbers and operations. A variable is a letter that stands for an unknown number. In the expression $m + 2$, m is a variable. An expression may contain one or more variables. The most common letters used for a variable in algebraic expressions are x, y, and z, or a, b, and c.

Word Expression	Algebraic Expression
four plus a number	$4 + n$
a number minus eighteen and nine tenths	$y - 18.9$
three and five tenths times a number	$3.5x$
a number times another number	xy
four fifths times a number	$\dfrac{4}{5}a$
three divided by a number	$\dfrac{3}{b}$

In algebra, it is more common to write division as a fraction, $\dfrac{3}{b}$.

When writing variables, the times sign, $\times$, is not used because it is easily confused with the variable x. Notice that two letters or a number and a letter can be written next to each other to show multiplication, as in $3.5x$ or xy.

Use These Steps

Write an algebraic expression for *twenty divided by a number*. Use x for the variable.

1. Write the number, 20, and the fraction bar.

$$\underline{20}$$

2. Write the variable, x, under the fraction bar.

$$\dfrac{20}{x}$$

Write an algebraic expression for each word expression. Use x, y, or z for the variable.

1. a number plus one
   $y + 1$

2. ten times a number

3. two times a number

4. a number minus seven

5. a number divided by twelve

6. twenty squared minus a number

Evaluating Algebraic Expressions

The value of an algebraic expression depends on what number is substituted for the variable. For example, if $n = 6$, then the value of the expression $4 + n$ is 10. Use the same order of operations when evaluating algebraic expressions as you do when you evaluate numerical expressions.

Order of Operations

1. Do operations within parentheses.

2. Do operations with powers and roots.

3. Do all multiplication and division operations from left to right.

4. Do all addition and subtraction operations from left to right.

Note: If expressions do not have parentheses or powers and roots, start with Rule 3.

Use These Steps

Evaluate the expression $27 - x \div 3$ if $x = 6$.

1. Substitute 6 for x in the expression.

$$27 - x \div 3$$
$$27 - 6 \div 3$$

2. Use the correct order of operations. Divide 6 by 3 first.

$$27 - \underbrace{(6 \div 3)}$$
$$27 - \quad 2$$

3. Subtract the answer from 27.

$$27 - 2 = 25$$

Evaluate each expression if $x = 5$. Use the correct order of operations.

1.
$$x + 3$$
$$5 + 3 = 8$$

2.
$$5 \div x$$

3.
$$\frac{x}{5} \cdot 4$$

4.
$$19 - x$$

5.
$$7 - x + 3$$
$$\underbrace{7 - 5} + 3$$
$$2 \quad + 3 = 5$$

6.
$$2 + x \div 1$$

7.
$$x + 10 + 3$$

8.
$$14x - 6$$

9.
$$5 \div x + \frac{20}{x}$$

10.
$$x \cdot 6 - 8$$

11.
$$3x + 5 \div x$$

12.
$$19 - 2 \cdot x$$

13.
$$23 + 12 \cdot x$$

14.
$$4x - 6$$

15.
$$\frac{10}{x}$$

16.
$$9x + \frac{x}{5}$$

Evaluating Algebraic Expressions with Exponents

Remember that you can write 10×10 as 10 to the second power, 10 squared, or 10^2. A variable can also be raised to a power. For example, y^2 is the same as y squared, y times y, or $y \cdot y$.

Refer to the rules for the correct order of operations on page 122.

Use These Steps

Evaluate the expression $y^2 + 3$ if $y = 2$.

1. Substitute 2 for y in the expression.

$$y^2 + 3$$
$$2^2 + 3$$

2. Use the correct order of operations. Raise 2 to the second power.

$$2^2 + 3$$
$$4 + 3$$

3. Add.

$$4 + 3 = 7$$

Evaluate each expression if $x = 4$. Use the correct order of operations.

1.
$6^2 + x$
$6^2 + 4$
$36 + 4 = 40$

2. $3^3 - x$

3. $10^2 \cdot x$

4. $9x \div 2^2$

5. $4x + 3^2$

6. $3x - 2^2$

7. $x^2 + 3$

8. $x^3 - 6$

9. $x^3 \cdot 2$

Evaluate each expression if $x = 8$. Use the correct order of operations.

10. $\dfrac{x^2}{8}$

$\dfrac{8^2}{8} = \dfrac{64}{8} = 8$

11. $100 - \dfrac{x^2}{2}$

12. $320 \div \dfrac{x^3}{16}$

13. $78 - x^2 + 7$

14. $256 \div 4 - x^2$

15. $6 + x^2 \cdot 4$

16. $10^2 - \dfrac{x^2}{4}$

17. $9^3 \div 3^2 + x^2$

18. $x^3 + 8^2 + 2x$

Evaluating Algebraic Expressions Using Parentheses

Parentheses are also used in algebraic expressions. Do the operation inside the parentheses first. Refer to the rules for the correct order of operations on page 122.

Use These Steps

Evaluate the expression $1 + (x - 3)$ if $x = 3$.

1. Substitute the given value of x into the expression.

$1 + (x - 3)$
$1 + (3 - 3)$

2. Do the operation inside the parentheses.

$1 + (3 - 3)$
$1 + 0$

3. Add.

$1 + 0 = 1$

Evaluate each expression if $x = 10$. Use the correct order of operations.

1.
$2 + (x - 1)$
$2 + (10 - 1)$
$2 + 9 = 11$

2.
$15 - (x + 3)$

3.
$4 \cdot (x - 5)$

4.
$20 \div (x - 6)$

5.
$32 - (5 + x)$

6.
$3 \cdot (x - 2)$

7.
$10 + (14 - x)$

8.
$66 \div (x - 4)$

9.
$19 - (x + 7)$

Evaluate each expression if $x = 12$. Use the correct order of operations.

10.
$(x + 9) \cdot 2$
$(12 + 9) \cdot 2$
$21 \cdot 2 = 42$

11.
$(x - 7) \div 5$

12.
$(x + 1) \cdot 3$

13.
$(x - 2) \div 2$

14.
$(3 + x) \cdot 6$

15.
$(20 - x) \div 4$

16.
$(13 + x) \div 5$

17.
$(x + 10) \cdot 10$

18.
$(32 - x) \div 10$

Equations

To solve an equation means to find the value of the variable that makes the equation true. The variable x stands for an unknown number that you can find by asking yourself *what number plus 2 equals 9?*

Use basic addition, subtraction, multiplication, and division facts to solve equations. Find the number that will make the equation true.

$$x + 2 = 9$$
$$\boxed{} + 2 = 9$$
$$\boxed{7} + 2 = 9$$
$$9 = 9$$

The number on the left side of the equation, 9, equals the number on the right side of the equation, 9. The value for x that makes the equation true is 7.

Use These Steps

Solve $n + 5 = 10$

1. To solve, find a value for n that makes this equation true.

   $$n + 5 = 10$$
   $$5 + 5 = 10$$

2. Write the solution.

   $$n = 5$$

Solve each equation.

1.
$$9 + x = 12$$
$$9 + 3 = 12$$
$$x = 3$$

2.
$$7 - x = 4$$

3.
$$x \div 2 = 2$$

4.
$$x \cdot 5 = 25$$

5.
$$x + 6 = 14$$

6.
$$x - 9 = 1$$

7.
$$\frac{8}{x} = 4$$

8.
$$12x = 36$$

9.
$$15 - x = 10$$

10.
$$1 - x = 0$$

11.
$$2 \cdot x = 0$$

12.
$$4x = 48$$

Equations

Some equations have two unknown numbers. However, you must know the value of one of the unknowns to find the solution.

$$x + y = 6$$

If you know that $y = 4$, then you can find the value of x. Substitute 4 in the equation for y. Then find the value for x that makes the equation true.

$$x + 4 = 6$$

Ask yourself *what number added to 4 equals 6?* Since $2 + 4 = 6$, the solution that makes this equation true is $x = 2$.

Use These Steps

Solve the equation $x - y = 1$ if $y = 9$.

1. Substitute 9 for y in the equation.

    $x - y = 1$
    $x - 9 = 1$

2. To find the solution, find a number for x that makes the equation true.

    $x - 9 = 1$
    $10 - 9 = 1$

3. Write the solution.

    $x = 10$

Find the solution for each equation if $y = 15$.

1.
$x + y = 20$
$x + 15 = 20$
$5 + 15 = 20$
$x = 5$

2.
$x - y = 5$

3.
$xy = 30$

4.
$\dfrac{x}{y} = 2$

5.
$y + x = 17$

6.
$y - x = 9$

7.
$y \div x = 5$

8.
$yx = 45$

9.
$x + y = 19$

10.
$x = 3 + y$

11.
$x = y - 5$

12.
$x = \dfrac{15}{y}$

13.
$y = x - 1$

14.
$y = 30 \div x$

15.
$y = x \cdot 3$

16.
$y = \dfrac{x}{5}$

Problem Solving: Using a Formula

In the United States, the Fahrenheit (F) scale is used to measure temperature. Most other countries in the world use the Celsius (C) or Centigrade scale. Scientists also use the Celsius scale.

You can change from one scale to the other scale by using a formula.

$$°F = \frac{9}{5}°C + 32 \qquad °C = \frac{5}{9}(°F - 32)$$

Example In winter, the temperature averages about 41°F in one southern state. What is the equivalent temperature using the Celsius scale?

Step 1. Write the formula for finding °C.

$$°C = \frac{5}{9}(°F - 32)$$

Step 2. Substitute 41 for °F.

$$°C = \frac{5}{9}(41 - 32)$$

Step 3. Evaluate the expression in parentheses.

$$°C = \frac{5}{9}(9)$$

Step 4. Multiply by $\frac{5}{9}$. Parentheses means to multiply.

$$°C = \frac{5}{9} \times 9 = \frac{5}{\cancel{9}} \times \frac{\cancel{9}^{1}}{1} = \frac{5}{1} = 5$$

41°F equals 5°C.

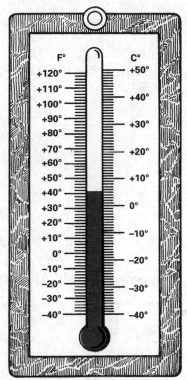

Solve.

1. The normal temperature for the human body is 98.6°F. What is the equivalent temperature in °C?

2. Peter recorded that a patient at the clinic had a temperature of 104°F. What is the equivalent temperature in °C?

Answer_____

Answer_____

Solve.

3. When making hard candy, you must boil the candy mixture to a temperature of about 302°F. What is the equivalent temperature in °C?

Answer_____

4. Water freezes at 0°C. What is the equivalent temperature in °F? (Hint: Use the formula for changing °F to °C.)

Answer_____

5. Water boils at 100°C. What is the equivalent temperature in °F?

Answer_____

6. If you set the thermostat on your heater for 20°C, what is the equivalent temperature in °F?

Answer_____

7. The average daily temperature in Miami during May was 77°F. What is the equivalent temperature in °C?

Answer_____

8. Denise found a recipe that gives a cooking temperature of 175°C. What is the equivalent cooking temperature in °F?

Answer_____

9. The recorded low temperature for the day was 59°F. What is the equivalent temperature in °C?

Answer_____

10. Horace took his dog to the veterinarian and was told the dog's temperature was 40°C. What was the equivalent temperature in F°?

Answer_____

Unit 4 *Review*

Find the corresponding letter or number for each problem.

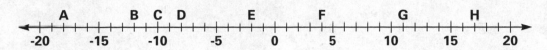

1. A _____
2. D _____
3. −10 _____
4. 17 _____

5. −12 _____
6. E _____
7. 4 _____
8. 11 _____

Find each answer.

9. $3^2 =$
10. $5^3 =$
11. $7^2 =$
12. $4^3 =$

13. $\sqrt{9} =$
14. $\sqrt{144} =$
15. $\sqrt{81} =$
16. $\sqrt{225} =$

Write a numerical expression for each problem. Evaluate.

17. seven plus twelve
18. nineteen divided by two

19. eighty times three
20. six plus nine minus four

Evaluate.

21. $2 + 4 - 6$
22. $9 - 3 \div 3$
23. $16 + 4 \div 2 - 9$

24. $1 + 3^2$
25. $10^3 - 500$
26. $8^2 + 4^2$

27. $(15 + 6) \div 3$
28. $40 \div (9 - 4)$
29. $(1 + 2) \cdot (5 \cdot 2)$

Write an algebraic expression for each problem. Use *x*, *y*, or *z*.

30. a number minus six
31. five times a number

32. a number divided by seven squared
33. two plus a number

Evaluate each expression if x = 3.

34.
$$18 \div x + 7$$

35.
$$30x$$

36.
$$\frac{x}{3} - 1$$

37.
$$5x + 9$$

38.
$$x^2 - 4$$

39.
$$x^3 - 2$$

40.
$$4 - (x + 1)$$

41.
$$25 \div (x + 2)$$

42.
$$(x - 2) \div 1$$

Solve each equation.

43.
$$6 + x = 10$$

44.
$$x - 19 = 7$$

45.
$$3x = 9$$

46.
$$9 \div x = 9$$

47.
$$\frac{18}{x} = 6$$

48.
$$x \cdot 10 = 100$$

Solve each equation if y = 1.

49.
$$x + y = 2$$

50.
$$xy = 5$$

51.
$$y = \frac{x}{7}$$

Below is a list of the problems in this review and the pages on which the skills are taught. If you missed any problems, turn to the pages listed and practice the skills. Then correct the problems you missed in the Unit Review.

Problems	Pages	Problems	Pages
1-8	110-111	30-33	121
9-16	113-114	34-42	122-124
17-20	115	43-48	125
21-29	116-118	49-51	126

Unit 5 ADDITION AND SUBTRACTION EQUATIONS

You work with positive and negative numbers when you balance your checkbook, figure how much sales figures are up or down, and see changes in the temperature outside. You will use the same ideas you did in working with positive and negative numbers when you solve equations using addition and subtraction.

In this unit, you will learn how to add and subtract positive and negative numbers and how to work addition and subtraction equations.

Getting Ready

You should be familiar with the skills on this page and the next before beginning this unit. To check your answers, turn to page 207.

 To write a numerical expression, change the words to numbers and math operations.

Write an expression. Then evaluate.

1. four plus two
   $4 + 2 = 6$

2. eight times three

3. thirty divided by five

4. twelve minus seven

5. six times nine

6. fifteen divided by three

For review, see Unit 4, page 115.   **131**

Getting Ready

 To evaluate numerical expressions, use the correct order of operations.

Evaluate. Use the correct order of operations.

7.
$3 + 7 \cdot 5$
$3 + 35 = 38$

8.
$8 - 2 \cdot 3$

9.
$6 + 7 \div 7$

10.
$18 - 9 \div 3$

11.
$9 + 2 - 3$

12.
$14 - 6 + 1$

13.
$70 - 15 \div 5$

14.
$100 - 44 \cdot 2$

For review see Unit 4, page 116.

 To evaluate algebraic expressions, use the correct order of operations.

Evaluate each expression if $x = 9$.

15.
$x + 4$
$9 + 4 = 13$

16.
$x - 2$

17.
$x + 3$

18.
$14 - x$

19.
$6x + (7 - 2)$

20.
$14 - x + 8$

21.
$(x + 5) + 2$

22.
$27 - x - 3$

For review, see Unit 4, pages 122-124.

To solve for the variable, use basic addition, subtraction, multiplication, and division.

Solve each equation.

23.
$x + 4 = 8$
$4 + 4 = 8$
$x = 4$

24.
$13 - x = 7$

25.
$10 + x = 15$

26.
$x - 9 = 1$

27.
$x - 2 = 6$

28.
$13 - x = 9$

29.
$19 - x = 0$

30.
$x + 10 = 11$

For review, see Unit 4, page 125.

Adding Signed Numbers

Numbers are either positive or negative. Positive numbers can show a gain or increase such as a price going up $5. Negative numbers can show a loss or decrease such as losing five pounds.

When adding positive and negative numbers, or signed numbers, follow these rules of addition. Remember that a positive number can be shown with or without the + sign.

> **Addition Rule 1.** To add two or more numbers with the same sign, add the numbers. Give the answer that sign.

For example, the temperature is -5 degrees at 10 P.M. By 11 P.M., it is 3 degrees colder. What is the temperature at 11 P.M.? To evaluate this expression, use Rule 1 for adding positive and negative numbers. Put parentheses around the -3 to keep the negative sign of the number from being confused with the addition operation sign, +.

$$-5 + (-3) = -8 \text{ degrees}$$

On the number line, find -5. Count 3 marks to the left. You can see that the new temperature is -8, or 8 degrees below zero.

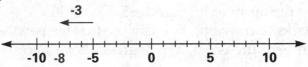

Use These Steps

Add $-6 + (-2)$

1. Add 6 and 2.

$$6 + 2 = 8$$

2. Since the numbers are both negative, give 8 a negative sign.

$$-6 + (-2) = -8$$

Add.

1.
$$7 + (+9)$$
$$7 + 9 = 16$$

2.
$$-12 + (-6)$$

3.
$$-20 + (-8)$$

4.
$$-15 + (-1) + (-4)$$

5.
$$-6 + (-10)$$

6.
$$1 + (+1)$$

7.
$$-8 + (-30)$$

8.
$$-11 + (-12) + (-3)$$

9. The temperature at 2 P.M. was 80°. It went up 5° by 5 P.M. What was the temperature at 5 P.M.?

10. The Samuels Company lost $200 in sales in May and $50 in June. Show their total loss in sales for May and June. (Hint: Show a loss in sales as a negative number. Add.)

Answer_____

Answer_____

Adding Signed Numbers

When you add numbers with different signs, use this rule.

> **Addition Rule 2.** To add numbers with different signs, find the difference between the numbers. Give the answer the sign of the larger number.

For example, yesterday morning at 6 A.M. the temperature was 5 degrees below zero. By 2 P.M. the temperature had risen 10 degrees. What was the temperature at 2 P.M.? To evaluate this expression, use Rule 2 for adding numbers.

$$-5 + 10 = 5 \text{ degrees}$$

The difference between 10 and 5 is 5. The answer is positive because the larger number, 10, is positive.

On the number line, find -5. Count 10 marks to the right. You can see that the new temperature is $+5$, or 5 degrees above zero.

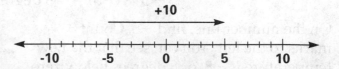

Use These Steps

Add $6 + (-8)$

1. **Find the difference between 8 and 6.**

$$8 - 6 = 2$$

2. **Since -8 is the larger number, give the answer a negative sign.**

$$6 + (-8) = -2$$

Add.

1.
$7 + (-2)$
$7 - 2 = 5$

2.
$-9 + 4$

3.
$4 + (-10)$

4.
$-12 + 6$

5.
$8 + (-9)$

6.
$-10 + 11$

7.
$-18 + 9$

8.
$15 + (-5)$

9.
$-22 + 7$

10.
$-40 + 70$

11.
$16 + (-32)$

12.
$25 + (-20)$

13.
$19 + (-20)$

14.
$-54 + 49$

15.
$-75 + 100$

16.
$68 + (-100)$

Adding Signed Numbers

When you add three or more numbers with different signs, use this rule.

> **Addition Rule 3.** To add three or more signed numbers, add the positive numbers. Add the negative numbers. Then add the two totals. Use Rule 2 to find the sign.

Knowing how to group positive and negative numbers together will be helpful when you balance a checking or savings account.

Use These Steps

Add $9 + (-10) + (-4) + 1$

1. Group the negative numbers and group the positive numbers.

$9 + 1 + (-10) + (-4)$

2. Add the positive numbers and add the negative numbers.

$9 + 1 + (-10) + (-4)$
  10 -14

3. Add the two totals. Since -14 is the larger number, give the answer a negative sign.

$10 + (-14) = -4$

Add.

1.
$-8 + (-2) + 6$
$-8 + (-2) + 6$
$-10 \quad + 6 = -4$

2.
$4 + (-1) + (-3)$

3.
$-6 + 4 + (-10)$

4.
$12 + (-7) + (-7)$

5.
$-22 + (-4) + 3 + 9$

6.
$40 + (-10) + (-20) + 10$

7.
$16 + (-25) + 25 + (-16)$

8.
$-20 + (-19) + (-14) + 8$

9.
$49 + (-54) + 6 + 9$

10.
$-22 + (-8) + (-7) + 32$

Add the following deposits (+) and withdrawals (−).

11.
$\$100 + (-\$50) + \$100 + (-\$60)$

12.
$-\$12 + (-\$38) + \$200 + (-\$25)$

13.
$\$125 + (-\$47) + (-\$23) + (-\$64)$

14.
$-\$15 + \$75 + \$56 + (-\$19)$

Subtracting Signed Numbers

When you subtract signed numbers, use the subtraction rule. Then use the addition rules you have already learned.

> **Subtraction Rule.** To subtract signed numbers, change the sign of the number being subtracted. Then add.

For example, yesterday afternoon at 6 P.M. the temperature was 2 degrees above zero. By 9 P.M. the temperature had fallen 10 degrees. What was the temperature at 9 P.M.? To find the answer, change the sign of the number being subtracted, 10. Positive 10 becomes -10. Then add.

$$2 - 10$$
$$2 + (-10) = -8 \text{ degrees}$$

On the number line, find $+2$. Count to the left 10 marks. You can see that the new temperature is -8, or 8 degrees below zero.

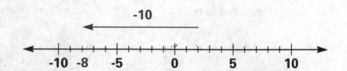

Use These Steps

Subtract $-11 - (+6)$

1. Change the sign of the number being subtracted.

$(+6)$ becomes (-6)

2. Add. Since the numbers are both negative, give 17 a negative sign.

$-11 + (-6) = -17$

Subtract.

1.
$3 - (+7)$
$3 + (-7) = -4$

2.
$-7 - (+6)$

3.
$-9 - (+2)$

4.
$10 - (+1)$

5.
$8 - (+9)$

6.
$-15 - (+12)$

7.
$-8 - (+6)$

8.
$17 - (+5)$

9.
$4 - (+4)$

10.
$20 - (+25)$

11.
$-14 - (+7)$

12.
$-30 - (+15)$

Write the following expressions in numbers. Subtract.

13. positive eleven minus positive seven

14. negative eight minus positive six

Subtracting Signed Numbers

Use the Subtraction Rule when you subtract positive or negative numbers.

Use These Steps

Subtract $10 - (-7)$

1. Change the sign of the number being subtracted.

   (-7) becomes $(+7)$

2. Add the two numbers. Since they are both positive, 17 is positive.

   $10 + (+7) = 17$

Subtract.

1.
$6 - (-1)$
$6 + (+1) = 7$

2.
$-15 - (-9)$

3.
$-18 - (-10)$

4.
$7 - (-3)$

5.
$-12 - (-13)$

6.
$11 - (-6)$

7.
$20 - (-10)$

8.
$-33 - (-4)$

9.
$25 - (-13)$

10.
$-46 - (-12)$

11.
$80 - (-40)$

12.
$54 - (-8)$

13.
$-17 - (-20)$

14.
$-39 - (-40)$

15.
$16 - (-16)$

16.
$-27 - (-27)$

Write the following expressions in numbers. Subtract.

17. positive twenty-seven minus negative seventeen

18. negative sixty minus negative sixteen

19. positive fifteen minus negative five

20. negative forty-six minus negative sixty-four

Adding with Zeros

Sometimes you need to add zeros. Remember the addition fact that zero plus any number equals that number.

$$3 + 0 = 3 \qquad\qquad 0 + 4 = 4$$
$$-5 + 0 = -5 \qquad\qquad 0 + (-7) = -7$$

When you add opposite numbers, the answer is always zero.

$$2 + (-2) = 0 \qquad\qquad -9 + 9 = 0$$

Use These Steps

Add $-5 + 5$

1. Use Addition Rule 2 since you are adding a positive and a negative number. Find the difference between 5 and 5.

$$5 - 5 = 0$$

2. Since the difference is zero, you do not need to put a sign in front of the answer.

$$-5 + 5 = 0$$

Write the opposite.

1. -6 __6__   2. 4 _____   3. -7 _____   4. 10 _____

5. 17 _____   6. 19 _____   7. -25 _____   8. -30 _____

Add.

9.
$$6 + (-6)$$
$$6 - 6 = 0$$
$$6 + (-6) = 0$$

10.
$$-4 + 0$$

11.
$$0 + 2$$

12.
$$0 + (-6)$$

13.
$$7 + (-7)$$

14.
$$-9 + 0$$

15.
$$0 + (-8)$$

16.
$$3 + 0$$

17.
$$-1 + 0$$

18.
$$10 + (-10)$$

19.
$$-12 + 12$$

20.
$$-15 + 0$$

21.
$$-20 + 20$$

22.
$$14 + (-14)$$

23.
$$0 + 3$$

24.
$$-36 + 36$$

Subtracting with Zeros

Sometimes you need to subtract zeros. Remember the subtraction fact that a number minus zero is that number.

$$6 - 0 = 6 \qquad\qquad (-5) - 0 = -5$$

Sometimes you may need to subtract from zero. Use the rule for subtraction.

$$0 - 5 \qquad\qquad\qquad 0 - (-7)$$
$$0 + (-5) = -5 \qquad\qquad 0 + (+7) = 7$$

When you subtract a number from itself, the answer is zero.

$$4 - 4 \qquad\qquad\qquad -9 - (-9)$$
$$4 + (-4) = 0 \qquad\qquad -9 + (+9) = 0$$

Use These Steps

Subtract $-6 - (-6)$

1. Use the Subtraction Rule. Change the sign of the number being subtracted.

   (-6) becomes $(+6)$

2. Add. Since the difference is zero, you do not need to put a sign in front of the answer.

   $-6 + (+6) = 0$

Subtract.

1.
$0 - (-6)$
$0 + (+6) = 6$

2.
$5 - 0$

3.
$-8 - 0$

4.
$0 - (+10)$

5.
$-9 - (-9)$

6.
$2 - (+2)$

7.
$0 - (-11)$

8.
$-13 - 0$

9.
$0 - 23$

10.
$-8 - (-8)$

11.
$15 - 0$

12.
$18 - (+18)$

13.
$-4 - (-4)$

14.
$0 - (-17)$

15.
$-9 - 0$

16.
$0 - 30$

17.
$12 - (+12)$

18.
$8 - 0$

19.
$-3 - (-3)$

20.
$0 - (-14)$

Mixed Review

Add or subtract.

1. $-4 + (+6)$

2. $8 - (+3)$

3. $-15 + 23$

4. $10 + (-25) + 15$

5. $4 - (+9)$

6. $8 + (-3)$

7. $-10 - (+7)$

8. $-43 + (-5) + (-2)$

9. $7 - (-2)$

10. $-8 - (+8)$

11. $-19 - (-6)$

12. $-9 + (-10) + (-6)$

13. $-2 + (-8) + 7$

14. $11 - (-8)$

15. $-1 + (-1)$

16. $-20 - (+17)$

17. $4 + 0$

18. $-9 + 0$

19. $-10 + 10$

20. $0 - (-15)$

21. $0 + 8$

22. $-4 - (+4)$

23. $-18 + 0$

24. $0 + (-16)$

25. $0 - (+10)$

26. $7 + (-7)$

27. $-6 - (-6)$

28. $-40 + 40$

29. $-3 - (+8)$

30. $14 - (+6)$

31. $29 - (+30)$

32. $0 - (+7)$

33. $-3 + 9 + (-6) + 4$

34. $-5 + (-6) + 6$

35. $10 + (-10) + (-2) + 2$

36. $8 - (-8)$

37. $76 - (+42)$

38. $-60 - (-50)$

39. $100 - (-50)$

Solving Addition Equations

To solve an addition equation means to find the value of the unknown, or variable. In an addition equation, subtract the same number from each side of the equation to leave the variable by itself on one side of the equal sign. You can check to see if the value for x is correct by substituting 2 for x in the equation.

$$x + 3 = 5$$
$$x(+ 3 - 3) = (5 - 3)$$
$$\quad 0 \qquad 2$$
$$x = 2$$

Check
$$x + 3 = 5$$
$$2 + 3 = 5$$
$$5 = 5, \text{ so } x = 2$$

Use These Steps

Solve $x + 9 = 10$

1. Subtract 9 from both sides of the equal sign.

$$x + 9 = 10$$
$$x + 9 - 9 = 10 - 9$$

2. $9 - 9 = 0$, so only x remains on the left side of the equation. $10 - 9 = 1$, so the value for x is 1.

$$x(+ 9 - 9) = (10 - 9)$$
$$\quad 0 \qquad\quad 1$$
$$x = 1$$

3. Check the answer by substituting the value of x into the original equation.

$$x + 9 = 10$$
$$1 + 9 = 10$$
$$10 = 10$$

Solve. Check.

1.
$$x + 4 = 7$$
$$x(+ 4 - 4) = (7 - 4)$$
$$\quad 0 \qquad\quad 3$$
$$x = 3$$
Check: $x + 4 = 7$
$$3 + 4 = 7$$
$$7 = 7$$

2.
$$x + 6 = 11$$

3.
$$x + 12 = 13$$

4.
$$x + 8 = 23$$

5.
$$19 + x = 27$$
$$(19 - 19) + x = (27 - 19)$$
$$\quad 0 \qquad\qquad 8$$
$$x = 8$$
Check: $19 + x = 27$
$$19 + 8 = 27$$
$$27 = 27$$

6.
$$35 + x = 70$$

7.
$$5 + x = 83$$

8.
$$40 + x = 99$$

9.
$$6 + x = 13$$

10.
$$x + 2 = 15$$

11.
$$x + 16 = 32$$

12.
$$25 + x = 50$$

Solving Addition Equations

Remember, use subtraction to solve an addition equation. Always subtract the same number from both sides of the equal sign.

Use These Steps

Solve $24 + x = -39$

1. Subtract 24 from both sides of the equal sign. $-39 - 24$ is the same as $-39 - (+24)$.

$$24 + x = -39$$
$$24 - 24 + x = -39 - 24$$

2. $24 - 24 = 0$, so only x remains on the left side of the equation. $-39 - 24 = -63$, so the value for x is -63.

$$\underbrace{24 - 24}_{0} + x = \underbrace{-39 - 24}_{-63}$$
$$x = -63$$

3. Check the answer by substituting the value of x into the original equation.

$$24 + x = -39$$
$$24 + (-63) = -39$$
$$-39 = -39$$

Solve. Check.

1.
$$15 + x = -6$$
$$\underbrace{15 - 15}_{0} + x = \underbrace{-6 - 15}_{-21}$$
$$x = -21$$
Check: $15 + x = -6$
$$15 + (-21) = -6$$
$$-6 = -6$$

2. $x + 8 = -10$

3. $x + 30 = -50$

4. $9 + x = -5$

5. $13 + x = -13$

6. $x + 42 = -12$

7. $x + 17 = -1$

8. $x + 4 = 0$

9. $50 + x = -10$

10. $21 + x = -4$

11. $16 + x = 0$

12. $x + 33 = -11$

Write an equation for each word expression. Use x for the variable. Solve. Check.

13. a number plus seven equals negative forty-two

14. eleven plus a number equals negative four

Solving Subtraction Equations

To solve a subtraction equation, add the same number to both sides of the equation. Make sure the variable is by itself on one side of the equation.

Use These Steps

Solve $x - 12 = 7$

1. Add 12 to both sides of the equal sign.

$$x - 12 = 7$$
$$x - 12 + 12 = 7 + 12$$

2. $-12 + 12 = 0$, so only x remains on the left side of the equation. $7 + 12 = 19$, so the value for x is 19.

$$x \underbrace{- 12 + 12}_{0} = \underbrace{7 + 12}_{19}$$
$$x = 19$$

3. Check the answer by substituting the value of x into the original equation.

$$x - 12 = 7$$
$$19 - 12 = 7$$
$$7 = 7$$

Solve. Check.

1.
$$x - 4 = 6$$
$$x \underbrace{- 4 + 4}_{0} = \underbrace{6 + 4}_{10}$$
$$x = 10$$
Check: $x - 4 = 6$
$$10 - 4 = 6$$
$$6 = 6$$

2.
$$x - 9 = 12$$

3.
$$x - 6 = 10$$

4.
$$x - 8 = 3$$

5.
$$x - 10 = 2$$

6.
$$x - 17 = 7$$

7.
$$x - 20 = 3$$

8.
$$x - 42 = 67$$

9.
$$x - 100 = 31$$

10.
$$x - 83 = 40$$

11.
$$x - 26 = 0$$

12.
$$x - 13 = 13$$

Solving Subtraction Equations

Sometimes the number on the right of the equal sign is negative. You can still use addition to solve subtraction equations.

Use These Steps

Solve $x - 6 = -3$

1. Add 6 to both sides of the equation.

$$x - 6 = -3$$
$$x - 6 + 6 = -3 + 6$$

2. $-6 + 6 = 0$, so only x remains on the left side of the equation. $-3 + 6 = 3$, so 3 is the value for x.

$$x \underbrace{- 6 + 6}_{0} = \underbrace{-3 + 6}_{3}$$
$$x = 3$$

3. Check.

$$x - 6 = -3$$
$$3 - 6 = -3$$
$$-3 = -3$$

Solve. Check.

1.
$$x - 4 = -4$$
$$x \underbrace{- 4 + 4}_{0} = \underbrace{-4 + 4}_{0}$$
$$x = 0$$
Check: $x - 4 = -4$
$$0 - 4 = -4$$
$$-4 = -4$$

2. $x - 9 = -1$ +9

3. $x - 7 = -6$ +7

4. $x - 10 = -11$

5. $x - 15 = -19$

6. $x - 14 = -3$

7. $x - 12 = -17$

8. $x - 23 = -30$

9. $x - 1 = -1$

10. $x - 30 = -15$

11. $x - 29 = -9$

12. $x - 51 = -27$

Write an equation for each word expression. Use x for the variable. Solve. Check.

13. a number minus eight equals negative four

14. a number minus twenty equals negative thirteen

Unit 5 Review

Add.

1. $8 + (-6)$

2. $-10 + 12$

3. $-16 + (-10)$

4. $-1 + (-1)$

5. $-59 + (-8) + (-1) + (-12)$

6. $75 + (-25) + (-5) + 20$

7. $-3 + (-6) + (-5) + 11$

8. $63 + 39 + (-36) + 3$

Subtract.

9. $6 - 4$

10. $-10 - 6$

11. $-12 - (-6)$

12. $15 - (-3)$

13. $17 - (+8)$

14. $32 - (+19)$

15. $-2 - (+16)$

16. $-40 - (+50)$

Add or subtract.

17. $0 + (-7)$

18. $-11 + 11$

19. $7 - 7$

20. $0 - 2$

Solve. Check.

21. $x + 5 = 10$

22. $12 + x = 16$

23. $x + 1 = 2$

24. $45 + x = 51$

25. $x + 6 = 0$

26. $x + 10 = -10$

27. $15 + x = 2$

28. $8 + x = -3$

Write an equation for each word expression. Use x for the variable. Solve. Check.

29. a number plus thirteen equals twenty-five

30. seven plus a number equals negative five

31. a number minus twenty-four equals twelve

32. a number minus ten equals zero

Solve. Check.

33.
$$x - 21 = -7$$

34.
$$x - 13 = 4$$

35.
$$x - 40 = 6$$

36.
$$x - 18 = 2$$

37.
$$x - 15 = -3$$

38.
$$x - 10 = -4$$

39.
$$x - 12 = -6$$

40.
$$x - 9 = -1$$

Below is a list of the problems in this review and the pages on which the skills are taught. If you missed any problems, turn to the pages listed and practice the skills. Then correct the problems you missed in the Unit Review.

Problems	Pages	Problems	Pages
1-8	133-135	21-30	141-142
9-16	136-137	31-40	143-144
17-20	138-139		

You may need to find some unknown information in order to build a garage, to put down tile or carpet, or to plant a garden. Knowing how to solve equations will help you find the missing information.

In this unit, you will learn how to multiply and divide positive and negative numbers. You will also learn how to solve multiplication and division equations as well as equations with all basic math operations.

Getting Ready

You should be familiar with the skills on this page and the next before beginning this unit. To check your answers, turn to page 210.

 To write a numerical expression, change the words to numbers and math operations.

Write an expression. Then evaluate.

1. five times seven
   $5 \times 7 = 35$

2. ten divided by two

3. eight times nine

4. sixteen divided by four

5. twenty-five divided by five

6. ten times ten

To evaluate numerical expressions, use the correct order of operations.

Evaluate. Use the correct order of operations.

7.

$\underbrace{(6 \times 4)}_{24} \div 3$

$24 \div 3 = 8$

8. $15 \div 3 \times 2$

9. $\dfrac{40}{8} \cdot 6$

10. $9 \cdot 8 \div 3$

11. $5 \times \dfrac{14}{7}$

12. $18 \div 9 \times 7$

13. $6 \cdot 8 \div 12$

14. $\dfrac{30}{5} \div 2$

For review, see Unit 4, pages 115–116.

 To evaluate algebraic expressions, substitute the given number for the variable.

Evaluate each expression if $x = 12$.

15.

$3x$

$3 \cdot 12 = 36$

16. $\dfrac{x}{4}$

17. $\dfrac{5x}{3}$

18. $2x \cdot 6$

19. $18 \div \dfrac{x}{4}$

20. $x \cdot \dfrac{1}{6}$

21. $7x \div 4$

22. $\dfrac{24}{x}$

For review, see Unit 4, page 122.

 To solve for the variable, use basic addition, subtraction, multiplication, and division.

Solve each equation.

23.

$3x = 9$

$3 \cdot 3 = 9$

$x = 3$

24. $\dfrac{x}{7} = 2$

25. $2x = 10$

26. $\dfrac{x}{4} = 3$

27. $5x = 20$

28. $\dfrac{x}{10} = 1$

29. $\dfrac{x}{3} = 6$

30. $4x = 12$

For review, see Unit 4, page 125.

Multiplying Signed Numbers

When you multiply signed numbers, follow the rules of multiplication. When multiplying two numbers with the same sign, use Rule 1.

Rule 1: To multiply numbers with the same sign, multiply and give the answer a positive sign.

$$-6 \cdot -3 = 18 \quad \text{or} \quad (-6)(-3) = 18$$
$$4(9) = 36 \quad \text{or} \quad (4)(9) = 36$$
$$(-4)(-3) = 12 \quad \text{or} \quad -4(-3) = 12$$

Notice that multiplication is shown using parentheses around one or both signed numbers in a problem. Parentheses are used with signed numbers to avoid confusing operation signs and negative number signs.

Use These Steps

Multiply $-7(-2)$

1. Multiply the two numbers.

2. Since both numbers have the same sign, the answer is positive.

$$7(2) = 14 \qquad\qquad -7(-2) = 14$$

Multiply.

1.
$(7)(3) = 21$

2.
$-10(-8)$

3.
$4(9)$

4.
$(-8)(-6)$

5.
$-12(-1)$

6.
$5(2)$

7.
$-15(-3)$

8.
$21(4)$

9.
$-1(-7)$

10.
$(36)(9)$

11.
$-13(-10)$

12.
$-40(-6)$

13.
$-103(-7)$

14.
$2(50)$

15.
$-17(-20)$

Write a multiplication problem using the words given. Multiply.

16. negative twenty-two multiplied by negative five

17. negative nineteen times negative thirty

Multiplying Signed Numbers

When you multiply two numbers with different signs, use this rule.

Rule 2: To multiply numbers with different signs, multiply and give the answer a negative sign.

$$(-5)(8) = -40 \qquad \text{or} \qquad -5(8) = -40$$
$$7(-1) = -7 \qquad \text{or} \qquad (7)(-1) = -7$$

Remember, zero times any number is always zero.

$$-10(0) = 0 \qquad\qquad (0)(-12) = 0$$

Use These Steps

Multiply $(6)(-10)$

1. Multiply the two numbers.

2. Since the numbers have different signs, the answer is negative.

$$(6)(10) = 60$$

$$(6)(-10) = -60$$

Multiply.

1.
$(-2)(3)$
(2)(3) = 6
(−2)(3) = −6

2.
$-5(4)$

3.
$(-9)(0)$

4.
$-7(2)$

5.
$-5(1)$

6.
$(10)(-5)$

7.
$(8)(-6)$

8.
$12(-3)$

9.
$-20(7)$

10.
$-16(2)$

11.
$(4)(-25)$

12.
$(-1)(30)$

Write a multiplication problem using the words given. Multiply.

13. negative three multiplied by positive twenty

14. positive forty-five times negative two

Dividing Signed Numbers

The rules for dividing signed numbers are the same as the rules for multiplying signed numbers. In algebra, division is usually shown with a fraction bar. Always divide the numerator by the denominator.

Rule 1: To divide numbers with the same sign, divide and give the answer a positive sign.

$$\frac{-6}{-3} = 2 \qquad \frac{24}{3} = 8$$

Use These Steps

Divide $\dfrac{-35}{-5}$

1. Divide the two numbers.

$$\frac{35}{5} = 7$$

2. Since both numbers have the same sign, the answer is positive.

$$\frac{-35}{-5} = 7$$

Divide.

1. $\dfrac{4}{2} = 2$

2. $\dfrac{-21}{-3}$

3. $\dfrac{-6}{-1}$

4. $\dfrac{12}{6}$

5. $\dfrac{-18}{-3}$

6. $\dfrac{27}{9}$

7. $\dfrac{-14}{-7}$

8. $\dfrac{-24}{-8}$

9. $\dfrac{30}{2}$

10. $\dfrac{-26}{-13}$

11. $\dfrac{49}{7}$

12. $\dfrac{-1}{-1}$

13. $\dfrac{63}{9}$

14. $\dfrac{70}{10}$

15. $\dfrac{-32}{-1}$

16. $\dfrac{100}{10}$

17. $\dfrac{-81}{-9}$

18. $\dfrac{-16}{-4}$

19. $\dfrac{72}{12}$

20. $\dfrac{-75}{-5}$

Write a division problem using the words given. Divide.

21. negative twenty-two divided by negative eleven

22. positive twelve divided by positive three

23. negative thirty-five divided by negative seven

24. positive sixteen divided by positive eight

Dividing Signed Numbers

When only one of the numbers in a division problem is negative, the answer is negative.

> **Rule 2:** To divide numbers with different signs, divide and give the answer a negative sign.

$$\frac{-70}{10} = -7 \qquad \frac{15}{-1} = -15$$

Notice that the negative sign may be shown in different places. The answer is the same.

$$\frac{-10}{2} = -5 \qquad -\frac{10}{2} = -5 \qquad \frac{10}{-2} = -5$$

Remember, zero divided by any number is always zero.

$$\frac{0}{-6} = 0$$

Use These Steps

Divide $\dfrac{36}{-9}$

1. Divide the two numbers.

$$\frac{36}{9} = 4$$

2. Since the numbers have different signs, the answer is negative.

$$\frac{36}{-9} = -4$$

Divide. Write remainders as fractions.

1. $\dfrac{-5}{2} = -2\dfrac{1}{2}$
2. $-\dfrac{0}{4}$
3. $\dfrac{18}{-6}$
4. $-\dfrac{84}{12}$

5. $\dfrac{-16}{2}$
6. $\dfrac{-25}{5}$
7. $\dfrac{21}{-4}$
8. $\dfrac{0}{-3}$

9. $-\dfrac{45}{9}$
10. $\dfrac{-50}{25}$
11. $-\dfrac{45}{2}$
12. $\dfrac{-100}{25}$

13. $\dfrac{33}{-8}$
14. $\dfrac{-15}{3}$
15. $-\dfrac{29}{7}$
16. $\dfrac{81}{-9}$

Write a division problem using the words given. Divide.

17. negative fifteen divided by positive one

18. positive twenty-three divided by negative five

Mixed Review

Multiply.

1. $(-6)(-7)$

2. $(-13)(-4)$

3. $(7)(9)$

4. $(-2)(6)$

5. $(1)(-7)$

6. $(-9)(3)$

7. $-11(-5)$

8. $8(-12)$

9. $-4(-10)$

10. $3(-8)$

11. $(4)(5)$

12. $(-6)(-3)$

Divide. Write remainders as fractions.

13. $\dfrac{-6}{-2}$

14. $\dfrac{-14}{-7}$

15. $\dfrac{-9}{-3}$

16. $\dfrac{36}{-6}$

17. $\dfrac{-40}{20}$

18. $-\dfrac{81}{9}$

19. $\dfrac{-33}{-5}$

20. $-\dfrac{17}{3}$

21. $\dfrac{51}{-4}$

22. $\dfrac{-11}{3}$

23. $\dfrac{-7}{-1}$

24. $\dfrac{45}{-5}$

Write a multiplication or division problem using the words given. Multiply or divide.

25. negative nine multiplied by negative ten

26. negative thirty-two divided by positive four

27. positive six times negative twelve

28. negative twenty divided by negative two

29. positive eighteen times positive three

30. positive twenty-nine divided by negative seven

31. negative thirteen multiplied by negative three

32. positive forty divided by negative nine

Solving Multiplication Equations

To solve a multiplication equation, use division in order to leave the variable by itself on one side of the equal sign. Divide the same number into each side of the equation.

$$5x = 10$$
$$\frac{5x}{5} = \frac{10}{5}$$
$$x = 2$$

Since 5 divided by 5 is 1, just write the variable by itself. The 1 is not shown in algebra.

Use These Steps

Solve $3x = 9$

1. Divide both sides of the equal sign by 3.

$$3x = 9$$
$$\frac{3x}{3} = \frac{9}{3}$$

2. $\frac{3}{3} = 1$, so only x remains on the left side of the equal sign. $\frac{9}{3} = 3$, so the value for x is 3.

$$\frac{3x}{3} = \frac{9}{3}$$
$$x = 3$$

3. Check the answer by substituting the value of x into the original equation.

$$3x = 9$$
$$3(3) = 9$$
$$9 = 9$$

Solve. Reduce fractions to lowest terms. Check.

1.
$$2x = 1 \quad \text{Check: } 2x = 1$$
$$\frac{2x}{2} = \frac{1}{2} \qquad 2\left(\frac{1}{2}\right) = 1$$
$$x = \frac{1}{2} \qquad\qquad 1 = 1$$

2.
$$9x = 3$$

3.
$$7x = 42$$

4.
$$8x = 48$$

5.
$$6x = 54$$

6.
$$7x = 4$$

7.
$$5x = 15$$

8.
$$12x = 8$$

9.
$$4x = 20$$

Solving Multiplication Equations

Some multiplication equations contain negative numbers. You can still use division to solve these equations. Follow the rules on pages 151 and 152 for dividing signed numbers.

Use These Steps

Solve $-12y = 36$

1. Divide both sides of the equation by -12.

$$-12y = 36$$
$$\frac{-12y}{-12} = \frac{36}{-12}$$

2. $\frac{-12}{-12} = 1$, so only y remains on the left side of the equation. $\frac{36}{-12} = -3$, so the value for y is -3.

$$\frac{-12y}{-12} = \frac{36}{-12}$$
$$y = -3$$

3. Check the answer by substituting the value of y into the original equation.

$$-12y = 36$$
$$-12(-3) = 36$$
$$36 = 36$$

Solve. Reduce fractions if possible. Check.

1.

$$-7x = 1 \quad \text{Check: } -7x = 1$$
$$\frac{-7x}{-7} = \frac{1}{-7} \quad -7\left(\frac{1}{-7}\right) = 1$$
$$x = \frac{1}{-7} \quad\quad 1 = 1$$

2.

$$5x = -25$$

3.

$$-4x = 48$$

4.

$$-9y = -18$$

5.

$$-6y = -6$$

6.

$$-8y = 2$$

7.

$$-10y = 20$$

8.

$$-3y = -12$$

9.

$$10y = -4$$

10.

$$-3x = -2$$

11.

$$-5x = -3$$

12.

$$-4x = -2$$

Solving Division Equations

To solve a division equation, multiply both sides of the equation by the same number.

Use These Steps

Solve $\dfrac{x}{4} = 5$

1. Multiply both sides of the equal sign by 4.

$$\dfrac{x}{4} = 5$$

$$4 \cdot \dfrac{x}{4} = 5 \cdot 4$$

2. $\dfrac{4}{4} = 1$, so only x remains on the left side. $5 \times 4 = 20$, so the value for x is 20.

$$\dfrac{4x}{4} = 20$$

$$x = 20$$

3. Check the answer by substituting the value of x into the original equation.

$$\dfrac{x}{4} = 5$$

$$\dfrac{20}{4} = 5$$

$$5 = 5$$

Solve. Check.

1.
$$\dfrac{x}{5} = 10 \quad \text{Check: } \dfrac{x}{5} = 10$$

$$5 \cdot \dfrac{x}{5} = 10 \cdot 5 \qquad \dfrac{50}{5} = 10$$

$$\dfrac{5x}{5} = 50 \qquad\qquad 10 = 10$$

$$x = 50$$

2.
$$\dfrac{y}{3} = 9$$

3.
$$\dfrac{x}{7} = 4$$

4.
$$\dfrac{x}{9} = 6$$

5.
$$\dfrac{y}{6} = 10$$

6.
$$\dfrac{x}{4} = 15$$

7.
$$\dfrac{y}{5} = 5$$

8.
$$\dfrac{y}{8} = 7$$

9.
$$\dfrac{x}{6} = 4$$

10.
$$\dfrac{x}{7} = 5$$

11.
$$\dfrac{y}{9} = 4$$

12.
$$\dfrac{y}{8} = 10$$

Solving Division Equations

Some division equations contain negative numbers. You can still use multiplication to solve division equations. If the expression with the variable has a negative sign, be sure to multiply by a negative number. Follow the rules on pages 149 and 150 for multiplying signed numbers.

Use These Steps

Solve $\dfrac{y}{-3} = 8$

1. Multiply both sides of the equation by -3.

$$\dfrac{y}{-3} = 8$$

$$-3\left(\dfrac{y}{-3}\right) = 8\,(-3)$$

2. $\dfrac{-3}{-3} = 1$, so only y remains on the left side.
$8(-3) = -24$, so the value for y is -24.

$$\dfrac{-3y}{-3} = -24$$

$$y = -24$$

3. Check the answer by substituting the value of y into the original equation.

$$\dfrac{y}{-3} = 8$$

$$\dfrac{-24}{-3} = 8$$

$$8 = 8$$

Solve. Check.

1.
$$\dfrac{y}{-2} = 2$$

Check: $\dfrac{y}{-2} = 2$

$$-2\left(\dfrac{y}{-2}\right) = 2\,(-2)$$

$$\dfrac{-4}{-2} = 2$$

$$\dfrac{-2y}{-2} = -4$$

$$2 = 2$$

$$y = -4$$

2. $\dfrac{x}{8} = -6$

3. $\dfrac{y}{-9} = 15$

4. $\dfrac{x}{-7} = 14$

5. $\dfrac{y}{-9} = 3$

6. $\dfrac{y}{5} = -7$

7. $\dfrac{x}{-3} = -1$

8. $\dfrac{y}{-6} = -10$

9. $\dfrac{x}{-10} = -9$

10. $\dfrac{y}{4} = -6$

11. $\dfrac{x}{8} = -20$

12. $\dfrac{x}{-9} = -32$

Mixed Review

Solve. Check.

1.
$$3x = 9$$

2.
$$5x = 15$$

3.
$$9x = 2$$

4.
$$16x = 32$$

5.
$$4x = 1$$

6.
$$10y = 7$$

7.
$$-12x = 24$$

8.
$$-10x = -3$$

9.
$$-5x = 15$$

10.
$$3x = -12$$

11.
$$-4x = 16$$

12.
$$-6x = -48$$

13.
$$\frac{x}{2} = 6$$

14.
$$\frac{y}{3} = 12$$

15.
$$\frac{x}{4} = 6$$

16.
$$\frac{x}{-3} = 15$$

17.
$$\frac{x}{-4} = -16$$

18.
$$\frac{y}{-5} = 25$$

19.
$$\frac{x}{4} = 3$$

20.
$$\frac{y}{6} = -10$$

21.
$$\frac{y}{9} = 4$$

Reciprocals

Some equations have a fraction before the variable. For example, in the equation $\frac{2}{3}x = 9$, the fraction is $\frac{2}{3}$.

To solve this kind of equation, multiply both sides of the equation by the *reciprocal* of the fraction. You can find the reciprocal of any fraction by inverting (turning upside down) the fraction. The reciprocal of $\frac{2}{3}$ is $\frac{3}{2}$ and the reciprocal of $-\frac{2}{3}$ is $-\frac{3}{2}$.

When you multiply an expression with a fraction by the reciprocal of the fraction, they cancel each other out and leave the variable by itself.

Use These Steps

Multiply $\frac{1}{5}x$ by the reciprocal of the fraction.

1. Find the reciprocal of $\frac{1}{5}$.

$$\frac{1}{5} \diagup\!\!\!\!\diagdown \frac{5}{1}$$

2. Multiply $\frac{5}{1}$ by $\frac{1}{5}x$. Cancel.

$$\frac{\overset{1}{\cancel{5}}}{1} \cdot \frac{1}{\cancel{5}}x = \frac{1}{1}x = x$$

Write the reciprocal of each fraction.

1. $\frac{1}{4}$

$$\frac{1}{4} \diagup\!\!\!\!\diagdown \frac{4}{1}$$

2. $-\frac{1}{6}$

3. $\frac{1}{8}$

4. $-\frac{1}{10}$

5. $\frac{1}{15}$

6. $\frac{2}{7}$

7. $-\frac{5}{6}$

8. $\frac{2}{5}$

9. $-\frac{3}{8}$

10. $\frac{7}{10}$

Multiply each expression by the reciprocal of the fraction. Cancel.

11. $\frac{4}{5}x$

$$\frac{\overset{1}{\cancel{5}}}{\cancel{4}} \cdot \frac{\overset{1}{\cancel{4}}}{\cancel{5}}x = \frac{1}{1}x = x$$

12. $-\frac{6}{7}x$

13. $\frac{2}{9}x$

14. $-\frac{7}{11}x$

15. $-\frac{2}{3}x$

16. $\frac{3}{5}y$

17. $\frac{1}{9}x$

18. $-\frac{3}{10}y$

19. $-\frac{7}{8}y$

20. $-\frac{1}{2}x$

Solving Fraction Equations

To solve a fraction equation, multiply each side of the equation by the reciprocal of the fraction. If the fraction is negative, be sure to put a negative sign in front of the reciprocal.

Use These Steps

Solve $\frac{2}{3}x = 4$

1. Multiply both sides by the reciprocal of $\frac{2}{3}$.

$$\frac{2}{3}x = 4$$

$$\frac{3}{2} \cdot \frac{2}{3}x = 4 \cdot \frac{3}{2}$$

2. $\frac{3}{2} \cdot \frac{2}{3}x = x$, so only x remains on the left side.

$4 \cdot \frac{3}{2} = \frac{12}{2}$, so the value for x is 6.

$$\frac{3}{2} \cdot \frac{2}{3}x = 4 \cdot \frac{3}{2}$$

$$x = \frac{12}{2}$$

$$x = 6$$

3. Check the answer by substituting the value of x into the original equation.

$$\frac{2}{3}x = 4$$

$$\frac{2}{3} \cdot 6 = 4$$

$$\frac{12}{3} = 4$$

$$4 = 4$$

Solve. Check.

1.

$$-\frac{7}{9}x = 14 \qquad \text{Check: } -\frac{7}{9}x = 14$$

$$-\frac{9}{7}\left(-\frac{7}{9}x\right) = 14\left(-\frac{9}{7}\right) \qquad -\frac{7}{9}(-18) = 14$$

$$x = -\frac{126}{7} \qquad\qquad \frac{126}{9} = 14$$

$$x = -18 \qquad\qquad\quad 14 = 14$$

2.

$$\frac{3}{4}y = -21$$

3.

$$\frac{3}{8}x = 9$$

4.

$$\frac{5}{6}x = 5$$

5.

$$\frac{4}{7}x = 8$$

6.

$$\frac{7}{10}x = -7$$

Solving Equations Using Two Operations

To solve some equations, you may need to use more than one operation. Add or subtract first. Then multiply or divide.

Use These Steps

Solve $3y + 4 = 10$

1. Subtract 4 from both sides.

$$3y + 4 = 10$$
$$3y + 4 - 4 = 10 - 4$$
$$0 \qquad 6$$
$$3y = 6$$

2. Divide both sides by 3.

$$\frac{3y}{3} = \frac{6}{3}$$
$$y = 2$$

3. Check the answer by substituting the value of y into the original equation.

$$3y + 4 = 10$$
$$3(2) + 4 = 10$$
$$6 + 4 = 10$$
$$10 = 10$$

Solve. Check.

1.

$$-3y + 8 = 2$$
$$-3y + 8 - 8 = 2 - 8$$
$$-3y = -6$$
$$\frac{-3y}{-3} = \frac{-6}{-3}$$
$$y = 2$$

Check: $-3y + 8 = 2$
$$-3(2) + 8 = 2$$
$$(-6) + 8 = 2$$
$$2 = 2$$

2.

$$10 + 5x = 20$$

3.

$$4y - 4 = 0$$

4.

$$3 - 6x = -39$$

5.

$$\frac{y}{2} - 6 = 4$$

6.

$$\frac{x}{2} + 6 = 3$$

7.

$$\frac{x}{3} - 1 = 3$$

8.

$$\frac{y}{4} - 5 = -15$$

Solving Equations Using Two Operations

When you solve equations, be sure to follow the rules for adding, subtracting, multiplying, and dividing signed numbers.

Use These Steps

Solve $\frac{3}{4}x - 12 = -12$

1. Add 12 to both sides.

$$\frac{3}{4}x - 12 = -12$$

$$\frac{3}{4}x \underbrace{(-12 + 12)}_{0} = \underbrace{(-12 + 12)}_{0}$$

$$\frac{3}{4}x = 0$$

2. Multiply both sides by $\frac{4}{3}$, the reciprocal of $\frac{3}{4}$.

$$\frac{4}{3} \cdot \frac{3}{4}x = 0 \cdot \frac{4}{3}$$

$$x = 0$$

3. Check the answer by substituting the value of x into the original equation.

$$\frac{3}{4}x - 12 = -12$$

$$\frac{3}{4} \cdot 0 - 12 = -12$$

$$0 - 12 = -12$$

$$-12 = -12$$

Solve. Check.

1.

$$\frac{2}{3}x + 2 = 10$$

$$\frac{2}{3}x + 2 - 2 = 10 - 2$$

$$\frac{2}{3}x = 8$$

$$\frac{3}{2} \cdot \frac{2}{3}x = 8 \cdot \frac{3}{2}$$

$$x = \frac{24}{2}$$

$$x = 12$$

Check: $\frac{2}{3}x + 2 = 10$

$$\frac{2}{3} \cdot 12 + 2 = 10$$

$$\frac{24}{3} + 2 = 10$$

$$8 + 2 = 10$$

$$10 = 10$$

2.

$$\frac{3}{10}x - 5 = -7$$

3.

$$\frac{2}{9}x - 6 = 44$$

4.

$$\frac{5}{7}x + 4 = -16$$

Unit 6 *Review*

Multiply.

1.
$(-6)(-4)$

2.
$(-1)(-10)$

3.
$-5(-4)$

4.
$(-7)(2)$

5.
$3(-8)$

6.
$-4(9)$

Divide.

7.
$\dfrac{-9}{-3}$

8.
$\dfrac{-5}{-1}$

9.
$\dfrac{-12}{-4}$

10.
$-\dfrac{6}{2}$

11.
$\dfrac{-18}{3}$

12.
$\dfrac{20}{-5}$

Solve. Check.

13.
$3x = 21$

14.
$8x = 56$

15.
$10x = 90$

16.
$-5x = 10$

17.
$-6x = -36$

18.
$4x = -16$

19.
$\dfrac{y}{4} = 6$

20.
$\dfrac{x}{3} = 8$

21.
$\dfrac{y}{2} = -10$

Write the reciprocal of each fraction.

22.
$\dfrac{1}{6}$

23.
$-\dfrac{9}{20}$

24.
$\dfrac{7}{12}$

Multiply each expression by the reciprocal of the fraction.

25.

$\dfrac{5}{9}x$

26.

$-\dfrac{2}{3}y$

27.

$\dfrac{7}{9}y$

Solve. Check.

28.

$\dfrac{3}{8}x = 15$

29.

$\dfrac{4}{5}x = -8$

30.

$\dfrac{2}{9}y = -6$

31.

$4x + 9 = 12$

32.

$\dfrac{y}{4} - 7 = 5$

33.

$-5x - 7 = 18$

34.

$\dfrac{3}{10}x - 4 = 20$

35.

$\dfrac{2}{3}x + 6 = 2$

36.

$\dfrac{9}{10}x - 9 = 0$

Below is a list of the problems in this review and the pages on which the skills are taught. If you missed any problems, turn to the pages listed and practice the skills. Then correct the problems you missed in the Unit Review.

Problems	Pages		Problems	Pages
1-6	149-150		22-27	159
7-12	151-152		28-30	160
13-18	154-155		31-36	161-162
19-21	156-157			

You have studied customary and metric measurement, basic geometry and formulas, and concepts of algebra. You have applied your understanding of measurement, geometry, and algebra in solving real-life problems and simple equations.

In this unit, you will study how to choose the correct formulas to solve problems in geometry. You will learn how to solve problems in geometry that require you to use more than one operation to find the answers. You will also learn how to work with the Pythagorean Theorem and similar triangles.

Getting Ready

You should be familiar with the skills on this page and the next before you begin this unit. To check your answers, turn to page 214.

 You should know how to square numbers and how to find the square root of numbers.

Find each answer.

1. $3^2 = 9$

2. $5^2 =$

3. $7^2 =$

4. $6^2 =$

5. $9^2 =$

6. $12^2 =$

7. $8^2 =$

8. $13^2 =$

9. $\sqrt{4} = 2$

10. $\sqrt{16} =$

11. $\sqrt{36} =$

12. $\sqrt{81} =$

13. $\sqrt{49} =$

14. $\sqrt{169} =$

15. $\sqrt{144} =$

16. $\sqrt{100} =$

You should be able to evaluate numerical expressions.

Evaluate each expression.

17.
$3^2 + 4^2$
$9 + 16 = 25$

18.
$9^2 - 2^2$

19.
$5^2 - 4^2$

20.
$1^2 + 8^2$

21.
$-3 + (-4) = -7$

22.
$9 - (-8)$

23.
$15 + (-10)$

24.
$-80 - 15$

For review, see Unit 4, pages 116-118, and Unit 5, pages 133-137.

 You should be able to evaluate algebraic expressions when the value for the variable is given.

Evaluate each expression if $x = 10$.

25.
$\dfrac{x}{2}$

$\dfrac{10}{2} = 5$

26.
$3 + x$

27.
$5x$

28.
$3x - 2$

29.
$19 - x$

30.
$-20 - x$

31.
$x - 6$

32.
$\dfrac{x}{2} - 1$

For review, see Unit 4, page 122.

You should be able to solve basic algebraic equations.

Solve.

33.
$9x = 45$
$\dfrac{9x}{9} = \dfrac{45}{9}$
$x = 5$

34.
$x - 2 = 10$

35.
$16 + x = 32$

36.
$x + 1 = 0$

37.
$\dfrac{3}{4}x = 15$

38.
$-10x = 100$

39.
$2x - 60 = 30$

40.
$\dfrac{1}{2}x + 2 = 1$

For review, see Unit 5, pages 141-144, and Unit 6, pages 154-157 and 160-162.

Choose a Formula: Finding Perimeter, Area, and Volume

You have used various formulas to find the perimeter, area, and volume of several geometric figures. Remember, a geometric formula shows the relationships among parts of a figure. The table lists these formulas. You will need to decide which formula to use to solve a problem.

	Perimeter	Area	Volume
■	$P = 4s$	$A = s^2$	$V = s^3$
▬	$P = 2l+2w$	$A = lw$	$V = lwh$
●	$C = \pi d$	$A = \pi r^2$	$V = \pi r^2 h$
▲		$A = \frac{1}{2}bh$	

Example Gail needs to know how many square feet are in the space in front of the seal pool at the zoo so that she can buy grass seed. The space is a rectangle that measures 20' by 45'. How many square feet is this?

Step 1. The problem asks for the number of square feet. To find square feet, use the formula for the area of a rectangle.

$$A = lw$$

Step 2. Substitute the numbers and multiply.

$$A = 45 \times 20$$
$$A = 900 \text{ square feet}$$

There are 900 square feet in the space in front of the seal pool.

Solve.

1. The employee lounge is shaped like a right triangle. One leg, or side, is 20' and the other leg is 30' long. How many square feet are in the employee lounge?

Answer_____

2. Haynes and Sons is building a fence around the circular fish pond at the capitol. The diameter of the area to be fenced is 10'. How many feet of fencing do they need?
(Hint: Use 3.14 for π.)

Answer_____

3. One side of the base of a packing box measures 2 feet. The box is 2 feet wide and 3 feet high. Circle the formula you would use to find how many cubic feet the box will hold.
   a. $V = lwh$ Solve for the answer.
   b. $P = 4s$
   c. $A = s^2$
   d. $V = s^3$

Answer_____

4. Jane is varnishing a door that is 3 feet by $6\frac{1}{2}$ feet. Circle the formula she would use to find the surface area of one side of the door.
   a. $P = 2l + 2w$ Solve for the answer.
   b. $A = lw$
   c. $V = lwh$
   d. $A = \pi r^2$

Answer_____

Sometimes you will be given the total perimeter, area, or volume and need to find one of the dimensions of the figure.

Example   Julius has to build a rectangular garden that covers an area of 120 square feet. The length of one side is 12 feet. What is the width of the garden?

Step 1.   Write the formula for the area of a rectangle.

$$A = lw$$

Step 2.   Substitute the given area and length.

$$120 = 12w$$

Step 3.   Since the unknown is usually on the left side of the equal sign, move 12w to the left side and 120 to the right side. Solve.

$$12w = 120$$
$$\frac{12w}{12} = \frac{120}{12}$$
$$w = 10$$

The width of the garden is 10 feet.

Solve.

5. Sabrina is making a rectangular patio cover that is 48 square feet in area. The length of one side is 4 feet. What is the length of the other side?

Answer_____

6. The circumference of a circular study area for the learning center is 154 feet. What is the diameter of the study area? (Hint: Use $\frac{22}{7}$ for π.)

Answer_____

7. The area of a triangular-shaped lot is 200 square feet. Circle the expression you would use to find the height of the triangle if the base is 20 feet.
   a. $200 = 20\,(h)$ Solve for the answer.
   b. $200 = \frac{1}{2}(20)(h)$
   c. $200 = \left(\frac{1}{2}\right)(h)$
   d. $200 = 2\,(20)(h)$

Answer_____

8. The area of the basement at Abe's Auto Parts is 225 square feet. Circle the expression you would use to find the length of each side if the basement is square.
   a. $225^2 = s$ Solve for the answer.
   b. $\frac{225}{4} = s$
   c. $\sqrt{225} = s$
   d. $\frac{225}{2} = 8$

Answer_____

Multi-Step Problems: Finding Area

Karen designs landscapes and gardens for construction companies. She often combines shapes to build patio areas or flower beds.

Example   Karen drew a sketch of a circle inside a square for a rose garden. Roses are to be planted only in the square outside the circle. What is the total area where she can plant roses?

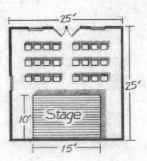

Step 1.   Find the area of the square.

$A = s^2$
$A = 28 \times 28 = 784$ square feet

Step 2.   Find the area of the circle. Since the diameter is 28 feet, the radius is 14 feet.

$A = \pi r^2$
$A = \dfrac{22}{7} \times \dfrac{14}{1} \times \dfrac{14}{1} = 616$ square feet

Step 3.   Subtract the area of the circle, 616 square feet, from the area of the square, 784 square feet, to find the total area where Karen can plant roses.

$$\begin{array}{r} 784 \\ -\ 616 \\ \hline 168 \end{array}$$

Karen can plant roses in an area of 168 square feet.

Solve.

1. Karen wants to put a 2-foot border around the outside of the rose garden. What will the area of the border be? (Hint: You will need to use the area of the square in the Example to find the answer.)

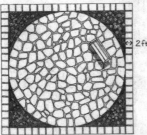

Answer_____

2. The meeting room at the Harper Hotel is being recarpeted. The room is square with 25-foot sides. The stage area, 10 feet by 15 feet, will not be carpeted. What is the total area being carpeted?

Answer_____

Solve.

3. Ted, an architect, drew this sketch for remodeling a garage. The total area of the garage is 360 square feet. If Ted changes the bedroom to 12' by 18', the office to 8' by 14', and the bath to 4' by 8', will the total area of the three rooms equal 360 square feet?

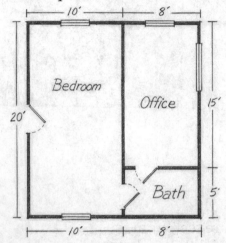

Answer_____

4. Gregorio has been hired to add a triangular-shaped cement area next to the driveway as shown in the drawing. What will be the total area of the driveway and the addition?

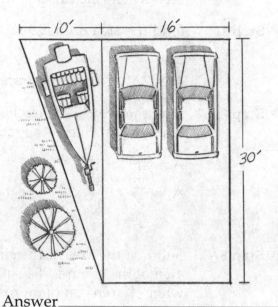

Answer_____

5. Petersons Painters are painting the 4 sides of this barn. They need to know the total surface area of the sides before they buy paint. Using the dimensions shown in the drawing, what is the total surface area they are painting?
(Hint: Find the surface area of the 4 sides including the door.)

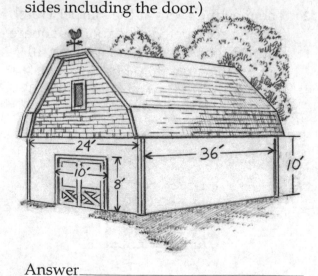

Answer_____

6. Alma will wallpaper a wall in this living room. Using the dimensions shown in the drawing, what is the area of the wall to be covered?
(Hint: Find the areas of the window and the door. Subtract these areas from the total area of the wall.)

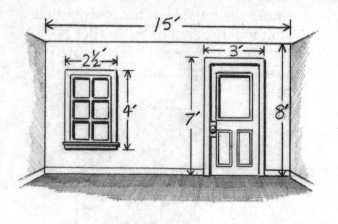

Answer_____

The Pythagorean Theorem

The Pythagorean Theorem shows how the lengths of the sides of a right triangle are related. If you know the lengths of the two shorter sides, called legs, you can find the length of the third side, called the hypotenuse. The hypotenuse is always opposite the right angle.

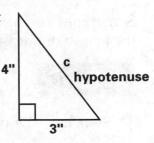

The formula shows that the sum of the squares of the two legs is equal to the square of the hypotenuse.

$$a^2 + b^2 = c^2$$

Example The right triangle above has legs that are 3 inches and 4 inches long. Find the length of the hypotenuse.

Step 1. Write the formula and substitute the correct numbers.

$$a^2 + b^2 = c^2$$
$$3^2 + 4^2 = c^2$$

Step 2. Simplify by finding the squares and adding.

$$9 + 16 = c^2$$
$$25 = c^2$$

Step 3. Since $c^2 = 25$, find c by finding the square root of 25.

$$c = \sqrt{25} = 5$$

The length of the third side is 5 inches.

Solve.

1. Find the hypotenuse of a right triangle with legs that are 12 inches and 5 inches long.

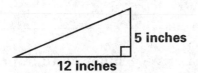

Answer_____

2. A part of the city park is shown in the drawing. A walking path will be made from point A to point B. How long will the path be?

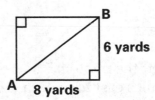

Answer_____

Sometimes you have the length of the hypotenuse and you need to find the length of one of the legs of the triangle. Use the same formula.

Example The bottom of a 15-foot ladder is placed 9 feet away from a wall. How high up will the ladder reach on the wall?

▶ **Step 1.** Draw a picture.

▶ **Step 2.** Write the formula and substitute the correct numbers.

$$a^2 + b^2 = c^2$$
$$9^2 + b^2 = 15^2$$

▶ **Step 3.** Solve.

$$81 + b^2 = 225$$
$$81 - 81 + b^2 = 225 - 81$$
$$b^2 = 144$$
$$b = \sqrt{144}$$
$$b = 12$$

The ladder will touch the wall at 12 feet.

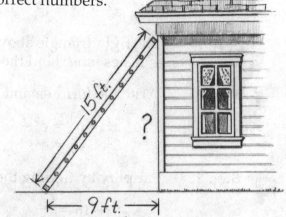

Solve. Make a drawing for each problem. Find the hypotenuse or the missing leg.

3. A ladder is placed against the side of a building at a height of 24'. If the ladder is 25' long, how far away from the building is the bottom of the ladder?

4. Jake wants to know the perimeter of his work area. If one leg is 5' and the other is 12', what is the perimeter of the space that is shaped like a right triangle?
(Hint: Add the lengths of the three sides to find the perimeter.)

Answer_____

Answer_____

5. Kwan left the photo lab and rode his bike 3 miles east to make a delivery. He turned south and rode 4 miles before making another delivery. If he rides in a straight line back to the lab, how far will he ride?

6. Martha drives 8 miles north from her home to work. She drives 6 miles east from work to the shopping center. How far does Martha drive from the shopping center straight to her home?

Answer_____

Answer_____

Multi-Step Problems: Similar Triangles

Similar triangles are the same shape and have equal corresponding angle measures. The corresponding sides form fractions or ratios that can be written as a proportion. This proportion can be used to find the length of corresponding sides of similar triangles.

Sides of similar triangles can be formed by the heights of objects and their shadows or by the distance across a lake or river. The unknown height or distance can be found by solving the proportion that is written using the corresponding sides.

Example   A flagpole casts an 8-foot shadow at 6 P.M. At the same time, a signpost 9 feet tall casts a 3-foot shadow. What is the height of the flagpole?

▶ **Step 1.**   Write a ratio for the height of the signpost to its shadow.

$$\frac{\text{height}}{\text{shadow}} = \frac{9}{3}$$

▶ **Step 2.**   Write an equal ratio for the height of the flagpole to its shadow. Use n for the height of the flagpole.

$$\frac{\text{height}}{\text{shadow}} = \frac{9}{3} = \frac{n}{8}$$

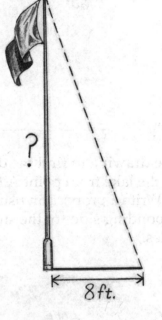

Step 3.   Cross-multiply to find n.

$$3n = 72$$
$$\frac{3n}{3} = \frac{72}{3}$$
$$n = 24$$

The height of the flagpole is 24 feet.

Solve.

1. A signpost 4 feet tall casts a shadow $1\frac{1}{2}$ feet long. At the same time of day, a nearby print shop casts a shadow $18\frac{3}{4}$ feet long. How tall is the shop?

2. The doghouse at Tuckers' Pet Supplies is beside their storage shed. The shed casts a shadow 9 feet long. At the same time of day, the 4-foot-high doghouse casts a shadow 3 feet long. How tall is the shed?

Answer_____   Answer_____

Use the similar triangles formed to set up a proportion. Solve.

3. Use the drawing to find the height of the taller tree.
    (Hint: Write equal ratios for the heights of the trees to their shadows.)

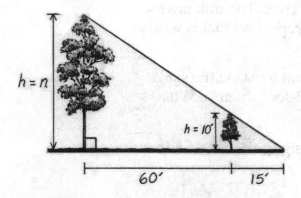

Answer_____

4. Use the drawing to find the distance across the pond. Use *d* for the distance.

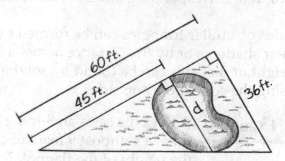

Answer_____

5. Use the drawing to find the distance across the lake from point A to point B. (Hint: Write a proportion using the corresponding sides of the similar triangles.)

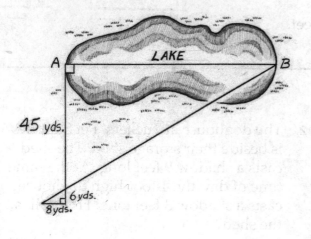

Answer_____

6. Use the drawing to find the length of the bridge across the river.

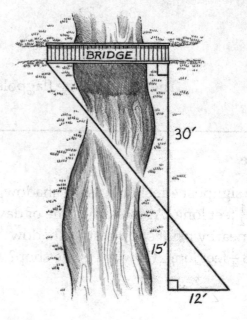

Answer_____

Skills Inventory

Write the equivalent measure.

1. 1 yard = _____ inches
2. _____ min. = 1 hr.
3. 1 pint = _____ quart

4. 1,000 lb. = _____ T.
5. 2 hr. = _____ min.
6. $\frac{1}{2}$ year = _____ weeks

7. 45 yd. = _____ ft.
8. 9 oz. = _____ c.
9. $3\frac{1}{4}$ gal. = _____ qt.

Change each measurement to the units given.

10. 9.5 miles = _____ miles _____ yards
11. 2 pints 1 cup = _____ pints

12. 3 feet 4 inches = _____ inches
13. 130 seconds = _____ min. _____ sec.

Add, subtract, multiply, or divide. Simplify the answer.

14.
$$\begin{array}{r} 5 \text{ days } 12 \text{ hours} \\ + 9 \text{ days } 18 \text{ hours} \\ \hline \end{array}$$

15.
$$\begin{array}{r} 4 \text{ feet} \\ + 1 \text{ yard} \qquad 6 \text{ inches} \\ \hline \end{array}$$

16.
$$\begin{array}{r} 5 \text{ tons } 100 \text{ pounds} \\ - 1 \text{ ton } \ 900 \text{ pounds} \\ \hline \end{array}$$

17.
$$\begin{array}{r} 2 \text{ quarts} \\ - \qquad 3 \text{ pints} \\ \hline \end{array}$$

18.
$$\begin{array}{r} 6 \text{ pounds } 5 \text{ ounces} \\ \times \qquad\qquad 10 \\ \hline \end{array}$$

19.
$$2\overline{)13 \text{ pints } 1 \text{ cup}}$$

Change each measurement.

20. 6 m = _____ cm

21. 450 mg = _____ g

Find the measure of each angle.

22. Find ∠ABD.

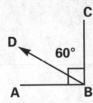

23. Find ∠DBA.

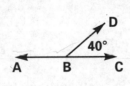

24. Find ∠c.

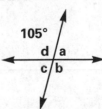

25. Find ∠a.

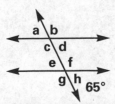

26. Find ∠ABC.

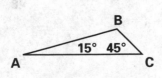

27. Find ∠EDF.

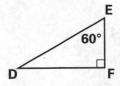

175

28. Find ∠HIJ.

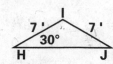

29. △ABC ~ △DEF   Find $\overline{AB}$.

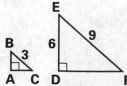

30. Find the perimeter.

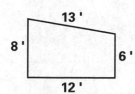

31. Find the circumference.

$C = \pi d \quad \pi = \frac{22}{7}$

32. Find the area.

$A = s^2$

33. Find the area.

$A = \pi r^2 \quad \pi = 3.14$

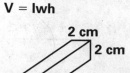

34. Find the volume.

$V = lwh$

Find each answer.

35.
$7^2 =$

36.
$3^3 =$

37.
$\sqrt{16} =$

38.
$\sqrt{25} =$

Evaluate each expression. Use 4 for x in problems 43-45.

39.
$3 \times 2 - 5$

40.
$21 + 6 \cdot 4$

41.
$4^2 - 10 + 3$

42.
$(8 + 4) \div 4$

43.
$\dfrac{24}{x}$

44.
$12x^3$

45.
$8 \cdot (x - 2)$

Add or subtract.

46.
$8 + (-4)$

47.
$-10 + (-6)$

48.
$-5 - (+7)$

49.
$20 - (-5)$

50.
$-9 + 0$

51.
$0 - 10$

Solve each equation.

52.
$$23 + x = 50$$

53.
$$x + 30 = -41$$

54.
$$2 + x + 7 = 12$$

55.
$$x - 6 = 4$$

56.
$$x - 3 = -5$$

57.
$$x - 12 = -3$$

Multiply or divide.

58.
$$(-6)(-4)$$

59.
$$-3(6)$$

60.
$$\frac{-5}{-1}$$

61.
$$\frac{-15}{5}$$

Solve each equation.

62.
$$4x = 16$$

63.
$$-5x = 20$$

64.
$$\frac{x}{4} = 3$$

65.
$$\frac{x}{-2} = -6$$

66.
$$3x - 2 = 7$$

67.
$$\frac{1}{3}x + 5 = 10$$

Below is a list of the problems in this Skills Inventory and the pages on which the skills are taught. If you missed any problems, turn to the pages listed and practice the skills. Then correct the problems you missed in the Skills Inventory.

Problem	Practice Page	Problem	Practice Page	Problem	Practice Page
Unit 1		24	80	43-45	121-124
1-9	24-35	25	81-82	*Unit 5*	
Unit 2		26-28	84-87	46-51	133-139
10-13	43-46	29	88-89	52-57	141-144
14-19	49-54, 57-58	30-34	93-99, 103-104	*Unit 6*	
20-21	60-66	*Unit 4*		58-61	149-152
Unit 3		35-38	113-114	62-65	154-157
22-23	78-79	39-42	115-118	66-67	160-162

Glossary

algebraic expression (page 121) - An expression with one or more variables, numbers, and math operations.

y + 4

angle (page 73) - Two lines that meet at a common point. The symbol for angle is ∠.

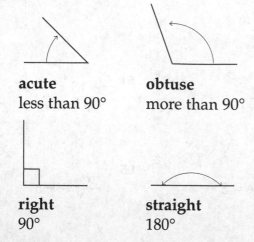

acute
less than 90°

obtuse
more than 90°

right
90°

straight
180°

area (page 96) - The measure of the space in square units of the inside of a flat figure.

base (page 113) - The number being taken or raised to a power.

3^2

circle (page 95) - A flat figure with all the points on its outer edge the same distance from the center.

circumference (page 95) - The distance around a circle's outer edge.

complementary angle (page 78) - Two angles are complementary if the sum of both angles is 90°.

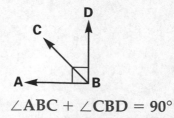

∠ABC + ∠CBD = 90°

corresponding angles (page 81) - The equal angles formed when a transversal cuts two parallel lines.

cube (page 102) - A solid figure with six square faces.

cylinder (page 102) - A solid figure with a circular top and base.

diameter (page 95) - The distance from one side of a circle through the center.

equation (page 109) - A number sentence with numbers, variables, and an equal sign.

x + 4 = 6

evaluate (page 115) - To find the answer.

exponent (page 113) - The number of times the base is multiplied.

3^2

formula (page 94) - A mathematical sentence that uses letters to show a relationship.

P = 2l + 2w

hypotenuse (page 171) - The long side of a right triangle that is always opposite the right angle.

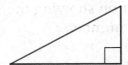

intersecting (page 74) - Lines that cross to form four angles with a point in common.

leg (page 167) - Any one of the sides of a right triangle other than the hypotenuse.

mixed measurement (page 43) - A measurement with two or more units.

2 gallons 2 quarts

negative number (page 109) - A number less than zero.

−10

number line (page 110) - A line with equally spaced points that are labeled with fractions, whole numbers, mixed numbers, or positive and negative numbers.

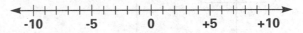

numerical expression (page 115) - An expression with one or more operations.

30 ÷ 5 + 6   (4 + 7) · 2

operation (page 107) - The process you use to solve a math problem. The basic operations are addition, subtraction, multiplication, and division.

parallel (page 74) - Two lines that run side-by-side the same distance apart and never cross. The symbol for parallel lines is ‖.

parallelogram (page 91) - A polygon with four sides and four angles. The opposite sides are equal and parallel. The opposite angles are equal.

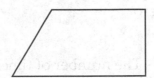

perimeter (page 93) - The measure of the distance around the outside of a figure.

perpendicular (page 74) - Two lines that cross forming four equal angles. The symbol for perpendicular lines is ⊥.

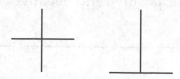

polygon (page 91) - A flat figure with many sides and angles. Regular polygons have equal sides and equal angles.

equilateral triangle
3 equal sides
3 equal angles

square
4 equal sides
4 equal angles

pentagon
5 equal sides
5 equal angles

hexagon
6 equal sides
6 equal angles

heptagon
7 equal sides
7 equal angles

octagon
8 equal sides
8 equal angles

positive number (page 109) - A number greater than zero.

10 or +10

power (page 113) - The number of times the base is multiplied. A number to the second power is squared, or 3^2. A number to the third power is cubed, or 3^3.

3^2 3^3

proportion (page 32) - Two equal ratios or fractions.

$$\frac{1 \text{ gallon}}{4 \text{ quarts}} = \frac{2 \text{ gallons}}{8 \text{ quarts}}$$

radius (page 95) - The distance from the center of a circle to any point on the edge.

ratio (page 32) - A fraction showing the relationship of two numbers.

$$\frac{1 \text{ yard}}{3 \text{ feet}}$$

reciprocal (page 159) - The inverted form of a fraction. A fraction multiplied by its reciprocal equals one.

$\frac{1}{4} \rightthreetimes \frac{4}{1}$

rectangle (page 91) - A polygon with four sides and four right angles. The opposite sides are parallel and equal.

rectangular solid (page 102) - A solid figure with equal opposite faces.

signed numbers (page 133) - Positive and negative numbers.

similar triangles (page 88) - Two triangles that have the same shape and equal corresponding angles. The symbol ~ means similar to.

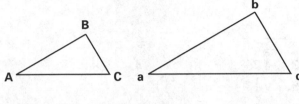

△ ABC~ △ abc

supplementary angle (page 79) - Two angles are supplementary if the sum of both angles is 180°.

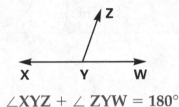

∠XYZ + ∠ ZYW = 180°

transversal (page 81) - A line that cuts two parallel lines.

trapezoid (page 91) - A polygon with four sides and four angles. Only one pair of opposite sides is parallel.

triangle (page 84) - A polygon with three sides and three angles. The sum of the angles is 180°. The symbol for a triangle is △.

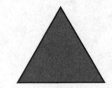 

equilateral triangle
3 equal sides
3 equal angles

isosceles triangle
2 equal sides
2 equal angles

right triangle
one 90° angle

scalene triangle
no equal sides or
equal angles

variable (page 121) - A letter that stands for an unknown number.

n + 5

vertex (page 73) - The point where two lines meet to form an angle.

vertical angles (page 80) - The equal opposite angles formed when two straight lines cross.

volume (page 103) - The measure of the space in cubic units of the inside of a three-dimensional or solid figure.

Answers & Explanations

The answer to the problem that was worked out for you in the lesson is written here in color. The next answer has an explanation written beneath it. The answers to the rest of the problems in the lesson follow in order.

Skills Inventory

Page 9

1. 210
2. 445

$$89$$
$$\times\ 5$$
$$\overline{445}$$

3. 4,768
4. 728
5. $9\frac{1}{2}$
6. $7\frac{1}{3}$

$$\begin{array}{r} 7\frac{2}{6} = 7\frac{1}{3} \\ 6\overline{)44} \\ -42 \\ \hline 2 \end{array}$$

7. $7\frac{6}{35}$
8. $14\frac{1}{20}$

Page 6

1. 12 inches
2. 60 seconds
3. $\frac{1}{4}$ or .25 gallon
4. $\frac{1}{16}$ or .0625 pound
5. 1,800 seconds
6. 42 months
7. 6 feet
8. $3\frac{1}{2}$ or 3.5 quarts
9. $4\frac{1}{2}$ or 4.5 feet
10. 2 miles 2,640 feet
11. $3\frac{1}{2}$ or 3.5 cups
12. 7 feet
13. 1 hr. 30 min.
14. 17 weeks
15. 2 yd. 2 ft. 7 in.
16. 2 lb. 10 oz.
17. 2 quarts
18. 16 T. 1,000 lb.
19. 3 qt. $1\frac{1}{2}$ pt.
20. 1,000 centimeters
21. .1 liter
22. 80°
23. 150°
24. 67°
25. 100°
26. 95°
27. 60°

Page 10

9. $6\frac{1}{2}$
10. 3

$$\begin{array}{r} 3 \\ 7\overline{)21} \\ -21 \\ \hline 0 \end{array}$$

11. $4\frac{3}{4}$
12. $4\frac{5}{12}$
13. $4\frac{1}{12}$
14. $\frac{1}{2}$
15. $\frac{1}{6}$

$$\frac{3}{18} = \frac{3 \div 3}{18 \div 3} = \frac{1}{6}$$

16. $\frac{2}{3}$
17. $\frac{5}{12}$
18. $\frac{3}{4}$
19. $\frac{1}{2}$
20. $9\frac{1}{2}$

$$10 = 9\frac{2}{2}$$
$$-\ \ \frac{1}{2} = \ \ \frac{1}{2}$$
$$\overline{9\frac{1}{2}}$$

Page 7

28. 90°
29. 4
30. 11 feet
31. 44 inches
32. 6 sq. cm.
33. 12.56 square miles
34. 704 cubic inches
35. 36
36. 8
37. 3
38. 8
39. 26
40. 27
41. 1
42. 8
43. 7
44. 15
45. 6
46. 1
47. −19
48. −10
49. 24
50. −10
51. −7

21. $3\frac{1}{9}$
22. $1\frac{13}{15}$
23. 8
24. 54

$$\frac{18}{1} \div \frac{1}{3} = \frac{18}{1} \times \frac{3}{1} = \frac{54}{1} = 54$$

Page 8

52. $x = 35$
53. $x = -82$
54. $x = 0$
55. $x = 16$
56. $x = -8$
57. $x = 7$
58. 54
59. −10
60. 3
61. −3
62. $x = 3$
63. $x = -6$
64. $x = 8$
65. $x = 35$
66. $x = 1$
67. $x = 12$

25. 12   **26.** 2

27. 2

28. 4

$$\frac{3}{n} \Large\bowtie \normalsize \frac{6}{8}$$

$$n \times 6 = 8 \times 3$$
$$6n = 24$$
$$n = 24 \div 6 = 4$$

29. 7   **30.** 1

Page 11

1. b. 20 inches

2. b. $31\frac{3}{10}$ miles

Because you travel farther distances in a car, the answer would be in the larger unit, miles.

3. a. 8 inches   **4.** a. 22 inches

5. b. 19 inches   **6.** a. $\frac{3}{16}$ inch

7. a. $1\frac{1}{4}$ inches   **8.** b. 4 inches

9. b. $14\frac{1}{2}$ inches   **10.** a. 7 inches

11. b. 25 miles   **12.** a. 9 inches

Page 12

1. $\frac{1}{2}$ inch

2. $1\frac{1}{2}$ inches

The nearest whole inch before the arrow is 1. The fraction of an inch that the arrow is pointing to is $\frac{1}{2}$. Write the measurement as the mixed number, $1\frac{1}{2}$.

3. $2\frac{1}{2}$ inches   **4.** $\frac{1}{4}$ inch

5. $1\frac{1}{4}$ inches

The nearest whole inch before the arrow is 1. The fraction of an inch that the arrow is pointing to is $\frac{1}{4}$. Write the measurement as the mixed number, $1\frac{1}{4}$.

6. $3\frac{3}{4}$ inches   **7.** $\frac{1}{8}$ inch

8. $\frac{5}{8}$ inch

Count the number of $\frac{1}{8}$-inch marks before the arrow. The fraction that the arrow is pointing to is $\frac{5}{8}$.

9. $4\frac{3}{8}$ inches   **10.** $\frac{1}{16}$ inch

11. $\frac{13}{16}$ inch

Count the number of $\frac{1}{16}$-inch marks before the arrow. The fraction that the arrow is pointing to is $\frac{13}{16}$.

12. $5\frac{7}{16}$ inches

Page 13

1. $\frac{3}{4}$ inch

2. $1\frac{5}{8}$ inches

Find the measurement shown by A. A = $1\frac{1}{2}$ inches. Find the measurement shown by C. C = $3\frac{1}{8}$ inches. Subtract A, the smaller number, from C, the larger number.

$$3\frac{1}{8} = 3\frac{1}{8} = 2\frac{9}{8}$$
$$-1\frac{1}{2} = 1\frac{4}{8} = 1\frac{4}{8}$$
$$\overline{\qquad\qquad 1\frac{5}{8} \text{ inches}}$$

3. $2\frac{1}{2}$ inches   **4.** $3\frac{1}{2}$ inches

5. $1\frac{3}{4}$ inches   **6.** $2\frac{5}{16}$ inches

7. $\frac{7}{8}$ inch   **8.** $1\frac{7}{16}$ inches

9. $1\frac{3}{16}$ inches

Page 14

1. a. 4 ounces

2. a. 4,000 pounds

Because a compact car weighs about one ton or 2,000 pounds, an ambulance would weigh about 4,000 pounds.

3. b. 20 pounds   **4.** b. 3 tons

5. b. 6 ounces   **6.** b. 5 pounds

7. b. 2 pounds   **8.** b. 18 pounds

9. a. 6 ounces   **10.** a. 11 ounces

11. a. 15 ounces   **12.** b. 6 pounds

13. b. 3 pounds   **14.** b. 7 tons

Page 15

Note: *If you have trouble finding the exact measurement on the scale, use a ruler or any straight edge (like a book or a sheet of paper) to line up the center dot on the arrow with the measurement the arrow is pointing to.*

1. $\frac{1}{2}$ pound

2. $\frac{3}{4}$ pound

The nearest whole pound before the weight the arrow is pointing to on the scale is zero. Count the number of $\frac{1}{4}$-pound marks after zero. You can also count the number of $\frac{1}{16}$-pound marks after zero, 12, and reduce to $\frac{3}{4}$.

3. 1 pound   **4.** $2\frac{1}{16}$ pounds

5. $2\frac{1}{2}$ pounds   **6.** 3 pounds

7. $3\frac{3}{8}$ pounds   **8.** $3\frac{3}{4}$ pounds

9. $3\frac{15}{16}$ pounds

Page 16

1. **1 ounce**

2. $2\frac{1}{2}$ ounces

Read down from zero to the nearest whole ounce, 2. The arrow is pointing to the $\frac{1}{2}$-ounce mark after 2. The total amount is read as $2\frac{1}{2}$ ounces.

3. 13 ounces   **4.** $6\frac{1}{2}$ ounces

5. 15 ounces   **6.** $9\frac{1}{2}$ ounces

Page 17

1. a. 12 gallons

2. b. 3 gallons

Because you use large amounts of water in a full bucket, you would use gallons.

3. b. 10 gallons   **4.** a. 1 fluid ounce

5. a. 4 fluid ounces   **6.** b. 4 gallons

7. a. 64 fluid ounces   **8.** a. 2 fluid ounces

9. b. 15 gallons   **10.** a. 8 fluid ounces

11. a. 16 fluid ounces   **12.** a. 6 fluid ounces

Page 18

1. $\frac{1}{4}$ **cup** = **2 ounces**

2. $1\frac{1}{2}$ cups = 12 ounces

Find the scale of measure marking the amount in the cup. You can see that 12 ounces is equal to $1\frac{1}{2}$ cups.

3. $\frac{3}{4}$ cup = 6 ounces   **4.** 2 cups = 16 ounces

5. $1\frac{1}{4}$ c. = 10 oz.   **6.** $1\frac{3}{4}$ c. = 14 oz.

Page 19

1. 1 tbsp.   **2.** $\frac{1}{2}$ fl. oz.

3. 2 tbsp.   **4.** 3 tsp.

5. 2 tsp.   **6.** 3 tsp.

7. $1\frac{1}{2}$ tsp.   **8.** 1 tsp.

9. teaspoon

Read across the chart to find that the dosage for a 7-year-old is 2 teaspoons.

10. $\frac{1}{2}$ oz.

The chart of equivalent measures shows that 3 teaspoons equal 1 tablespoon and that 1 tablespoon equals $\frac{1}{2}$ ounce, so 3 teaspoons equal $\frac{1}{2}$ ounce.

Page 20

1. a. 4 hours

2. a. 8 hours

Because most work shifts are fulltime jobs, it would probably take hours, the larger unit, to work one shift.

3. b. 30 minutes   **4.** a. $3\frac{1}{2}$ hours

5. a. 10 minutes   **6.** b. 6 hours

7. b. 40 minutes   **8.** a. 5 minutes

9. a. 18 months   **10.** a. 10 seconds

11. a. 20 minutes   **12.** a. 45 minutes

Page 21

1. 0830

2. 1300

Add 1 to 12 to get 13. Add zeros to make a 4-digit number, 1300. 1:00 P.M. is read as 1300, or 1300 hours, on a 24-hour clock.

3. 1025   **4.** 1525

5. 0400   **6.** 1630

7. 2215   **8.** 2030

9. 6:30 P.M.

10. 6:00 A.M.

The sixth hour of the new day is 6. Zeros are added to make a 4-digit number, 0600. Therefore, 0600 is the sixth hour after midnight, or 6:00 A.M.

11. 9:45 P.M.   **12.** 2:15 P.M.

13. 6:00 P.M.

Since Martin punched out at 1800, subtract 12 from 18 to get the hour on a 12-hour clock. $18 - 12 = 6$. Add a colon and two zeros to get 6:00 in the evening, or 6:00 P.M. Martin left work at 6:00 P.M.

14. 1:50 P.M.

Since the receipt shows 1350, subtract 12 from 13 to change to a 12-hour clock. $13 - 12 = 1$. The minutes stay the same. Add a colon between the 1 and the 50 and write P.M. after 1:50 since the time was after 1 P.M. or 1300. Carla was in the store at 1:50 P.M.

Page 22

1. 1 hour
2. 1 hour 20 minutes
   Read clockwise from the top to the 1-hour mark. The arrow is pointing to 20 minutes past the 1-hour mark, or 1 hour and 20 minutes.
3. 1 hour 50 minutes   **4.** 30 minutes
5. 12 minutes   **6.** 45 minutes

Page 23

1. $5\frac{5}{16}$ inches   **2.** $3\frac{1}{4}$ inches
3. $1\frac{1}{8}$ inches   **4.** $\frac{1}{2}$ inch
5. 2 inches   **6.** $\frac{13}{16}$ inch
7. $2\frac{11}{16}$ inches   **8.** $\frac{9}{16}$ pound
9. $3\frac{1}{4}$ pounds   **10.** $1\frac{1}{2}$ pounds
11. $1\frac{1}{2}$ c. = 12 oz.   **12.** $\frac{3}{4}$ c. = 6 oz.
13. $\frac{1}{2}$ cup = 4 ounces   **14.** 0730
15. 1915   **16.** 2305
17. 0525

Page 24

1. 12 inches
2. 60 minutes
   Use the Measures of Time table. Find 1 hour. The equivalent time in minutes will be to the right of the equal sign.
3. 16 ounces   **4.** 7 days
5. 4 cups   **6.** 2,000 pounds
7. 5,280 feet   **8.** 3 feet
9. 8 ounces
10. 4 quarts
    Use the Measures of Capacity table. Find 1 gallon. The equivalent capacity in quarts will be to the right of the equal sign.
11. 24 hours   **12.** 12 months
13. 52 weeks   **14.** 36 inches
15. 60 seconds   **16.** 2 cups

Page 25

1. $\frac{1}{3}$ yard
2. $\frac{1}{4}$ gallon
   Find the number of quarts in 1 gallon from the table on page 24. 4 quarts = 1 gallon. Write a fraction with 1 quart as the numerator and 4 quarts as the denominator, $\frac{1}{4}$.
3. $\frac{1}{60}$ hour   **4.** $\frac{1}{24}$ day

5. $\frac{1}{12}$ year   **6.** $\frac{1}{2}$ quart
7. $\frac{1}{2}$ foot
8. $\frac{1}{2}$ hour
   Find the number of minutes in 1 hour from the table on page 24. 60 minutes = 1 hour. Write a fraction with 30 minutes as the numerator and 60 minutes as the denominator, $\frac{30}{60}$. Reduce the fraction to lowest terms. $\frac{30}{60} = \frac{1}{2}$.
9. $\frac{1}{2}$ gallon   **10.** $\frac{3}{7}$ week
11. $\frac{1}{4}$ year   **12.** $\frac{2}{3}$ yard
13. $\frac{1}{2}$ pound   **14.** $\frac{1}{3}$ year

Page 26

1. 9 inches < 1 foot   **2.** 1 yard > 20 inches
3. 1 mile = 5,280 feet
4. 12 " = 1'
   Use the table on page 24 to find how many inches are in 1 foot. 12 in. = 1 ft. Compare. 12 inches = 12 inches, so 12 in. = 1 ft.
5. 1 foot > 8 inches   **6.** 6 inches < 1 foot
7. 5 days < 1 week   **8.** 1 yd. > 2 ft.
9. 2 qt. < 1 gal.   **10.** 36 inches = 1 yard
11. 6 mo. < 1 yr.   **12.** 3,000 lb. > 1 ton
13. No
   Use the table on page 24 to compare 3 feet and 30 inches. 1 yard equals 36 inches. 30 inches < 36 inches, so 30 inches < 3 feet. Susanna does not have enough cord.
14. No
   Use the table on page 24 to compare 6 quarts and 1 gallon. 1 gallon = 4 quarts. 4 quarts < 6 quarts, so 1 gallon < 6 quarts. Jake does not have enough oil.

Page 27

1. 60 seconds   **2.** $\frac{1}{60}$ min.
3. 2 pt.   **4.** 1 quart
5. 1 foot   **6.** 1 lb.
7. 2 cups   **8.** $\frac{1}{4}$ hr.
9. 1 ton   **10.** 12"
11. $\frac{1}{2}$ pound   **12.** 1 week
13. 36 in.   **14.** 2 pints
15. $\frac{1}{3}$ day   **16.** 1 hour
17. 8 cups > 1 quart   **18.** 1,780 feet < 1 mile
19. 16 oz. = 1 lb.   **20.** 60 sec. = 1 min.
21. 1 yd. > 32 in.   **22.** 4 ounces < 1 cup

23. 1 quart = 4 cups   **24.** 5,260 feet < 1 mile
25. 16 pints > 1 cup
26. Less than a pound
16 ounces = 1 pound. 12 ounces < 16 ounces, so 12 ounces < 1 pound.
27. Quinton
7 days = 1 week
7 days > 5 days, so 1 week > 5 days

Page 28

1. **288 ounces**
2. 18 pints
Write the number of pints in 1 quart.
1 quart = 2 pints. Multiply 9 quarts by 2 pints.
$9 \times 2 = 18$
3. 120 min.   **4.** 21 ft.
5. 6,000 pounds   **6.** 900 sec.
7. 288 inches   **8.** 96 hours
9. 168 "   **10.** 80 oz.
11. 36 months   **12.** 29,920 yards
13. 49 days   **14.** 156 weeks
15. 36 cups
16. 40 quarts
1 gallon = 4 quarts. $10 \times 4 = 40$ quarts
17. 60 inches
1 foot = 12 inches. $5 \times 12 = 60$ inches

Page 29

1. **5 cups**
2. 100 oz.
Write the number of ounces in 1 pound.
1 lb. = 16 oz. Multiply $6\frac{1}{4}$ lb. by 16 oz.
$$6\frac{1}{4} \times 16 = \frac{25}{\cancel{4}} \times \frac{\overset{4}{\cancel{16}}}{1} = \frac{100}{1} = 100 \text{ oz.}$$
3. 90 minutes   **4.** 112 inches
5. 7 pt.   **6.** 86 ounces
7. 204 inches   **8.** 18 mo.
9. 12 ounces   **10.** 64,944 feet
11. 31 qt.   **12.** 46 feet
13. 195 min.
1 hour = 60 minutes
$$3\frac{1}{4} \times 60 = \frac{13}{\cancel{4}} \times \frac{\overset{15}{\cancel{60}}}{1} = \frac{195}{1} = 195 \text{ minutes}$$
14. 5,000 pounds
1 ton = 2,000 pounds
$$2\frac{1}{2} \times 2,000 = \frac{5}{\cancel{2}} \times \frac{\overset{1000}{\cancel{2000}}}{1} = \frac{5000}{1} = 5,000 \text{ lb.}$$

Page 30

1. **2 pounds**
2. 4 c.
Write the number of ounces in 1 cup.
8 oz. = 1 c. Divide 32 ounces by 8 ounces.
$32 \div 8 = 4$ c.
3. 4 hrs.   **4.** 5 '
5. 4 days   **6.** 2 T.
7. 4 gallons   **8.** 2 mi.
9. 6 pints   **10.** 4 yr.
11. 15 min.   **12.** 4 yards
13. 3 weeks
7 days = 1 week
$21 \div 7 = 3$ weeks
14. 6 tons
2,000 lb. = 1 T.
$12,000 \div 2,000 = 6$ T.

Page 31

1. $2\frac{1}{4}$ **gal.**
2. $5\frac{3}{4}$ pounds
Write the number of ounces in one pound.
16 ounces = 1 pound. Divide 92 ounces by 16 ounces. Show the remainder as a fraction of a pound. Reduce.
$92 \div 16 = 5\frac{12}{16} = 5\frac{3}{4}$ pounds
3. $1\frac{1}{3}$ ft.   **4.** $\frac{5}{8}$ T.
5. $3\frac{1}{3}$ min.   **6.** $3\frac{1}{3}$ yards
7. $8\frac{1}{2}$ lb.   **8.** $2\frac{1}{4}$ cups
9. $1\frac{3}{22}$ miles   **10.** $\frac{1}{2}$ mi.
11. $1\frac{1}{2}$ tons   **12.** $9\frac{1}{2}$ quarts
13. $5\frac{2}{3}$ hr.   **14.** $4\frac{6}{7}$ weeks
15. $4\frac{1}{2}$ pt.
16. $3\frac{1}{2}$ years
12 mo. = 1 yr.
$42 \div 12 = 3\frac{6}{12} = 3\frac{1}{2}$ yr.
17. $4\frac{1}{2}$ ft.
12 inches = 1 foot
$54 \div 12 = 4\frac{6}{12} = 4\frac{1}{2}$

Page 32

1. 192 oz.
2. 30 pt.
   Since you are changing quarts to pints, write the ratio that shows 1 quart to 2 pints. Write a proportion with n for the missing number of pints.

   $\dfrac{1\,\text{qt.}}{2\,\text{pt.}} = \dfrac{15\,\text{qt.}}{n\,\text{pt.}}$

   Cross-multiply to find n.

   $\dfrac{1}{2} \,\diagdown\!\!\!\!\diagup\, \dfrac{15}{n}$

   $n \times 1 = 2 \times 15$
   $n = 2 \times 15 = 30\,\text{pt.}$

3. 720 sec.   4. 21 ft.
5. 10,000 lb.   6. 64 oz.
7. 35 days   8. 14,080 yd.
9. 480 oz.
10. 72 in.

    $\dfrac{1\,\text{foot}}{12\,\text{inches}} = \dfrac{6\,\text{feet}}{n\,\text{inches}}$

    $\dfrac{1}{12} \,\diagdown\!\!\!\!\diagup\, \dfrac{6}{n}$

    $n \times 1 = 12 \times 6$
    $n = 12 \times 6 = 72\,\text{inches}$

11. 420 minutes

    $\dfrac{1\,\text{hour}}{60\,\text{minutes}} = \dfrac{7\,\text{hours}}{n\,\text{minutes}}$

    $\dfrac{1}{60} \,\diagdown\!\!\!\!\diagup\, \dfrac{7}{n}$

    $n \times 1 = 60 \times 7$
    $n = 60 \times 7 = 420\,\text{minutes}$

Page 33

1. 40 oz.
2. 27 qt.
   Since you are changing gallons to quarts, write the ratio that shows 1 gallon to 4 quarts. Write a proportion with n for the missing number of quarts.

   $\dfrac{1\,\text{gallon}}{4\,\text{quarts}} = \dfrac{6\frac{3}{4}\,\text{gallons}}{n\,\text{quarts}}$

   Cross-multiply to find n.

   $\dfrac{1}{4} \,\diagdown\!\!\!\!\diagup\, \dfrac{6\frac{3}{4}}{n}$

   $n \times 1 = 4 \times 6\frac{3}{4}$

   $n = \dfrac{\overset{1}{\cancel{4}}}{1} \times \dfrac{27}{\underset{1}{\cancel{4}}} = \dfrac{27}{1} = 27\,\text{qt.}$

3. 78 wk.   4. 15 in.
5. 9 mo.   6. 200 min.

7. 100 ounces

   $\dfrac{1\,\text{pound}}{16\,\text{ounces}} = \dfrac{6\frac{1}{4}\,\text{pounds}}{n\,\text{ounces}}$

   $\dfrac{1}{16} \,\diagdown\!\!\!\!\diagup\, \dfrac{6\frac{1}{4}}{n}$

   $n \times 1 = 16 \times 6\frac{1}{4}$

   $n \times 1 = \dfrac{\overset{4}{\cancel{16}}}{1} \times \dfrac{25}{\cancel{4}} = \dfrac{100}{1} = 100\,\text{ounces}$

8. 26 cups

   $\dfrac{1\,\text{quart}}{4\,\text{cups}} = \dfrac{6\frac{1}{2}\,\text{quarts}}{n\,\text{cups}}$

   $\dfrac{1}{4} \,\diagdown\!\!\!\!\diagup\, \dfrac{6\frac{1}{2}}{n}$

   $n \times 1 = 4 \times 6\frac{1}{2}$

   $n = \dfrac{\overset{2}{\cancel{4}}}{1} \times \dfrac{13}{\underset{1}{\cancel{2}}} = \dfrac{26}{1} = 26\,\text{cups}$

Page 34

1. 3 c.
2. 4 yd.
   Since you are changing feet to yards, write the ratio that shows 3 feet to 1 yard. Then write a proportion with n for the missing number of yards.

   $\dfrac{3\,\text{feet}}{1\,\text{yard}} = \dfrac{12\,\text{feet}}{n\,\text{yards}}$

   Cross-multiply and divide to find n.

   $\dfrac{3}{1} \,\diagdown\!\!\!\!\diagup\, \dfrac{12}{n}$

   $n \times 3 = 1 \times 12$
   $3n = 12$
   $n = 12 \div 3 = 4\,\text{yd.}$

3. 3 lb.   4. 4 wk.
5. 6 qt.   6. 7 T.
7. 5 yr.   8. 5 gal.
9. 3 mi.
10. 15 pounds

    $\dfrac{16\,\text{ounces}}{1\,\text{pound}} = \dfrac{240\,\text{ounces}}{n\,\text{pounds}}$

    $\dfrac{16}{1} = \dfrac{240}{n}$

    $n \times 16 = 1 \times 240$
    $16n = 240$
    $n = 240 \div 16 = 15\,\text{pounds}$

11. 2 gallons

    $\dfrac{4\,\text{quarts}}{1\,\text{gallon}} = \dfrac{8\,\text{quarts}}{n\,\text{gallons}}$

    $\dfrac{4}{1} = \dfrac{8}{n}$

    $n \times 4 = 1 \times 8$
    $4n = 8$
    $n = 8 \div 4 = 2\,\text{gallons}$

Page 35

1. $5\frac{2}{3}$ yd.

2. $\frac{3}{4}$ min.

   Since you are changing seconds to minutes, write the ratio that shows 60 seconds to 1 minute. Write a proportion with n for the missing number of minutes.

   $$\frac{60 \text{ seconds}}{1 \text{ minute}} = \frac{45 \text{ seconds}}{n \text{ minutes}}$$

   Cross-multiply and divide to find n. Write the answer as a fraction and reduce to lowest terms.

   $$\frac{60}{1} \diagup\!\!\!\!\diagdown \frac{45}{n}$$

   $n \times 60 = 1 \times 45$

   $\qquad 60n = 45$

   $\qquad n = 45 \div 60 = \frac{45}{60} = \frac{3}{4}$ min.

3. $5\frac{1}{2}$ pt.   4. $1\frac{3}{4}$ T.

5. $12\frac{1}{3}$ yd.   6. $2\frac{1}{2}$ gal.

7. $2\frac{1}{2}$ lb.   8. $\frac{1}{3}$ yr.

9. $10\frac{1}{2}$ qt.   10. $\frac{25}{44}$ mi.

11. $\frac{5}{6}$ ft.   12. $\frac{1}{4}$ yr.

13. $1\frac{7}{12}$ feet

   $$\frac{12 \text{ inches}}{1 \text{ foot}} = \frac{19 \text{ inches}}{n \text{ feet}}$$

   $$\frac{12}{1} \diagup\!\!\!\!\diagdown \frac{19}{n}$$

   $n \times 12 = 1 \times 19$

   $\qquad 12n = 19$

   $\qquad n = 19 \div 12 = 1\frac{7}{12}$ feet

14. $\frac{7}{12}$ day

   $$\frac{24 \text{ hours}}{1 \text{ day}} = \frac{14 \text{ hours}}{n \text{ days}}$$

   $$\frac{24}{1} \diagup\!\!\!\!\diagdown \frac{14}{n}$$

   $n \times 24 = 1 \times 14$

   $\qquad 24n = 14$

   $\qquad n = 14 \div 24 = \frac{14}{24} = \frac{7}{12}$ day

Page 36

1. 8 cups

   4 cups = 1 quart

   4 quarts = 1 gallon

   $4 \times 4 = 16$ cups in 1 gallon

   16 cups $\times \frac{1}{2}$ gallon = 8 cups

   They can get 8 1-cup servings.

2. 150 inches or $4\frac{1}{6}$ yards

   1 yard = 36 inches

   5 yards $\times$ 36 inches = 180 inches

   180 inches $-$ 30 inches = 150 inches

   She needs to buy 150 inches more trim.

3. 20 servings

   4 cups = 1 quart

   5 quarts $\times$ 4 cups = 20 cups

   There are 20 1-cup servings in 5 quarts.

4. 7 days

   14 months $\times$ 4 hours = 56 hours

   56 hours $\div$ 8 hours = 7 days

   Jalissa has earned 7 8-hour vacation days.

Page 37

5. 15 strings

   12 inches = 1 foot

   60 feet $\times$ 12 inches = 720 inches

   720 inches $\div$ 48 inches = 15 strings

   Trina needs 15 strings of lights.

6. 1 gallon

   $$\frac{2}{3} \text{ c.} \times 24 \text{ hr.} = \frac{2}{\cancel{3}_1} \times \frac{\cancel{24}^8}{1} = \frac{16}{1} = 16 \text{ c.}$$

   4 cups = 1 quart

   4 quarts = 1 gallon

   4 cups $\times$ 4 quarts = 16 cups in 1 gallon

   The faucet leaks 1 gallon of water in a 24-hour day.

7. 40 meatballs

   1 pound = 16 ounces

   16 ounces $\times$ 5 pounds = 80 ounces

   80 ounces $\div$ 2 ounces = 40 meatballs

   She got 40 meatballs.

8. $20\frac{1}{16}$ tons

   16 ounces = 1 pound

   2,000 pounds = 1 ton

   $16 \times 2,000 = 32,000$ ounces in 1 ton

   642,000 ounces $\div$ 32,000 ounces = $20\frac{1}{16}$ ton

   The post office handled $20\frac{1}{16}$ tons of mail.

9. 8 gallons

   8 ounces = 1 cup

   2 cups = 1 pint

   8 ounces $\times$ 2 cups = 16 ounces in 1 pint

   16 ounces $\div$ 2 ounces = 8

   He will need 8 gallons of gas if he uses the whole pint of oil.

10. 16 servings

4 cups = 1 quart

4 cups × 3 quarts = 12 cups in 3 quarts

$$12 \text{ c.} \div \frac{3}{4} \text{ c.} = \frac{\overset{4}{\cancel{12}}}{1} \times \frac{4}{\underset{1}{\cancel{3}}} = \frac{16}{1} = 16 \text{ servings}$$

He gets 16 servings from 3 quarts of soup.

Unit 1 Review, page 38

1. $2\frac{7}{8}$ inches   **2.** $5\frac{1}{4}$ inches

3. $\frac{3}{16}$ inch   **4.** $4\frac{1}{2}$ inches

5. $1\frac{1}{8}$ inches   **6.** $3\frac{9}{16}$ inches

7. $3\frac{1}{2}$ inches   **8.** $3\frac{1}{16}$ inches

9. $1\frac{3}{8}$ inches   **10.** $3\frac{1}{2}$ pounds

11. $1\frac{3}{4}$ pounds   **12.** $2\frac{1}{8}$ pounds

13. $3\frac{1}{2}$ ounces   **14.** 12 ounces

15. 8 ounces

Page 39

16. $1\frac{3}{4}$ c. = 14 oz.   **17.** 1 cup = 8 ounces

18. $\frac{1}{4}$ cup = 2 ounces   **19.** 0645

20. 1315   **21.** 1835

22. 50 minutes   **23.** 22 minutes

24. 1 hr. 15 min.   **25.** 24 months > 1 year

26. 1 day < 48 hours   **27.** 1' < 24 "

28. 1 lb. = 16 oz.   **29.** 1,200 lb. < 1 T.

30. 8 qt. > 1 gal.   **31.** 4 c. > 1 pt.

32. 1 yd. = 36 in.   **33.** 1 year < 56 weeks

Page 40

34. 48 ounces   **35.** 5 c.

36. 182 weeks   **37.** $1\frac{1}{3}$ feet

38. 14 pints   **39.** $1\frac{1}{2}$ minutes

40. 5 qt.   **41.** $1\frac{1}{4}$ tons

42. 1,000 pounds   **43.** 72 hours

44. 5 pints   **45.** 36 inches

46. $2\frac{1}{2}$ gallons   **47.** 360 seconds

48. $1\frac{1}{3}$ years   **49.** 60 hours

50. $3\frac{1}{3}$ days   **51.** $\frac{1}{4}$ mile

52. $2\frac{3}{4}$ years   **53.** 27 feet

54. $3\frac{3}{4}$ pounds   **55.** 1,200 min.

56. 16 qt.   **57.** 42 days

Unit 2

Page 41

1. $1\frac{1}{2}$

2. $\frac{1}{5}$

$$.2 = \frac{2}{10} = \frac{2 \div 2}{10 \div 2} = \frac{1}{5}$$

3. $\frac{1}{100}$ **4.** $6\frac{3}{4}$

5. $3\frac{1}{4}$ **6.** $10\frac{4}{5}$

7. $\frac{7}{20}$ **8.** $15\frac{3}{5}$

Page 42

9. 8.2

10. .25

$$
\begin{array}{r}
.25 \\
4\overline{)1.00} \\
-\ 8 \\
\hline
20 \\
-\ 20 \\
\hline
0
\end{array}
$$

11. .7   **12.** 3.375

13. 4.5   **14.** .875

15. 12.75   **16.** .03

17. 33.37

18. 121.6

$$
\begin{array}{r}
118.0 \\
+\ \ 3.6 \\
\hline
121.6
\end{array}
$$

19. 1.5   **20.** 60.09

21. 14.4

22. 60.33

$$
\begin{array}{r}
72.03 \\
-\ 11.70 \\
\hline
60.33
\end{array}
$$

23. 104.74   **24.** 12.8

25. 9.24

26. .05

$$
\begin{array}{r}
.5 \\
\times\ .1 \\
\hline
.05
\end{array}
$$

27. 5.1   **28.** .1325

29. 17

30. 100

$$
\begin{array}{r}
10\ 0. \\
.5\overline{)50.0} \\
-\ 5 \\
\hline
00 \\
-\ 0 \\
\hline
00 \\
-\ 0
\end{array}
$$

31. 30.5   **32.** 930

Page 43

1. 2 feet 3 inches
2. 3 ft. 6 in.
   Change .5 feet to inches. 12 in. = 1 ft.
   .5 ft. = .5 × 12 = 6 in. Write the number of feet, 3, and the number of inches, 6.
3. 2 yards 1 foot   **4.** 1 mile 2,640 feet
4. 3 days 12 hours   **6.** 3 lb. 2 oz.
5. 1 year 26 weeks   **8.** 7 hr. 45 min.
6. 3 hours 15 minutes
   Change .25 hour to minutes. 60 min. = 1 hr.
   .25 hour = .25 × 60 = 15 min.
7. 3 feet 6 inches
   Change $\frac{1}{2}$ foot to inches. 12 in. = 1 ft.
   $\frac{1}{2}$ foot = $\frac{1}{2}$ × 12 = 6 in.

Page 44

1. $5\frac{1}{2}$ quarts
2. $3\frac{1}{2}$ c.
   Change 4 ounces to cups. 8 oz. = 1 c.
   4 oz. = $\frac{4}{8}$ = $\frac{1}{2}$ c. Add the number of cups to the fraction of cups. $3 + \frac{1}{2} = 3\frac{1}{2}$
3. $7\frac{1}{2}$ pints   **4.** $2\frac{3}{4}$ gal.
4. $3\frac{2}{3}$ yd.   **6.** $1\frac{1}{4}$ miles
5. $6\frac{2}{3}$ ft.   **8.** $3\frac{1}{3}$ days
6. $7\frac{1}{2}$ pounds
   Change 8 ounces to pounds. 16 oz. = 1 lb.
   8 oz. = $\frac{8}{16}$ = $\frac{1}{2}$ lb. Add the number of pounds to the fraction of pounds.
   $7 + \frac{1}{2} = 7\frac{1}{2}$
7. $3\frac{1}{2}$ hours
    Change 30 minutes to hours. 60 min. = 1 hr.
    30 min. = $\frac{30}{60}$ = $\frac{1}{2}$ hr. Add the number of hours to the fraction of hours. $3 + \frac{1}{2} = 3\frac{1}{2}$

Page 45

1. 68 inches
2. 34 in.
   Change 2 feet to inches. 1 ft. = 12 in.
   2 ft. = 2 × 12 = 24 in.
   Add the answer, 24, to 10.
   24 + 10 = 34 in.
3. 4 ft.   **4.** 222 inches
4. 86 oz.   **6.** 2,500 lb.

7. 255 minutes   **8.** 58 weeks
8. 12 ounces   **10.** 6 quarts
9. 14 feet
    Change 4 yards to feet.
    1 yard = 3 feet
    4 yards = 4 × 3 = 12 feet
    Add the answer, 12, to 2. 12 + 2 = 14 feet
10. 32 months
    Change 2 years to months.
    1 year = 12 months
    2 years = 2 × 12 = 24 months
    Add the answer, 24, to 8.
    24 + 8 = 32 months

Page 46

1. 1 hour 40 minutes
2. 3 c. 4 oz.
   Change 28 ounces to cups. 1 c. = 8 oz.
   28 oz. = 28 ÷ 8 = 3 c. R 4. Write the remainder as the number of ounces.
   3 c. R 4 = 3 c. 4 oz.
3. 7 pt. 1 c.   **4.** 2 gal. 3 qt.
4. 5 yards 2 feet   **6.** 1 mi. 1,320 ft.
5. 6 ft. 8 in.   **8.** 2 weeks 5 days
6. 4 days 8 hours   **10.** 7 hr. 15 min.
7. 1 yr. 13 wk.   **12.** 2 years 6 months
8. 4 pounds 6 ounces
    Change 70 ounces to pounds. 1 lb. = 16 oz.
    70 oz. = 70 ÷ 16 = 4 lb. R 6. Write the remainder as the number of ounces.
    4 lb. R 6 = 4 lb. 6 oz.
9. 12 minutes 30 seconds
    Change 750 seconds to minutes.
    1 min. = 60 sec.
    750 sec. = 750 ÷ 60 = 12 min. R 30. Write the remainder as the number of seconds.
    12 min. R 30 = 12 min. 30 sec.

Page 47

1. 19 feet = 6 yards 1 foot
2. 18 cups = 4 quarts 2 cups
   Change 18 cups to quarts and cups or change 4 quarts 2 cups to cups. Compare.
   18 c. = 18 ÷ 4 = 4 qt. 2 c.
   or
   4 qt. = 4 × 4 = 16 c.
   16 c. + 2 c. = 18 c.
   18 c. = 4 qt. 2 c.
3. $6\frac{1}{2}$ gallons > 6 gallons 1 quart

4. $8'9'' > 8\frac{2}{3}$ feet

   8 ft. 9 in. $= 8\frac{9}{12}$ ft. $= 8\frac{3}{4}$ ft.

   or

   $8\frac{2}{3}$ ft. $= 8$ ft. 8 in.

   8 ft. 9 in. $>$ 8 ft. 8 in., so $8'9'' > 8\frac{2}{3}$ ft.

   or

   $8\frac{3}{4}$ ft. $> 8\frac{2}{3}$ ft., so $8'9'' > 8\frac{2}{3}$ ft.

5. 7 hours 15 min. $<$ 7.5 hours

6. 10.75 pounds $>$ 10 pounds 7 ounces

   10.75 pounds $= 10\frac{3}{4}$ pounds $=$

   10 pounds 12 ounces

   or

   10 pounds 7 ounces $= 10\frac{7}{16}$ pounds $=$

   10.4375 pounds

   10 pounds 12 ounces $>$ 10 pounds 7 ounces,

   so 10.75 pounds $>$ 10 pounds 7 ounces.

   10.75 pounds $>$ 10.4375 pounds, so

   10.75 pounds $>$ 10 pounds 7 ounces.

7. Bright brand

   12 cups $= 12 \div 4 = 3$ quarts

   or

   2 quarts $= 2 \times 4 = 8$ cups

   8 cups $+$ 3 cups $=$ 11 cups

   12 cups $>$ 11 cups,

   so 12 cups $>$ 2 quarts

   3 cups

   or

   3 quarts $>$ 2 quarts 3 cups,

   so 12 cups $>$ 2 quarts 3 cups

8. the pear tree

   5 feet 8 inches $= 5\frac{8}{12}$ feet $= 5\frac{2}{3}$ feet

   or

   $5\frac{3}{4}$ feet $=$ 5 feet 9 inches

   5 feet 8 inches $<$ 5 feet 9 inches, so

   5 feet 8 inches $< 5\frac{3}{4}$ feet

   or

   $5\frac{2}{3}$ feet $< 5\frac{3}{4}$ feet, so

   5 feet 8 inches $< 5\frac{3}{4}$ feet

Page 48

1. b. 34 inches
   Change 2 feet to inches. 1 foot $=$ 12 inches.
   2 feet $= 2 \times 12 = 24$ inches.
   Add the answer, 24, to 10.
   $24 + 10 = 34$.

2. b. .75 pound
   Change $\frac{3}{4}$ pound to a decimal. Divide the numerator, 3, by the denominator 4.

   $$4\overline{)3.00}$$
   $$\frac{-28}{20}$$
   $$\frac{-20}{0}$$
   with quotient .75

3. c. 1 hr. 25 min.
   Change 85 minutes to hours.
   1 hr. $=$ 60 min.
   85 min. $= 85 \div 60 = 1$ hour R 25 $=$
   1 hr. 25 min.

4. c. 8 cups
   Change 64 ounces to cups.
   8 ounces $=$ 1 cup
   64 ounces $= 64 \div 8 = 8$ cups

5. a. $1\frac{1}{2}$ lb.
   Change .5 pound to a fraction of a pound.
   1.5 lb. $= 1\frac{5}{10} = 1\frac{1}{2}$ lb.

6. b. $2\frac{5}{8}$ lb.
   Change 42 ounces to pounds. 16 oz. $=$ 1 lb.
   42 oz. $= 42 \div 16 = 2\frac{10}{16} = 2\frac{5}{8}$ lb.

7. c. 5 years
   Change 60 months to years.
   1 year $=$ 12 months
   60 months $= 60 \div 12 = 5$ years

8. a. 4.5 feet
   Change 54 inches to feet. 1 foot $=$ 12 inches
   54 inches $= 54 \div 12 = 4\frac{6}{12} = 4\frac{1}{2} = 4.5$ feet

Page 49

1. **9 feet 6 inches**
2. **3 feet 9 inches**
   Add the inches. Add the feet.

   $$\begin{array}{r} 7 \text{ inches} \\ + \ 3 \text{ feet 2 inches} \\ \hline 3 \text{ feet 9 inches} \end{array}$$

3. 10 ft. 9 in.   4. 7 wk. 6 days
5. 32 min. 25 sec.   6. 13 lb. 12 oz.
7. 10 hr. 45 min.   8. 17 gal. 3 qt.
9. 7 c. 5 oz.   10. 65 yd. 2 ft.
11. 18 hr. 50 min.   12. 20 T. 1,500 lb.
13. 5 ft. 10 in.
    Add 2 ft. 8 in. and 3 ft. 2 in. Add the inches.
    Add the feet.

    $$\begin{array}{r} 2 \text{ ft.} \ \ 8 \text{ in.} \\ + \ 3 \text{ ft.} \ \ 2 \text{ in.} \\ \hline 5 \text{ ft. 10 in.} \end{array}$$

191

14. 3 gallons 3 quarts
Add 2 gallons 2 quarts and 1 gallon 1 quart.
Add the quarts. Add the gallons.

2 gallons 2 quarts
+ 1 gallon 1 quart
3 gallons 3 quarts

Page 50

1. 6 feet
2. 11 yards 1 foot
Change 13 feet to yards.
13 feet = 13 ÷ 3 = 4 yards 1 foot
Add the answer to 7 yards.
7 yards + 4 yards 1 foot = 11 yards 1 foot
3. 7 pounds **4.** 5 tons
5. 5 cups **6.** 8 quarts 1 pint
7. 6 gallons 2 quarts **8.** 4 pints 1 cup
9. 3 hr. 30 min. **10.** 4 days 18 hours
11. 4 miles 2,640 feet **12.** 2 pounds
13. 14 minutes **14.** 7 years

Page 51

1. 4 c. 1 oz.
2. 8 wk. 1 day
Add the days. Add the weeks. Simplify the answer.

4 wk. 2 days
+ 3 wk. 6 days
7 wk. 8 days

8 days = 8 ÷ 7 = 1 wk. 1 day

7 wk.
+ 1 wk. 1 day
8 wk. 1 day

3. 3 ft. 4 in. **4.** 8 hr. 5 min.
5. 12 lb. 14 oz. **6.** 13 yd.
7. 10 gal. **8.** 6 T. 200 lb.
9. 14 min. 5 sec.
10. 22 pounds
Add 14 pounds 4 ounces and 7 pounds 12 ounces. Add the ounces. Add the pounds. Simplify the answer.

14 pounds 4 ounces
+ 7 pounds 12 ounces
21 pounds 16 ounces

16 oz. = 16 ÷ 16 = 1 lb.
1 lb. + 21 lb. = 22 lb.

11. 8 feet 4 inches
Add 3 feet 6 inches and 4 feet 10 inches.
Add the inches. Add the feet. Simplify the answer.

3 feet 6 inches
+ 4 feet 10 inches
7 feet 16 inches

16 in. = 16 ÷ 12 = 1 foot 4 inches

7 feet
+ 1 foot 4 inches
8 feet 4 inches or 2 yards 2 feet 4 inches

Page 52

1. 5 yd. 2 ft. 9 in.
2. 7 gal. 1 pt.
Set up the problem. Change 5 gallons to quarts. Add and simplify. Since 4 quarts = 1 gallon, the answer can be simplified again.

5 gal.   2 pt. = 20 qt. 2 pt.
+   6 qt. 3 pt. = 6 qt. 3 pt.
26 qt. 5 pt. =
28 qt. 1 pt. = 7 gal. 1 pt.

3. 10 pt. 1 c. 2 oz. or 5 qt. 1 c. 2 oz.
4. 4 days 45 min. **5.** 5 gallons
6. 3 T. 1,001 lb. 2 oz. **7.** 5 yd. 1 ft. 4 in.
8. 2 yr. 27 wk.

Page 53

1. 1 hr. 30 min.
2. 7 ft. 8 in.
Borrow 1 foot. Change 1 foot to 12 inches.
Add 12 inches to 6 inches. Write 18 above the 6. Subtract.

  7   18
  8 ft. 6 in.
−   10 in.
  7 ft.   8 in.

3. 3 pt. 1 c. **4.** 9 hr. 45 min.
5. 5 oz. **6.** 1 min. 40 sec.
7. 1 hr. 7 sec.
8. 5 qt. 1 pt.
Borrow 1 quart. Change 1 quart to 2 pints. Subtract.

  6   2 pt.
  7 qt.
− 1 qt. 1 pt.
  5 qt. 1 pt.

9. 2 yd. 1 ft.

10. 52 pounds 10 ounces

Subtract 4 pounds 6 ounces from 57 pounds to find the weight of the computer. Borrow 1 pound. Change 1 pound to 16 ounces. Subtract.

```
     56      16 oz.
    5̶7̶ lb.
  −  4 lb.  6 oz.
    52 lb. 10 oz.
```

11. 33 feet 8 inches

Subtract 16 feet 4 inches from 50 feet to find how much wire was left. Borrow 1 foot. Change 1 foot to 12 inches. Subtract.

```
     49      12 inches
    5̶0̶ feet
  − 16 feet 4 inches
    33 feet 8 inches
```

Page 54

1.– 8. You can simplify some of the answers.

1. 9 ft. 4 in.

2. 5,500 lb.

Set up the problem. Change 3 tons to pounds. Subtract.

```
    3 T.      = 6,000 lb.
  −   500 lb. =   500 lb.
               5,500 lb.
```

3. 4 pt. **4.** 4 qt. 1 pt.

5. 1 c. 6 oz. **6.** 255 min. 20 sec.

7. 2 quarts 1 pint

Subtract 5 quarts 1 pint from 2 gallons to find how much disinfectant was left. Change 2 gallons to quarts. Borrow 1 gallon. Subtract.

```
                    7      2 pt.
    2 gal.        = 8̶ qt.
  −     5 qt. 1 pt. = 5 qt. 1 pt.
                     2 qt. 1 pt.
```

8. 7 feet 2 inches

Subtract 1 foot 10 inches from 3 yards to find how much hose was left. Change 3 yards to feet. Borrow 1 foot. Subtract.

```
                        8       12 inches
    3 yards            = 9̶ feet
  −       1 foot 10 inches = 1 foot 10 inches
                        7 feet   2 inches
```

Page 55

1. 2 hours 40 minutes

Subtract the starting time for the movie, 5:35, from the ending time, 8:15. Since 15 minutes is less than 35 minutes, borrow 1 hour. Change the hour to 60 minutes and add to the 15 minutes. Subtract the minutes. Subtract the hours.

```
     7  75
    8̶:1̶5̶
  − 5:35
    2:40
```

2. 2 hours 28 minutes

```
     8  77
    9̶:1̶7̶
  − 6:49
    2:28
```

3. 1 hour 30 minutes

```
     11  70
    1̶2̶:1̶0̶
  − 10:40
     1:30
```

4. 55 minutes

```
      9  85
    1̶0̶:2̶5̶
  −  9:30
       55
```

Page 56

5. 6 hours 15 minutes

Subtract the time Beatrice started work, 7:15 A.M., from the time she stopped work, 1:30 P.M. Since 7:15 is in the morning and 1:30 is in the afternoon, add 12 hours to 1. Subtract the minutes. Subtract the hours.

```
     13
    1̶:30
  − 7:15
    6:15
```

6. 4 hours 25 minutes

```
     14
    2̶:55
  − 10:30
     4:25
```

7. 5 hours 40 minutes

```
     16
    1̶7̶ 85
    5̶:2̶5̶
  − 11:45
     5:40
```

8. 6 hours 45 minutes

```
     17
    1̶8̶ 75
    6̶:1̶5̶
  − 11:30
     6:45
```

Page 57

1. **19 lb. 8 oz.**
2. 41 gal. 1 qt.
   Multiply the quarts. Multiply the gallons. Simplify the answer.

   $$\begin{array}{r} 8 \text{ gal. 1 qt.} \\ \times \qquad 5 \\ \hline 40 \text{ gal. 5 qt.} = 41 \text{ gal. 1 qt.} \end{array}$$

3. 29 ft.
4. 28 yd. 1 ft.
5. 11 qt.
6. 4 hr. 15 min.
7. 52 lb. 8 oz.
8. 7 days
9. 11 pt. 1 oz.
10. 25 feet 6 inches
    Multiply 4 feet 3 inches by 6. Multiply the inches. Multiply the feet. Simplify the answer.

    $$\begin{array}{r} 4 \text{ feet 3 inches} \\ \times \qquad 6 \\ \hline 24 \text{ feet 18 inches} = 25 \text{ feet 6 inches} \end{array}$$

11. 13 hours
    Multiply 4 hours 20 minutes by 3. Multiply the minutes. Multiply the hours. Simplify the answer.

    $$\begin{array}{r} 4 \text{ hr. 20 min.} \\ \times \qquad 3 \\ \hline 12 \text{ hr. 60 min.} = 13 \text{ hr.} \end{array}$$

Page 58

1. **2 qt. $1\frac{1}{2}$ pt.**
2. 1 hr. 15 min.
   Divide 3 into 3 hours. Then divide 3 into 45 min. $45 \div 3 = 15$.

   $$\begin{array}{r} 1 \text{ hr. 15 min.} \\ 3\overline{)3 \text{ hr. 45 min.}} \\ -3 \\ \hline 0 \quad 4 \\ -3 \\ \hline 15 \\ -15 \end{array}$$

3. 3 ft. 11 in.
4. 3 lb. 14 oz.
5. 1 T. 1,300 lb.
6. 2 yd. 1 ft.
7. 4 min. 50 sec.
8. 3 gal. 2 qt.
9. 1 ft. 6 in.

Page 59

1. 4 gallons 3 quarts
2. 332 in.
3. 5 min. 40 sec.
4. 4 quarts 2 cups
5. 74 oz.
6. 4,200 lb.
7. $9\frac{1}{2}$ pt.
8. $5\frac{2}{3}$ years
9. 3 ft. 6 in.
10. 6 lb. 4 oz.
11. 1 ft. 3 in.
12. 1 hr. 30 min.
13. 1 gallon 1 quart < 6 quarts

14. $3\frac{1}{2}$ pounds > 3 pounds 2 ounces
15. 6 cups 1 ounce
16. 15 feet 8 inches
17. 11 pt.
18. 7 ft. 4 in.
19. 2 hr. 50 min.
20. 14 T. 1,300 lb.
21. 23 gal.
22. 4 hours 18 min.
23. 1 pound 6 ounces
    Divide 24 pounds 12 ounces by 18 to find the number of pounds for each basket.

    $$\begin{array}{r} 1 \text{ pound} \qquad 6 \text{ ounces} \\ 18\overline{)24 \text{ pounds}} \qquad 12 \text{ ounces} \\ -18 \\ \hline 6 \text{ pounds} = + \ 96 \text{ ounces} \\ \hline 108 \text{ ounces} \\ -108 \\ \hline 0 \end{array}$$

24. 3 hours 30 minutes
    Multiply 1 hour 10 minutes by 3. Multiply minutes. Multiply hours.

    $$\begin{array}{r} 1 \text{ hour} \quad 10 \text{ minutes} \\ \times \qquad\qquad 3 \\ \hline 3 \text{ hours 30 minutes} \end{array}$$

Page 60

1. **b. gram**
2. a. meters
   Meters are used to measure length. Material is usually bought by the yard.
3. c. liter
4. b. grams
5. c. liters
6. a. meters
7. c. liters
8. a. meters
9. c. liters
10. b. grams

Page 61

1. **c. kilometers**
2. a. milliliter
   Milliliter is the smallest unit of measurement for capacity. Medicine would be measured in small units.
3. a. milligrams
4. b. grams
5. b. liters
6. a. centimeters

Page 62

1. **50 m**
2. 90 cm
   Find *meter* in the table. Find *centi-* in the table. Count the number of steps, 2, from meter to centi. Move the decimal 2 places to the right.
   .9 m = .90 = 90 cm
3. 1.4 mm
4. 6 mL
5. 83 dL
6. 1,200 mg
7. 13,000 g
8. 5,300 L
9. 5,000 mg
10. 5,000 m

11. 45,250 g

Page 63
1. 170 cm
2. 8.2 kiloliters
   Find *liter* in the table. Find *kilo-* in the table. Count the number of steps, 3, from liters to kilo-. Move the decimal point 3 places to the left.
   8,200 liters = 8200 = 8.2 kiloliters
3. .009 grams
4. 50 meters
5. 65 liters
6. 20 kg
7. 32 km
8. 100 L
9. .8 kilometers
   Count the number of steps in the table from meters to kilo-. There are 3 steps. Since you are changing from smaller to larger units, move the decimal point 3 places to the left.
   800 meters = 800 = .8 km
10. .34 liters
    Count the number of steps in the table from milli- to liters. There are 3 steps. Move the decimal point 3 places to the left.
    340 mL = 340 = .34 L

Page 64
1. 2 L > 20 mL
2. 35 cm < 35 km
   Change 35 cm to kilometers or change 35 km to centimeters.
   35 cm = 00035 = .00035 km
   or
   35 km = 3500000 = 3,500,000 cm
   Compare.
   .00035 km < 35 km
   or 35 cm < 3,500,000 cm
3. 750 mg < 7.5 hg
4. 3.6 kL < 36,000 L
5. 39 cg = 390 mg
6. 4 km > 400 m
7. 8 L < 8 daL
8. 9.5 dam = 95 m
9. 11 mL < .00011 kL
10. 3 kg > 30 g
11. .7 g = 700 mg
12. 10 cm > 10 mm
13. 14 g < 14 kg
14. 1,800 mm < 18 m
15. .2 dg = .02 g

Page 65
1. 45.03 g
2. 2.19 kL
   Change 190 L to kiloliters, the larger unit.
   190 L = 190 = .19 kL. Add the kiloliters.
   2 + .19 = 2.19 kL
3. 83 cm
4. 15.19 L
5. 89.6 dag
6. 2.5 km

7. 24.84 mL
8. 94 cm
   Change 10 mm to centimeters, the larger unit. 10 mm = 10 = 1.0 cm. Subtract the result, 1.0 cm, from 95 cm. 95 − 1 = 94 cm.
9. 16.95 hL
10. 9.99 kg
11. 3.4 km
12. 5.5 g
13. 6 km
    Change 3,000 m to kilometers, the larger unit. 3000 m = 3000 = 3.0 km. Then add the kilometers. 3 + 3 = 6. Sami rode 6 kilometers.
14. 81.5 kg
    Change 9,000 grams to kilograms, the larger unit. 9000 g = 9000 = 9.0 kg.
    Subtract the result from 90.5 kg.
    90.5 − 9 = 81.5 kg. The air conditioning unit weighed 80.5 kg.

Page 66
1. 13.5 kL
2. 6.25 g
   Set up the problem. Multiply. Change the answer in milligrams to the larger unit, grams.
   $$\begin{array}{r} 625 \text{ mg} \\ \times\ 10 \\ \hline 6250 \text{ mg} \end{array}$$ = 6250 = 6.25 g
3. .584 km
4. 1.2 L
5. 17.5 cg
6. 175 dam
7. 600 L
8. 60 cm
   Set up the problem. Divide. Change the answer in meters to a smaller unit, centimeters.
   $$\begin{array}{r} .6 \text{ m} \\ 100\overline{)60.0 \text{ m}} \\ -\underline{60\ 0} \\ 0 \end{array}$$
   .6 m = 60 = 60 cm
9. 15 mg

Page 67
1. less than a mile
   1 km ≈ .62 mile
2. Yes
   From the table find the relationship of kilometers to miles. 1 km ≈ 0.62 mile. Change $\frac{6}{10}$ to a decimal, .6.
   .6 ≈ .62

Page 68

3. No

From the table find the relationship,
1 liter ≈ 1.06 quarts. Since 4 qt. = 1 gal.,
multiply each side of the relationship by 4.
22 liters ≈ 23.32 quarts. Compare.
Since 4 liters ≈ 1 gallon, 22 liters will not fill
a 22-gallon gas tank.

4. Yes

Find the relationship of kilograms and
pounds in the table. 1 kilogram ≈ 2.2
pounds. Compare the two measures. Since
1 kilogram is more than 2 pounds, Mariana
has enough meat for her meat loaf.

5. Yes

Find the relationship of meters to yards in
the table. 1 meter ≈ 39.37 inches. Since you
know that 36 inches = 1 yard, 1 meter ≈
1 yard. Since 1 meter is more than 1 yard
and Gwen needs 10 yards of wire fence, 10
meters will be enough wire fence.

6. more than a kilogram

Find the relationship of kilograms and
pounds in the table. 1 kilogram ≈ 2.2
pounds. Compare. Since 1 kilogram ≈ 2.2
pounds, 1 kilogram is less than 3 pounds.
Penny's patient should gain more than
1 kilogram a month.

7. No

Find the relationship of kilometers and
miles in the table. 1 kilometer ≈ 0.62 mile.
Compare. Since 1 kilometer is less than 1
mile, 40 kilometers is less than 40 miles.
Ken will be driving less than 40 miles per
hour if he drives 40 kilometers per hour.

8. too short

Find the relationship of centimeters to
inches in the table. 1 inch = 2.54
centimeters. Compare. Since 1 inch is more
than 2 centimeters, the 2-centimeter screw
will be too short to fix the chair.

9. Yes

Find the relationship of kilograms to
pounds. 1 kilogram ≈ 2.2 pounds. Multiply
both sides of the relationship by 5.
5 × 1 kilogram ≈ 5 × 2.2 pounds.
5 kilograms ≈ 11.0 pounds. Compare. Since
11 pounds is less than 15 pounds, 5
kilograms is less than 15 pounds. Casey's
package weighs less than the 15-pound
limit.

10. more

Find the relationship of liters to quarts.
1 liter ≈ 1.06 quarts. Since 4 quarts = 1
gallon, 1 gallon is more than 1 liter. A
gallon of ice cream is more than a liter of
ice cream.

Unit 2 Review, page 69

1. 2 days 12 hours
2. 3 miles 3,960 feet
3. $9\frac{2}{3}$ yards
4. $6\frac{3}{4}$ hours
5. 40 inches
6. 5,000 pounds
7. 2 T. 1,000 lb.
8. 5 cups 5 ounces
9. 5' 5" < $5\frac{1}{2}$ feet
10. 3.6 hr. > 3 hr. 10 min.
11. 5 gallons 1 quart
12. 14 yards
13. 17 pt.
14. 22 qt.
15. 3 miles 4,480 feet
16. 9 hr. 20 min. 40 sec.
17. 90 feet 5 inches
18. 4 pounds 5 ounces
19. b. grams
20. a. meters
21. c. kilometers
22. a. milligrams

Page 70

23. 2,000 meters
24. 1,700 centimeters
25. 40,000 milligrams
26. .5 decaliters
27. .015 kiloliters
28. .2 kilograms
29. 3 cm
30. 3 grams
31. 97 L < 2 kL
32. 3.6 m = 3,600 mm
33. 470 g > 5 dag
34. 2 km < 5,000 m
35. 35.15 grams or 35,150 milligrams
36. 56.8 kL or 56,800 L
37. 131.4 m
38. 40 cm

Unit 3

Page 71

1. 30
2. 196

```
    14
  × 14
    56
  + 14
   196
```

3. 60
4. 46
5. 90
6. 96
7. 55
8. 180
9. 55
10. 120

Page 72

11. $\frac{1}{2}$

12. $23\frac{3}{4}$

$17\frac{3}{4}$

$+\ 6$

$23\frac{3}{4}$

13. $74\frac{1}{2}$ 14. 6

15. 45   16. 21

17. $9\frac{7}{10}$ 18. $\frac{8}{21}$

19. 61   20. 15.3

21. 59.5

8.5

$\times\ \ 7$

59.5

22. 6.5   23. 7

24. .5   25. .18

26. 2   27. 8.18

28. 155.8

Page 73

1. $\angle$h   2. $\angle$Y or $\angle$XYZ

3. $\angle$b   4. $\angle$G or $\angle$FGH

5. $\angle$d   6. $\angle$c

7.   8.

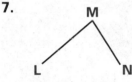

9.

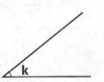

10. *Angle may vary in size and direction.*

10.

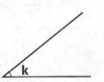

Page 74

1. perpendicular, intersecting
2. parallel
3. perpendicular, intersecting
4. parallel
5. intersecting   6. none of these
7. parallel   8. perpendicular
9. parallel
10. perpendicular, intersecting
11. parallel
12. perpendicular

Page 75

1. 30°
2. 90°
   The bottom or base side of the angle crosses at 0° on the outside scale. The mark on the outside scale where the other side of the angle crosses the protractor is 90. Write 90 with the symbol for degrees.
3. 145°   4. 110°

Page 76

1. 120°
2. 20°
   The bottom or base side of the angle crosses at 0° on the inside scale. The mark on the inside scale where the other side of the angle crosses the protractor is 20. Write 20 with the symbol for degrees.
3. 150°   4. 75°

Page 77

1. 45°, acute
2. 100°, obtuse
   The bottom or base side of the angle crosses at 0° on the outside scale. The mark on the outside scale where the other side of the angle crosses the protractor is 100. Since 100 is between 90° and 180°, the angle is obtuse.
3. 30°, acute   4. 125°, obtuse

Page 78

1. $\angle$**XYZ = 80°**
2. $\angle$w = 55°
   Subtract 35°, the given angle, from 90°, the total degrees in the right angle.
   90° − 35° = 55°
3. $\angle$d = 40°   4. $\angle$PQR − 70°
5. $\angle$m = 45°   6. $\angle$x = 15°
7. $\angle$a = 63°   8. $\angle$ABD = 78°
9. $\angle$e = 10°

Page 79

1. $\angle$**LMN = 35°**
2. $\angle$a = 80°
   Subtract 100°, the given angle, from 180°, the total degrees in a straight angle.
   180° − 100° = 80°
3. $\angle$r = 45°   4. $\angle$n = 143°
5. $\angle$g = 140°   6. $\angle$SRQ = 100°

Page 80

1. $\angle$**c = 60°**
   $\angle$**b = $\angle$d = 120°**

2. ∠l = ∠n = 80°
   ∠o = 100°
   ∠m and ∠o are vertical angles, so ∠m = ∠o. ∠m and ∠l are supplementary angles and equal 180°. ∠l and ∠n are vertical angles, so ∠l = ∠n.
   ∠m = 100°
   ∠m = ∠o, so ∠o = 100°
   ∠l = 180° − 100°
   ∠l = 80°
   ∠l = ∠n
   ∠l = 80°, so ∠n = 80°
3. ∠k = ∠m = 150°
   ∠n = 30°

Page 81
1. ∠1 = 60°
2. ∠4 = 60°
   ∠1 and ∠4 are vertical angles, so ∠4 = ∠1.
   ∠1 = 60°, so ∠4 = 60°.
3. ∠3 = 120°   4. ∠7 = 120°
5. ∠6 = 120°   6. ∠5 = 60°

Page 82
1. ∠a = ∠d = ∠e = ∠h = 45°
   ∠b = ∠c = ∠f = ∠g = 135°
   Since ∠a and the given angle are supplementary angles, subtract to find ∠a.
   ∠a = 180° − 135°
   ∠a = 45°
   The four acute angles are equal.
   ∠a = ∠d = ∠e = ∠h = 45°
   The four obtuse angles are equal.
   ∠b = ∠c = ∠f = ∠g = 135°
2. ∠a = ∠d = ∠e = ∠h = 140°
   ∠f = ∠b = ∠c = ∠g = 40°
3. ∠a = 45°
   Since ∠a and the given angle are alternate interior angles, ∠a = 45°.
4. 60°
   Since the horizontal and vertical boards make a right angle, the two angles are complementary angles.
   Complement = 90° − given angle
   Complement = 90° − 30° = 60°

Page 83
1. right   2. acute
3. obtuse   4. right
5. 55°   6. 130°
7. 24°   8. 65°
9. 45°   10. 150°
11. 90°   12. 63°

13. ∠h = ∠j = 30°   14. ∠r = ∠t = 125°
    ∠i = 150°   ∠s = 55°
15. ∠n = ∠o = ∠r = ∠s = 80°
    ∠m = ∠p = ∠q = ∠t = 100°

Page 84
1. ∠a = 63°
2. ∠ABC = 60°
   Add the two given angles. Subtract the sum from 180°.
   60° + 60° = 120°
   180° − 120° = 60°
3. ∠c = 33°   4. ∠DEF = 90°
5. ∠e = 60°   6. ∠f = 45°

Page 85
1. ∠a = 16°
2. ∠b = 24°
   Since the triangle is a right triangle, add 90° plus the given angle, 66°. Subtract the sum, 156°, from 180°.
   66° + 90° = 156°
   180° − 156° = 24°
3. ∠c = 61°   4. ∠d = 20°
5. ∠e = 60°   6. ∠f = 42°

Page 86
1. ∠R = ∠S = 45°
   ∠Q = 90°
2. ∠T = ∠U = 50°
   ∠V = 80°
   TV = UV, so ∠T = ∠U
   ∠U = 50°, so ∠T = 50°
   50° + 50° = 100°
   180° − 100° = 80°, so ∠V = 80°
3. ∠X = ∠Z = 75°
   ∠Y = 30°
4. ∠L = ∠M = ∠N = 60°
5. ∠A = ∠C = 45°
   ∠B = 90°
6. ∠D = ∠E = ∠F = 60°

Page 87
1. ∠A = ∠C = 74°
2. ∠D = ∠F = 65°
   Subtract the given angle, E, from 180°. Divide the result by 2. Check by adding the three angles.
   180° − 50° = 130°
   130° ÷ 2 = 65°
   50° + 65° + 65° = 180°
3. ∠G = ∠I = 45°, ∠H = 90°
4. ∠J = ∠L = 45°, ∠K = 90°
5. ∠M = ∠O = 60°

6. $\angle P = \angle R = 45°$, $\angle Q = 90°$

7. $\angle S = \angle U = 63°$

8. $\angle W = \angle Y = 45°$, $\angle X = 90°$

9. $\angle X = \angle Z = 40°$

Page 88

1. $\angle H = 80°$

$\angle J = 40°$

$\triangle GHI \sim \triangle JKL$

2. $\angle A = 30°$

$\angle N = 60°$

$\triangle ABC \sim \triangle LMN$

Find the unknown angle in each triangle.

$\triangle ABC : 60° + 90° = 150°$

$\angle A = 180° - 150° = 30°$

$\triangle LMN : 30° + 90° = 120°$

$\angle N = 180° - 120° = 60°$

Compare the corresponding angles.

$\angle A = \angle L = 30°$

$\angle B = \angle M = 90°$

$\angle C = \angle N = 60°$

Page 89

1. $\overline{LM} = 10$

2. $\overline{QS} = 15$

Write a proportion using the pairs of corresponding sides. Substitute the length of the sides in the proportion. Use n for the length of QS. Cross-multiply to find the unknown side.

$$\frac{\overline{QS}}{\overline{TV}} = \frac{\overline{RS}}{\overline{UV}} \qquad \frac{n}{25} \times \frac{12}{20}$$

$$n \times 20 = 12 \times 25$$

$$20n = 300$$

$$\overline{QS} = 300 \div 20 = 15$$

3. $\overline{AC} = 8$ **4.** $\overline{JH} = 12.5$

Page 90

1. $\angle a = 50°$ **2.** $\angle b = 30°$

3. $\angle c = 88°$ **4.** $\angle d = 32°$

5. $\angle e = 45°$ **6.** $\angle f = 80°$

7. $\angle B = \angle C = 60°$ **8.** $\angle F = \angle D = 40°$

                                $\angle E = 100°$

9. $\angle G = \angle I = 64°$ **10.** $n = 30$

11. $n = 20$

Page 91

1. rectangle

2. triangle

A triangle has three sides and three angles.

3. parallelogram   **4.** rectangle

5. trapezoid   **6.** triangle

7. rectangle   **8.** trapezoid

9. parallelogram

Page 92

1. pentagon   **2.** square

3. hexagon   **4.** heptagon

5. triangle   **6.** octagon

7. hexagon   **8.** pentagon

Note: *8. is not a regular pentagon.*

9. square

Page 93

1. 13 in.

2. 17.2 '

Add the lengths of the four sides.

$3 + 3 + 5 + 6.2 = 17.2'$

3. 47 cm   **4.** 50.5 m

5. 16 ft.   **6.** 44 mi.

7. 15 feet

Add the lengths of the three sides of the shawl to find the perimeter.

$5\frac{1}{2} + 5\frac{1}{2} + 4 = 14\frac{2}{2} = 15$

8. 75 feet

$20 + 15 + 18 + 22 = 75$

Page 94

1. 50 '

2. 20.8 cm

Use the formula for the perimeter of a square, $P = 4s$. Substitute 5.2 cm for the side. Multiply.

$P = 4s$

$P = 4 \times 5.2$

$P = 20.8$ cm

3. 21 ft.   **4.** 25.2 m

5. $157\frac{1}{2}$ in.   **6.** 4 mi.

Page 95

1. 396 "

2. 220 cm

Use the formula $C = \pi d$. Substitute 70 cm for d and $\frac{22}{7}$ for π in the formula. Cancel and multiply.

$C = \pi d$

$C = \frac{22}{7} \times 70$ cm

$C = \frac{22}{7} \times \frac{\overset{10}{\cancel{70}}}{1}$

$C = \frac{220}{1}$

$C = 220$ cm

3. 44 m   **4.** 125.6 ft.

5. 25.12 mi.
$C = 2\pi r$
$C = 2 \times 3.14 \times 4$
$C = 25.12$ mi.

6. 31.4 '

Page 96

1. **9 square units**
2. **12 square units**
Count the number of square units inside the figure, 12. Multiply the length times the width.
$4 \times 3 = 12$ square units
3. 8 square units　　**4.** 10 square units
5. 12 square units　　**6.** 16 square units

Page 97

1. 14 sq. ft.
2. 9.61 sq. m
Use the formula for the area of a square, $A = s^2$. Substitute 3.1 m for the length of any side. Multiply. Write the answer in square units.
$A = s^2$
$A = 3.1^2$
$A = 3.1 \times 3.1$
$A = 9.61$ square meters
3. 72 sq. yd.　　**4.** $30\frac{1}{4}$ sq. "
5. 76.125 sq. cm　　**6.** 144 sq. mi.
7. 540 square feet
Use the formula for the area of a rectangle, $A = lw$. Substitute 30 feet for the length and 18 feet for the width. Multiply. Write the answer in square units.
$A = lw$
$A = 30 \times 18$
$A = 540$ square feet
8. $56\frac{1}{4}$ square feet
Use the formula for the area of a square, $A = s^2$. Substitute $7\frac{1}{2}$ feet for the length of a side.
$A = s^2$
$A = 7\frac{1}{2}^2$
$A = \frac{15}{2} \times \frac{15}{2} = \frac{225}{4}$
$A = 56\frac{1}{4}$ square feet

Page 98

1. $76\frac{1}{2}$ sq. ft.
2. 15 sq. cm
Use the formula for the area of a triangle. Substitute 3 cm for the base, b, and 10 cm for the height, h. Multiply. Write the answer in square units.
$A = \frac{1}{2}bh$
$A = \frac{1}{\overset{}{\underset{1}{2}}} \times \frac{3}{1} \times \frac{\overset{5}{10}}{1} = \frac{15}{1}$
$A = 15$ sq. cm
3. 84 sq. yd.　　**4.** 180 sq. "
5. 36 sq. '　　**6.** 30 sq. m

Page 99

1. 616 sq. m
2. 3, 850 sq. cm
Use the formula for the area of a circle. Substitute 35 cm for r and $\frac{22}{7}$ for π. Multiply.
$A = \pi r^2$
$A = \frac{22}{7} \times 35^2$
$A = \frac{22}{\underset{1}{7}} \times \frac{\overset{5}{35}}{1} \times \frac{35}{1} = 3,850$ sq. cm
3. 18,634 sq. in.　　**4.** 3.14 sq. mi.
5. 78.5 sq. '
$A = \pi r^2$
$A = 3.14 \times 5^2$
$A = 3.14 \times 25 = 78.5$ square '
6. 28.26 sq. in.

Page 100

1. – 8. Your pictures should be similar to these.

1. $58\frac{1}{2}$ square miles

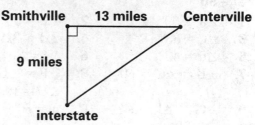

The area formed by connecting these 3 points is a triangle. Find the area of a triangle.
$A = \frac{1}{2}bh$
$A = \frac{1}{2} \times 13 \times 9$
$A = 58\frac{1}{2}$ square miles

2. $\overline{YZ}$ = 18 inches

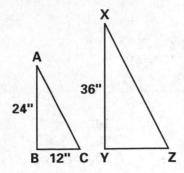

Write a proportion using the pairs of corresponding sides. Substitute the given values in the proportion. Use n for the length of YZ. Cross-multiply.

$$\frac{\overline{AB}}{\overline{XY}} = \frac{\overline{BC}}{\overline{YZ}}$$

$$\frac{24}{36} \diagdown \frac{12}{n}$$

$$24 \times n = 36 \times 12$$
$$24n = 432$$
$$n = 432 \div 24$$
$$\overline{YZ} = 18$$

Page 101

3. 1,080 square feet

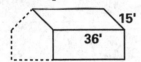

Each half of the roof is a rectangle. Find the area of one side. Add the areas of both sides.
Area = lw
A = 36 × 15
A = 540 square feet
Area of both sides = 540 + 540 = 1,080 square feet

4. 31 feet

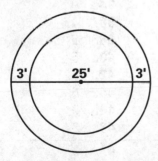

Add the diameter of the garden and the width of the border on each side of the circular garden.
25 feet + 3 feet + 3 feet = 31

5. 180 square feet

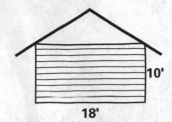

Each side of the shed is a rectangle. Find the area of a rectangle to find the number of square feet for each side.
A = lw
A = 10 × 18 = 180 square feet

6. 154 square feet

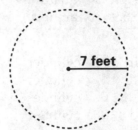

The area covered by the water sprinkler is a circle. The distance from the center of the circle to the edge of the circle, 7 feet, is the radius. Find the area of the circle.
A = πr²

$$A = \frac{22}{\overset{1}{\cancel{7}}} \times \frac{\overset{1}{\cancel{7}}}{1} \times \frac{7}{1} = \frac{154}{1}$$

A = 154 square feet

7. 3 miles

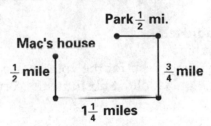

Add the distance walked in each direction to find the total distance to the park.
$\frac{1}{2} + 1\frac{1}{4} + \frac{3}{4} + \frac{1}{2} = 3$ miles

8. 36.96 square feet

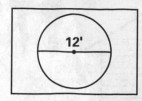

Use the formula for the area of a circle to find the area of the sign. Subtract the answer from 150 square feet to find the area of the side not covered by the sign. Divide the diameter, 12, by 2 to get the radius.

$A = \pi r^2$
$A = 3.14 \times 6^2$
$A = 3.14 \times 36 = 113.04$ square feet
$150 - 113.04 = 36.96$ square feet

Page 102

1. rectangular solid **2.** cylinder
3. rectangular solid **4.** cylinder
5. cube **6.** cylinder
7. rectangular solid **8.** cylinder
9. rectangular solid

Page 103

1. 12 cubic units
2. 9 cubic units
Count the number of cubic units, 9. Multiply the length times the width times the height. Write the answer in cubic units.
$3 \times 1 \times 3 = 9$
3. 4 cubic units **4.** 8 cubic units
5. 12 cubic units **6.** 24 cubic units

Page 104

1. 8 cubic feet
2. 16 cubic "
Use the formula for the volume of a rectangular solid. Substitute the correct numbers.
$V = lwh$
$V = 4 \times 2 \times 2 = 16$ cubic "
3. 3,080 cubic m **4.** 18,480 cubic inches
5. 27 cubic cm **6.** 10 cubic yd.

Unit 3 Review, page 105

1. 55° **2.** 40°
3. ∠c = 20° **4.** ∠d = 55°
5. ∠a = 60° **6.** ∠e = 90°
7. ∠f = ∠h = 80°
∠g = 100°
8. ∠i = ∠k = ∠l = ∠n = 120°
∠j = ∠m = ∠o = ∠60°
9. ∠x = 91° **10.** ∠y = 60°

11. ∠z = 45°
12. ∠B = 70°
∠C = 40°
13. ∠Z = ∠Y = 75°
14. ∠M = ∠N = 45°
∠L = 90°

Page 106

15. x = 4 **16.** y = 7
17. 24 cm **18.** 33 '
19. 26 " **20.** 44 cm
21. 77 square ' **22.** 36 square m
23. 30 square inches **24.** 153.86 sq. mi.
25. 512 cubic ' **26.** $38\frac{1}{2}$ cubic inches
27. 5 cubic m

Unit 4

Page 107

1. 12 **2.** 7
3. 13 **4.** 6
5. 5 **6.** 3
7. 11 **8.** 6
9. 8 **10.** 8
11. 7 **12.** 4

Page 108

13. 7 **14.** 2
15. 8 **16.** 5
17. 6 **18.** 7
19. 9 **20.** 12
21. 15 **22.** 9
23. 7 **24.** 4
25. 49 **26.** 8
27. 36 **28.** 4
29. 30 **30.** 0
31. 9 **32.** 5
33. 8 **34.** 9
35. 9 **36.** 45
37. 9 **38.** 7
39. 9 **40.** 5
41. 0 **42.** 42
43. 9 **44.** 5
45. 49 **46.** 7
47. 20 **48.** 3

Page 109

1. negative number
2. equation
3. positive number
4. solving an equation
5. four times a number equals seven equation
6. negative number

7. unknown number
8. positive number
9. unknown number
10. equation
11. solving an equation
12. four times a number equals seven equation

Page 110

1. $-20°$
2. $+98°$ or $98°$
   Write the number of degrees with the degree sign. Because the word *above* is used, put a plus sign in front of the number.
3. $+5°$ or $5°$
4. $-5°$
5. $-16°$
6. $+65°$ or $65°$
7. $+30°$
8. $+25°$ or $25°$
   Write the number of degrees the arrow is pointing to. Since the number is above zero, put a plus sign in front of the number. The number is understood to be positive without the plus sign.
9. $+18°$ or $18°$
10. $+10°$ or $10°$
11. $0°$
12. $-5°$
13. $-10°$
14. $-16°$
15. $-26°$

Page 111

1. I
2. K
   Find zero on the number line. Since positive numbers are to the right of zero, move to the right by counting 6 marks. Write the letter that corresponds to 6, K.
3. F
4. E
5. C
6. O
7. N
8. D
9. H
10. J
11. G
12. B
13. M
14. A
15. L
16. -20
17. -12
   Find zero on the number line. Count the number of marks to get to the letter C. Since C is 12 marks to the left of zero, it is a negative number. Write a minus sign in front of the number.
18. -3
19. 0
20. 5
21. -9
22. -16
23. 3
24. 12
25. 20
26. 19
27. 14

28. -5
29. 9
30. 16

Page 112

1. $-6 < -5$
2. $-12 > -15$
   Find -12 and -15 on the number line. Since -12 is to the right of -15, -12 is greater than -15. Write $>$ between the numbers to show that -12 is greater than -15.
3. $-7 < -1$
4. $-20 < -10$
5. $-2 < 2$
6. $7 > -3$
7. $-9 < 10$
8. $15 > -18$
9. $-3 < 0$
10. $-15 < 6$
11. $-13 < -8$
12. $-1 < 5$
13. $4 > -4$
14. $1 > -2$
15. $5 > -8$
16. $20 > -20$
17. $-9 > -10$
18. $-11 > -15$
19. $9 > -17$
20. $-19 < 0$
21. $13 > -6$
22. $-1 < 1$
23. $8 > -18$
24. $10 > -10$
25. $-15°$
   Find -15 and 5 on the number line. Since -15 is to the left of 5, $-15°$ is colder than $5°$.
26. 2,500 feet
    2,500 is to the right of $-3,000$ on a number line, so 2,500 feet is more than or higher than $-3,000$ feet.
27. $1°$
    1 is to the right of -10 on the number line, so $1°$ is warmer than $-10°$.
28. -200 feet
    -200 is to the left of -130 on a number line, so -200 feet is less than or lower than $-130°$ feet.

Page 113

1. 1
2. 4
   Write a multiplication problem. The exponent, 2, tells you to multiply two twos. $2 \times 2 = 4$.
3. 9
4. 0
5. 25
6. 36
7. 49
8. 64
9. 81
10. 100
11. 1
12. 8
13. 27
14. 64
15. 125
16. 121
17. 1,000
18. 225
19. 0
20. 144

21. 121 square inches
The exponent in s^2, 2, tells you to multiply side by side. Since each side is 11 inches, multiply 11 by 11. $11 \times 11 = 121$.

22. 16
A number squared is the same as a number to the second power. Since the radius is 4 feet, $r^2 = 4 \times 4 = 16$.

Page 114

1. 4

2. 2
What number times itself equals 4?
$2 \times 2 = 4$. The square root of 4 is 2.

3.	3	**4.**	6
5.	7	**6.**	8
7.	9	**8.**	10
9.	12	**10.**	5
11.	11	**12.**	15
13.	13	**14.**	1
15.	14	**16.**	0

17. 15 feet
Find the square root of 225.
Since $15 \times 15 = 225$, $\sqrt{225} = 15$.

18. 12 yards
Find the square root of 144.
Since $12 \times 12 = 144$, $\sqrt{144} = 12$.

Page 115

1. $6 + 90 = 96$

2. $12 - 7 = 5$
Write a numerical expression. $12 - 7$.
Evaluate by subtracting. $12 - 7 = 5$.

3. 19×3 or $19 \cdot 3 = 57$

4. $4 \div 10$ or $\frac{4}{10} = .4$ or $\frac{2}{5}$

5. $8 + 6 + 2 = 16$

6. $100 \times 7 \times 2$ or $100 \cdot 7 \cdot 2 = 1,400$

7. $2,000 \div 4$ or $\frac{2,000}{4} = 500$

8. $25 - 0 = 25$

9. $3 \cdot 4 \cdot 3 = 36$

10. $55 \div 11$ or $\frac{55}{11} = 5$

Page 116

1. $3 + 28 = 31$

2. 9
First divide 5 by 1. Then add the result to 4.
$(5 \div 1) + 4$
$\quad 5 \quad + 4 = 9$

3.	5	**4.**	100
5.	12	**6.**	7
7.	6	**8.**	31

9. 4

10. 20
First multiply 11 by 2. Add the result to 12. Subtract 14 from 34.
$12 + (11 \cdot 2) - 14$
$(12 + 22) - 14$
$\quad 34 \quad - 14 = 20$

11.	0	**12.**	15

Page 117

1. 3

2. 145
Evaluate the number with an exponent.
$6^2 = 6 \times 6$. Multiply. Add.
$1 + 6^2 \cdot 4$
$1 + (36 \cdot 4)$
$1 + \quad 144 = 145$

3.	81	**4.**	28
5.	183	**6.**	10
7.	89	**8.**	50
9.	48	**10.**	72
11.	36	**12.**	33
13.	100	**14.**	46
15.	339	**16.**	74
17.	2,714	**18.**	68

19. 20
$4^2 - 3 + 7$
$16 - 3 + 7 = 20$

20. 241
$25 + 6^3$
$25 + 216 = 241$

21. 80
$8^2 + 4^2$
$64 + 16 = 80$

22. 24
$4^3 - 40$
$64 - 40 = 24$

Page 118

1. 22

2. 160
Do the operation in parentheses first.
Multiply the result, 40, by 4.
$(36 + 4) \cdot 4$
$40 \cdot 4 = 160$

3.	1	**4.**	5
5.	17	**6.**	10
7.	14	**8.**	4
9.	16	**10.**	7
11.	32	**12.**	7
13.	200	**14.**	5
15.	40	**16.**	2

17. 7

18. 6
First add 10 and 8 to get the total number of pencils. Then divide the total by 3.
$(10 + 8) \div 3$
$18 \div 3 = 6$

19. 72 bottles

First subtract 6 bottles from 24 bottles to find how many bottles in each case can be sold. Then multiply the result by 4 cases.

$(24 - 6) \cdot 4$

$18 \cdot 4 = 72$

Page 119

1. 132 square feet

Find the total area of the side. Subtract the area of the door.

total area − door area

$(20 \cdot 9) - (6 \cdot 8)$

$180 - 48 = 132$

2. 260 square feet

area of each end + triangular roof area

$(20 \cdot 9) + 80$

$180 + 80 = 260$

3. 1,020 square feet

area of first section + area of second section

$(30 \cdot 14) + (30 \cdot 20)$

$420 + 600 = 1,020$

4. 256 square feet

area of each side × number of sides

$(8^2) \cdot 4$

$64 \cdot 4 = 256$

Page 120

1. $-2°$ **2.** $+50°$ or $50°$
3. $+32°$ or $32°$ **4.** $-14°$
5. C **6.** F
7. A **8.** G
9. I **10.** -16
11. 0 **12.** $+10$ or 10
13. -5 **14.** $+19$ or 19
15. $-3 < 3$ **16.** $-9 > -11$
17. $7 > -2$ **18.** $0 > -1$
19. $-15 < 14$ **20.** $-5 < 5$
21. $1 > -12$ **22.** $10 > -3$
23. 81 **24.** 64
25. 169 **26.** 125
27. 100 **28.** 4
29. 7 **30.** 11
31. 2 **32.** $12 - 9 = 3$
33. $8 + 10 = 18$ **34.** $3 \times 7 \times 2 = 42$
35. 20 **36.** 5
37. 12 **38.** 2
39. 232 **40.** 20
41. 63 **42.** 6
43. 2

Page 121

1. – 6. Answers may vary.

1. $y + 1$

2. $10x$

Write the number, 10, and the variable, x, next to each other.

3. $2y$ **4.** $z - 7$
5. $x \div 12$ or $\dfrac{x}{12}$ **6.** $20^2 - x$

Page 122

1. 8
2. 1

Substitute 5 for x in the expression. Divide 5 by 5.

$5 \div x$

$5 \div 5 = 1$

3. 4 **4.** 14
5. 5
6. 7

Substitute 5 for x in the expression. Divide 5 by 1. Add 2 to 5. $2 + 5 = 7$.

$2 + x \div 1$

$2 + \underbrace{5 \div 1}$

$2 + \quad 5 = 7$

7. 18 **8.** 64
9. 5 **10.** 22
11. 16 **12.** 9
13. 83 **14.** 14
15. 2 **16.** 46

Page 123

1. 40
2. 23

Substitute 4 for x in the expression. Raise 3 to the third power. Subtract.

$3^3 - x$

$3^3 - 4$

$27 - 4 = 23$

3. 400 **4.** 9
5. 25 **6.** 8
7. 19 **8.** 58
9. 128 **10.** 8
11. 68

$100 - \dfrac{x^2}{2}$

$100 - \dfrac{8^2}{2}$

$100 - \dfrac{64}{2}$

$100 - 32 = 68$

12. 10 **13.** 21
14. 0 **15.** 262
16. 84 **17.** 145
18. 592

Page 124

1. 11
2. 2

   Substitute 10 for x in the expression. Do the operation inside the parentheses first. Subtract the result from 15.
   $15 - (x + 3)$
   $15 - (10 + 3)$
   $15 - 13 = 2$

3. 20
4. 5
5. 17
6. 24
7. 14
8. 11
9. 2
10. 42
11. 1

   Substitute 12 for x in the expression. Do the operation inside the parentheses. Divide.
   $(x - 7) \div 5$
   $(12 - 7) \div 5$
   $5 \div 5 = 1$

12. 39
13. 5
14. 90
15. 2
16. 5
17. 220
18. 2

Page 125

1. $x = 3$
2. $x = 3$

   Find a value for x that makes this equation true. Write the solution.
   $7 - x = 4$
   $7 - 3 = 4$
   $x = 3$

3. $x = 4$
4. $x = 5$
5. $x = 8$
6. $x = 10$
7. $x = 2$
8. $x = 3$
9. $x = 5$
10. $x = 1$
11. $x = 0$
12. $x = 12$

Page 126

1. $x = 5$
2. $x = 20$

   Substitute 15 for y in the equation. Find a number for x that makes the equation true. Write the solution.
   $x - y = 5$
   $x - 15 = 5$
   $20 - 15 = 5$
   $x = 20$

3. $x = 2$
4. $x = 30$
5. $x = 2$
6. $x = 6$
7. $x = 3$
8. $x = 3$
9. $x = 4$
10. $x = 18$
11. $x = 10$
12. $x = 1$

13. $x = 16$
14. $x = 2$
15. $x = 5$
16. $x = 75$

Page 127

1. 37°C

   Use the formula for finding °C. Substitute 98.6 for °F. Evaluate the expression. Use the correct order of operations.
   $°F = \frac{5}{9}(98.6 - 32)$

   $°F = \frac{5}{9}(66.6)$

   $°F = \frac{5}{9} \times \frac{\overset{7.4}{\cancel{66.6}}}{1} = \frac{37}{1} = 37$

2. 40°C
   $°C = \frac{5}{9}(104 - 32)$

   $°C = \frac{5}{9}(72)$

   $°C = \frac{5}{9} \times \frac{\overset{8}{\cancel{72}}}{1} = \frac{40}{1} = 40$

Page 128

3. 150°C
   $°C = \frac{5}{9}(302 - 32)$

   $°C = \frac{5}{9}(270)$

   $°C = \frac{5}{9} \times \frac{\overset{30}{\cancel{270}}}{1} = \frac{150}{1} = 150$

4. 32°F

   Use the formula for finding °F. Substitute 0 for °C. Evaluate the expression.
   $°F = \frac{9}{5}(0) + 32$

   $°F = 0 + 32$
   $°F = 32$

5. 212°F
   $°F = \frac{9}{5}(100) + 32$

   $°F = \frac{9}{5} \times \frac{\overset{20}{\cancel{100}}}{1} + 32$

   $°F = 180 + 32 = 212$

6. 68°F

$$°F = \frac{9}{5}(20) + 32$$

$$°F = \frac{9}{\cancel{5}} \times \frac{\overset{4}{\cancel{20}}}{1} + 32$$
$${}_{1}$$

$$°F = 36 + 32 = 68$$

7. 25°C

$$°C = \frac{5}{9}(77 - 32)$$

$$°C = \frac{5}{9}(45)$$

$$°C = \frac{5}{\cancel{9}} \times \frac{\overset{5}{\cancel{45}}}{1} = \frac{25}{1} = 25$$
$${}_{1}$$

8. 347°F

$$°F = \frac{9}{5}(175) + 32$$

$$°F = \frac{9}{\cancel{5}} \times \frac{\overset{35}{\cancel{175}}}{1} + 32$$
$${}_{1}$$

$$°F = 315 + 32 = 347$$

9. 15°C

$$°C = \frac{5}{9}(59 - 32)$$

$$°C = \frac{5}{9}(27)$$

$$°C = \frac{5}{\cancel{9}} \times \frac{\overset{3}{\cancel{27}}}{1} = \frac{15}{1} = 15$$
$${}_{1}$$

10. 104°F

$$°F = \frac{9}{5}(40) + 32$$

$$°F = \frac{9}{\cancel{5}} \times \frac{\overset{8}{\cancel{40}}}{1} + 32$$
$${}_{1}$$

$$°F = 72 + 32 = 104$$

Unit 4 Review, page 129

1.	−18	**2.**	−8
3.	C	**4.**	H
5.	B	**6.**	−2
7.	F	**8.**	G
9.	9	**10.**	125
11.	49	**12.**	64
13.	3	**14.**	12
15.	9	**16.**	15
17.	$7 + 12 = 19$	**18.**	$19 \div 2$ or $\frac{19}{2} =$

18. $9\frac{1}{2}$ or 9.5

19.	$80 \times 3 = 240$	**20.**	$6 + 9 - 4 = 11$
21.	0	**22.**	8
23.	9	**24.**	10
25.	500	**26.**	80
27.	7	**28.**	8
29.	30		

30. – 33. Answers may vary.

30.	$x - 6$	**31.**	$5x$
32.	$\frac{z}{7^2}$	**33.**	$2 + x$

Page 130

34.	13	**35.**	90
36.	0	**37.**	24
38.	5	**39.**	25
40.	0	**41.**	5
42.	1	**43.**	$x = 4$
44.	$x = 26$	**45.**	$x = 3$
46.	$x = 1$	**47.**	$x = 3$
48.	$x = 10$	**49.**	$x = 1$
50.	$x = 5$	**51.**	$x = 7$

Unit 5

Page 131

1.	$4 + 2 = 6$	**2.**	8×3 or $8 \cdot 3 = 24$
3.	$30 \div 5$ or $\frac{30}{5} = 6$	**4.**	$12 - 7 = 5$
5.	6×9 or $6 \cdot 9 = 54$	**6.**	$15 \div 3$ or $\frac{15}{3} = 5$

Page 132

7. 38

8. 2

$$8 - 2 \cdot 3$$
$$8 - 6 = 2$$

9.	7	**10.**	15
11.	8	**12.**	9
13.	67	**14.**	12
15.	13		

16. 7

$$x - 2$$
$$9 - 2 = 7$$

17.	12	**18.**	5
19.	59	**20.**	13
21.	16	**22.**	15
23.	$x = 4$		

24. $x = 6$

$$13 - x = 7$$
$$13 - 6 = 7$$
$$x = 6$$

25.	$x = 5$	**26.**	$x = 10$
27.	$x = 8$	**28.**	$x = 4$
29.	$x = 19$	**30.**	$x = 1$

Page 133

1. 16
2. −18
   Add 12 and 6. 12 + 6 = 18. Since the numbers are both negative, give the answer, 18, a negative sign.
   −12 + (−6) = −18
3. −28
4. −20
5. −16
6. 2
7. −38
8. −26
9. 85°
   Add 80 and 5. 80 + 5 = 85
10. −$250
    Add 200 and 50. 200 + 50 = 250. Since the company had a loss in sales, add a negative sign to the answer.

Page 134

1. 5
2. −5
   Find the difference between 9 and 4. 9 − 4 = 5. Since −9 is the larger number, give the answer a negative sign.
   −9 + 4 = −5
3. −6
4. −6
5. −1
6. 1
7. −9
8. 10
9. −15
10. 30
11. −16
12. 5
13. −1
14. −5
15. 25
16. −32

Page 135

1. −4
2. 0
   Group the negative numbers and group the positive numbers. Add the positive numbers and add the negative numbers. Add the two totals.
   4 + (−1) + (−3)
   4 + (−4) = 0
3. −12
4. −2
5. −14
6. 20
7. 0
8. −45
9. 10
10. −5
11. $90
12. $125
13. −$9
14. $97

Page 136

1. −4

2. −13
   Change the sign of +6 to −6. Add. Since the numbers are both negative, give the answer a negative sign.
   −7 − (+6)
   −7 + (−6) = −13
3. −11
4. 9
5. −1
6. −27
7. −14
8. 12
9. 0
10. −5
11. −21
12. −45
13. 11 − (+7) = 4
14. −8 − (+6) = −14

Page 137

1. 7
2. −6
   Change the sign of −9 to 9. Find the difference between 15 and 9. Since −15 is the larger number, the answer is negative.
   −15 − (−9)
   −15 + 9 = −6
3. −8
4. 10
5. 1
6. 17
7. 30
8. −29
9. 38
10. −34
11. 120
12. 62
13. 3
14. 1
15. 32
16. 0
17. 27 − (−17) = 27 + 17 = 44
18. −60 − (−16) = −60 + 16 = −44
19. 15 − (−5) = 15 + 5 = 20
20. −46 − (−64) = −46 + 64 = 18

Page 138

1. 6
2. −4
   The opposite of negative 4 is positive 4.
3. 7
4. −10
5. −17
6. −19
7. 25
8. 30
9. 0
10. −4
    Zero plus any number equals that number.
    −4 + 0 = −4
11. 2
12. −6
13. 0
14. −9
15. −8
16. 3
17. −1
18. 0
19. 0
20. −15
21. 0
22. 0
23. 3
24. 0

Page 139

1. 6
2. 5
   Any number minus zero is that number.
   $5 - 0 = 5$

3.	−8	4.	−10
5.	0	6.	0
7.	11	8.	−13
9.	−23	10.	0
11.	15	12.	0
13.	0	14.	17
15.	−9	16.	−30
17.	0	18.	8
19.	0	20.	14

Page 140

1.	2	2.	5
3.	8	4.	0
5.	−5	6.	5
7.	−17	8.	−50
9.	9	10.	−16
11.	−13	12.	−25
13.	−3	14.	19
15.	−2	16.	−37
17.	4	18.	−9
19.	0	20.	15
21.	8	22.	−8
23.	−18	24.	−16
25.	−10	26.	0
27.	0	28.	0
29.	−11	30.	8
31.	−1	32.	−7
33.	4	34.	−5
35.	0	36.	16
37.	34	38.	−10
39.	150		

Page 141

1. $x = 3$
2. $x = 5$
   Subtract 6 from both sides of the equal sign so only x remains on the left side of the equation. $11 - 6 = 5$, so the value for x is 5. Check by substituting the value of x into the original equation.
   Solve: $x + 6 = 11$
   $$x + 6 - 6 = 11 - 6$$
   $$0 \qquad 5$$
   $$x = 5$$
   Check: $x + 6 = 11$
   $$5 + 6 = 11$$
   $$11 = 11$$

3. $x = 1$ 4. $x = 15$

5. $x = 8$
6. $x = 35$
   Solve: $35 + x = 70$
   $$35 - 35 + x = 70 - 35$$
   $$0 \qquad 35$$
   $$x = 35$$
   Check: $35 + x = 70$
   $$35 + 35 = 70$$
   $$70 = 70$$

7.	$x = 78$	8.	$x = 59$
9.	$x = 7$	10.	$x = 13$
11.	$x = 16$	12.	$x = 25$

Page 142

1. $x = -21$
2. $x = -18$
   Subtract 8 from both sides of the equal sign so only x remains on the left side of the equation. $-10 - 8 = -18$, so the value for x is -18. Check by substituting the value of x into the original equation.
   Solve: $x + 8 = -10$
   $$x + 8 - 8 = -10 - 8$$
   $$0 \qquad -18$$
   $$x = -18$$
   Check: $x + 8 = -10$
   $$-18 + 8 = -10$$
   $$-10 = -10$$

3.	$x = -80$	4.	$x = -14$
5.	$x = -26$	6.	$x = -54$
7.	$x = -18$	8.	$x = -4$
9.	$x = -60$	10.	$x = -25$
11.	$x = -16$	12.	$x = -44$

13. $x + 7 = -42$
    $$x = -49$$
14. $11 + x = -4$
    $$x = -15$$

Page 143

1. $x = 10$
2. $x = 21$
   Add 9 to both sides of the equal sign so only x remains on the left side of the equation. $12 + 9 = 21$, so the value for x is 21. Check by substituting the value of x into the original equation.
   Solve: $x - 9 = 12$ Check: $x - 9 = 12$
   $$x - 9 + 9 = 12 + 9 \qquad 21 - 9 = 12$$
   $$0 \qquad 21 \qquad 12 = 12$$
   $$x = 21$$

3.	$x = 16$	4.	$x = 11$
5.	$x = 12$	6.	$x = 24$
7.	$x = 23$	8.	$x = 109$

9. $x = 131$ **10.** $x = 123$
11. $x = 26$ **12.** $x = 26$

Page 144

1. $x = 0$
2. $x = 8$

Add 9 to both sides of the equation, so only x remains on the left side of the equation. $-1 + 9 = 8$, so the value for x is 8. Check.

Solve: $x - 9 = -1$ Check: $x - 9 = -1$
$$x\underbrace{(-9 + 9)} = \underbrace{(-1 + 9)}$$
$$0 \qquad\qquad 8$$
$$x = 8$$
$$8 - 9 = -1$$
$$-1 = -1$$

3. $x = 1$ **4.** $x = -1$
5. $x = -4$ **6.** $x = 11$
7. $x = -5$ **8.** $x = -7$
9. $x = 0$ **10.** $x = 15$
11. $x = 20$ **12.** $x = 24$
13. $x - 8 = -4$ **14.** $x - 20 = -13$
     $x = 4$ $x = 7$

Unit 5 Review, page 145

1. 2   **2.** 2
3. -26 **4.** -2
5. -80 **6.** 65
7. -3 **8.** 69
9. 2   **10.** -16
11. -6 **12.** 18
13. 9   **14.** 13
15. -18 **16.** -90
17. -7 **18.** 0
19. 0   **20.** -2
21. $x = 5$ **22.** $x = 4$
23. $x = 1$ **24.** $x = 6$
25. $x = -6$ **26.** $x = -20$
27. $x = -13$ **28.** $x = -11$

Page 146

29. $x + 13 = 25$ **30.** $7 + x = -5$
     $x = 12$ $x = -12$
31. $x - 24 = 12$ **32.** $x - 10 = 0$
     $x = 36$ $x = 10$
33. $x = 14$ **34.** $x = 17$
35. $x = 46$ **36.** $x = 20$
37. $x = 12$ **38.** $x = 6$
39. $x = 6$ **40.** $x = 8$

Unit 6

Page 147

1. 5×7 or $5 \cdot 7 = 35$ **2.** $10 \div 2$ or $\frac{10}{2} = 5$

3. 8×9 or $8 \cdot 9 = 72$ **4.** $16 \div 4$ or $\frac{16}{4} = 4$

5. $25 \div 5$ or $\frac{25}{5} = 5$

6. 10×10 or $10 \cdot 10 = 100$

Page 148

7. 8
8. 10
$$\underbrace{(15 \div 3)} \times 2$$
$$5 \quad \times 2 = 10$$

9. 30   **10.** 24
11. 10   **12.** 14
13. 4   **14.** 3
15. 36   **16.** 3
                      $\frac{12}{4} = 3$
17. 20   **18.** 144
19. 6   **20.** 2
21. 21   **22.** 2
23. $x = 3$ **24.** $x = 14$
                      $\frac{x}{7} = 2$
                      $\frac{14}{7} = 2$
25. $x = 5$ **26.** $x = 12$
27. $x = 4$ **28.** $x = 10$
29. $x = 18$ **30.** $x = 3$

Page 149

1. 21
2. 80

Multiply the two numbers. $10 \times 8 = 80$. Since both numbers have the same sign, the answer is positive. $-10(-8) = 80$.

3. 36   **4.** 48
5. 12   **6.** 10
7. 45   **8.** 84
9. 7   **10.** 324
11. 130   **12.** 240
13. 721   **14.** 100
15. 340   **16.** $-22 \, (-5) = 110$
17. $-19 \, (-30) = 570$

Page 150

1. -6
2. -20

Multiply the two numbers. $(5)(4) = 20$. Since the numbers have different signs, the answer is negative. $-5(4) = -20$.

3. 0   **4.** -14
5. -5 **6.** -50
7. -48 **8.** -36
9. -140 **10.** -32
11. -100 **12.** -30
13. $-3 \, (20) = -60$ **14.** $45 \, (-2) = -90$

Page 151

1. 2
2. 7

   Divide the two numbers. $\frac{21}{3} = 7$. Since the numbers have the same sign, the answer is positive. $\frac{-21}{-3} = 7$.

3. 6 **4.** 2
5. 6 **6.** 3
7. 2 **8.** 3
9. 15 **10.** 2
11. 7 **12.** 1
13. 7 **14.** 7
15. 32 **16.** 10
17. 9 **18.** 4
19. 6 **20.** 15
21. $\frac{-22}{-11} = 2$ **22.** $\frac{12}{3} = 4$
23. $\frac{-35}{-7} = 5$ **24.** $\frac{16}{8} = 2$

Page 152

1. $-2\frac{1}{2}$
2. 0

   Zero divided by any number is always zero.

3. -3 **4.** -7
5. -8 **6.** -5
7. $-5\frac{1}{4}$ **8.** 0
9. -5 **10.** -2
11. $-22\frac{1}{2}$ **12.** -4
13. $-4\frac{1}{8}$ **14.** -5
15. $-4\frac{1}{7}$ **16.** -9
17. $\frac{-15}{1} = -15$ **18.** $\frac{23}{-5} = -4\frac{3}{5}$

Page 153

1. 42 **2.** 52
3. 63 **4.** -12
5. -7 **6.** -27
7. 55 **8.** -96
9. 40 **10.** -24
11. 20 **12.** 18
13. 3 **14.** 2
15. 3 **16.** -6
17. -2 **18.** -9
19. $6\frac{3}{5}$ **20.** $-5\frac{2}{3}$

21. $-12\frac{3}{4}$ **22.** $-3\frac{2}{3}$
23. 7 **24.** -9
25. $-9\,(-10) = 90$ **26.** $\frac{-32}{4} = -8$
27. $6\,(-12) = -72$ **28.** $\frac{-20}{-2} = 10$
29. $(18)(3) = 54$ **30.** $\frac{29}{-7} = -4\frac{1}{7}$
31. $-13\,(-3) = 39$ **32.** $\frac{40}{-9} = -4\frac{4}{9}$

Page 154

1. $x = \frac{1}{2}$
2. $x = \frac{1}{3}$

   Divide both sides of the equal sign by 9. $\frac{9}{9} = 1$, so only x remains on the left side of the equal sign. $\frac{3}{9} = \frac{1}{3}$, so the value for x is $\frac{1}{3}$.
   Check the answer by substituting the value of x into the original equation.

   Solve: $9x = 3$ Check: $9x = 3$
   $\frac{9x}{9} = \frac{3}{9}$ $9\left(\frac{1}{3}\right) = 3$
   $x = \frac{1}{3}$ $3 = 3$

3. $x = 6$ **4.** $x = 6$
5. $x = 9$ **6.** $x = \frac{4}{7}$
7. $x = 3$ **8.** $x = \frac{2}{3}$
9. $x = 5$

Page 155

1. $x = \frac{1}{-7}$
2. $x = -5$

   Divide both sides of the equation by 5. $\frac{5}{5} = 1$, so only x remains on the left side of the equation. $\frac{-25}{5} = -5$, so the value of x is -5. Check the answer by substituting the value of x into the original equation.

   Solve: $5x = -25$ Check: $5x = 25$
   $\frac{5x}{5} = \frac{-25}{5}$ $5(-5) = -25$
   $x = -5$ $-25 = -25$

3. $x = -12$ **4.** $y = 2$
5. $y = 1$ **6.** $y = \frac{1}{-4}$

7. $y = -2$
8. $y = 4$
9. $y = \dfrac{-2}{5}$
10. $x = \dfrac{2}{3}$
11. $x = \dfrac{3}{5}$
12. $x = \dfrac{1}{2}$

Page 156

1. $x = 50$
2. $y = 27$

Multiply both sides of the equal sign by 3. $\dfrac{3}{3} = 1$, so only y remains on the left side.

$9 \times 3 = 27$, so the value for y is 27. Check the answer by substituting the value of y into the original equation.

Solve: $\dfrac{y}{3} = 9$ Check: $\dfrac{y}{3} = 9$

$3 \cdot \dfrac{y}{3} = 9 \cdot 3$ $\dfrac{27}{3} = 9$

$y = 27$ $9 = 9$

3. $x = 28$
4. $x = 54$
5. $y = 60$
6. $x = 60$
7. $y = 25$
8. $y = 56$
9. $x = 24$
10. $x = 35$
11. $y = 36$
12. $y = 80$

Page 157

1. $y = -4$
2. $x = -48$

Multiply both sides of the equation by 8. $\dfrac{8}{8} = 1$, so only x remains on the left side.

$(-6)\,8 = -48$, so the value for x is -48. Check the answer by substituting the value of x into the original equation.

Solve: $\dfrac{x}{8} = -6$ Check: $\dfrac{x}{8} = -6$

$8\left(\dfrac{x}{8}\right) = (-6)\,8$ $\dfrac{-48}{8} = -6$

$\dfrac{8x}{8} = -48$ $-6 = -6$

$x = -48$

3. $y = -135$
4. $x = -98$
5. $y = -27$
6. $y = -35$
7. $x = 3$
8. $y = 60$
9. $x = 90$
10. $y = -24$
11. $x = -160$
12. $x = 288$

Page 158

1. $x = 3$
2. $x = 3$
3. $x = \dfrac{2}{9}$
4. $x = 2$
5. $x = \dfrac{1}{4}$
6. $y = \dfrac{7}{10}$

7. $x = -2$
8. $x = \dfrac{3}{10}$
9. $x = -3$
10. $x = -4$
11. $x = -4$
12. $x = 8$
13. $x = 12$
14. $y = 36$
15. $x = 24$
16. $x = -45$
17. $x = 64$
18. $y = -125$
19. $x = 12$
20. $y = -60$
21. $y = 36$

Page 159

1. $\dfrac{4}{1}$
2. $-\dfrac{6}{1}$

Invert the fraction $-\dfrac{1}{6}$ to find its reciprocal.

3. $\dfrac{8}{1}$
4. $-\dfrac{10}{1}$
5. $\dfrac{15}{1}$
6. $\dfrac{7}{2}$
7. $-\dfrac{6}{5}$
8. $\dfrac{5}{2}$
9. $-\dfrac{8}{3}$
10. $\dfrac{10}{7}$
11. $\dfrac{5}{4} \cdot \dfrac{4}{5}x = x$
12. $-\dfrac{7}{6} \cdot -\dfrac{6}{7}x = x$

Find the reciprocal of $-\dfrac{6}{7}$ by inverting. The reciprocal is $-\dfrac{7}{6}$. Multiply and cancel.

$-\dfrac{\overset{1}{\cancel{7}}}{\cancel{6}} \cdot -\dfrac{\overset{1}{\cancel{6}}}{\cancel{7}}x = \dfrac{1}{1}x = x$

13. $\dfrac{9}{2} \cdot \dfrac{2}{9}x = x$
14. $-\dfrac{11}{7} \cdot -\dfrac{7}{11}x = x$
15. $-\dfrac{3}{2} \cdot -\dfrac{2}{3}x = x$
16. $\dfrac{5}{3} \cdot \dfrac{3}{5}y = y$
17. $\dfrac{9}{1} \cdot \dfrac{1}{9}x = x$
18. $-\dfrac{10}{3} \cdot -\dfrac{3}{10}y = y$
19. $-\dfrac{8}{7} \cdot -\dfrac{7}{8}y = y$
20. $-\dfrac{2}{1} \cdot -\dfrac{1}{2}x = x$

Page 160

1. $x = -18$
2. $y = -28$

   Multiply both sides by the reciprocal of $\frac{3}{4}$.

   $\frac{4}{3} \cdot \frac{3}{4}y = y$, so only y remains on the left side.

   $-21 \cdot \frac{4}{3} = \frac{-84}{3}$, so the value for y is -28.

   Check by substituting the value of y into the original equation.

   Solve: $\frac{3}{4}y = -21$ Check: $\frac{3}{4}y = -21$

   $\frac{4}{3} \cdot \frac{3}{4}y = (-21) \cdot \frac{4}{3}$ $\frac{3}{4}(-28) = -21$

   $y = \frac{-84}{3}$ $-21 = -21$

   $y = -28$

3. $x = 24$ 4. $x = 6$
5. $x = 14$ 6. $x = -10$

Page 161

1. $y = 2$
2. $x = 2$

   Subtract 10 from both sides. Divide both sides by 5. Check by substituting the value of x into the original equation.

   Solve: $10 + 5x = 20$

   $10 + 5x - 10 = 20 - 10$

   $5x = 10$

   $\frac{5x}{5} = \frac{10}{5}$

   $x = 2$

   Check: $10 + 5x = 20$

   $10 + 5(2) = 20$

   $10 + 10 = 20$

   $20 = 20$

3. $y = 1$ 4. $x = 7$
5. $y = 20$ 6. $x = -6$
7. $x = 12$ 8. $y = -40$

Page 162

1. $x = 12$

2. $x = -6\frac{2}{3}$

   Add 5 to both sides. Multiply both sides by the reciprocal of $\frac{3}{10}$, $\frac{10}{3}$. Check by substituting the value of x into the original equation.

   Solve: $\frac{3}{10}x - 5 = -7$

   $\frac{3}{10}x - 5 + 5 = -7 + 5$

   $\frac{3}{10}x = -2$

   $\frac{10}{3} \cdot \frac{3}{10}x = (-2)\left(\frac{10}{3}\right)$

   $x = \frac{-20}{3}$

   $x = -6\frac{2}{3}$

   Check:

   $\frac{3}{10}x - 5 = -7$

   $\frac{3}{10}\left(-6\frac{2}{3}\right) - 5 = -7$

   $\frac{3}{10}\left(-\frac{20}{3}\right) - 5 = -7$

   $(-2) - 5 = -7$

   $-7 = -7$

3. $x = 225$ 4. $x = -28$

Unit 6 Review, page 163

1. 24   2. 10
3. 20   4. -14
5. -24 6. -36
7. 3   8. 5
9. 3   10. -3
11. -6 12. -4
13. $x = 7$ 14. $x = 7$
15. $x = 9$ 16. $x = -2$
17. $x = 6$ 18. $x = -4$
19. $y = 24$ 20. $x = 24$
21. $y = -20$ 22. $\frac{6}{1}$
23. $-\frac{20}{9}$ 24. $\frac{12}{7}$

Page 164

25. $\frac{9}{5} \cdot \frac{5}{9}x = x$ 26. $-\frac{3}{2} \cdot -\frac{2}{3}y = y$

27. $\frac{9}{7} \cdot \frac{7}{9}y = y$ 28. $x = 40$

29. $x = -10$ 30. $y = -27$

31. $x = \dfrac{3}{4}$ **32.** $y = 48$

33. $x = -5$ **34.** $x = 80$

35. $x = -6$ **36.** $x = 10$

Unit 7

1. 9   **2.** 25

3. 49   **4.** 36

5. 81   **6.** 144

7. 64   **8.** 169

9. 2   **10.** 4

11. 6   **12.** 9

13. 7   **14.** 13

15. 12   **16.** 10

17. 25   **18.** 77
$81 - 4 = 77$

19. 9   **20.** 65

21. -7 **22.** 17
$9 + 8 = 17$

23. 5   **24.** -95

25. 5   **26.** 13
$3 + 10 = 13$

27. 50   **28.** 28

29. 9   **30.** -30

31. 4   **32.** 4

33. $x = 5$

34. $x = 12$
$x - 2 = 10$
$x - 2 + 2 = 10 + 2$
$x = 12$

35. $x = 16$ **36.** $x = -1$

37. $x = 20$ **38.** $x = -10$

39. $x = 45$ **40.** $x = -2$

1. 300 sq. ft.
The problem asks for square feet. Use the formula for the area of a triangle, $A = \frac{1}{2}bh$. Substitute the numbers and multiply.
$A = \frac{1}{2}bh$
$A = \frac{1}{2} \times 20 \times 30$
$A = \frac{1}{\cancel{2}} \times \frac{\cancelto{10}{20}}{1} \times \frac{30}{1} = \frac{300}{1}$
$A = 300$ sq. ft.

2. 31.4'
Use the formula for the circumference of a circle, $C = \pi d$. Substitute and multiply.
$C = \pi d$
$C = 3.14 \times 10$
$C = 31.4'$

3. a. $V = lwh$, 12 cubic feet
Use the formula for the volume of a rectangular solid, $V = lwh$. Substitute and multiply.
$V = lwh$
$V = 2 \times 2 \times 3$
$V = 12$ cubic feet

4. b. $A = lw$, $19\frac{1}{2}$ sq. ft.

Use the formula for the area of a rectangle, $A = lw$. Substitute and multiply.
$A = lw$
$A = 3 \times 6\frac{1}{2}$
$A = \frac{3}{1} \times \frac{13}{2} = \frac{39}{2} = 19\frac{1}{2}$ square feet

5. 12 feet
Use the formula for the area of a rectangle, $A = lw$. Substitute 48 square feet for the area and 4 feet for the length. Solve.
$A = lw$
$48 = 4w$
$4w = 48$
$\dfrac{4w}{4} = \dfrac{48}{4}$
$w = 12$ feet

6. 49 feet
Use the formula for the circumference of a circle, $C = \pi d$. Substitute 154 feet for the circumference and $\frac{22}{7}$ for π. Solve.
$C = \pi d$
$154 = \frac{22}{7}d$
$\frac{22}{7}d = 154$
$\frac{7}{22} \cdot \frac{22}{7}d = \frac{154}{1} \cdot \frac{7}{22}$
$d = \frac{\cancelto{7}{154}}{1} \cdot \frac{7}{\cancel{22}} = \frac{49}{1} = 49$
$d = 49$ feet

7. b. $200 = \frac{1}{2}(20)(h)$, 20 feet

Use the formula for the area of a triangle, $A = \frac{1}{2}bh$. Substitute and solve.

$$A = \frac{1}{2}bh$$
$$200 = \frac{1}{2} \times 20 \times h$$
$$200 = \frac{1}{2} \times \frac{\overset{10}{\cancel{20}}}{1} \times h$$
$$\phantom{200 = \frac{1}{2} \times }_{1}$$
$$200 = 10h$$
$$\frac{10h}{10} = \frac{200}{10}$$
$$h = 20 \text{ feet}$$

8. c. $\sqrt{225} = s$, 15 feet

Use the formula for the area of a square, $A = s^2$. Substitute the given area. Move the unknown to the left side. Solve.

$$A = s^2$$
$$225 = s^2$$
$$s^2 = 225$$
$$s = \sqrt{225}$$
$$s = 15 \text{ feet}$$

Page 169

1. 240 square feet

The area of the square without the border is 784 square feet. Find the area of the square with the border. Add 2 feet to the length of each side of the square. $28 + 2 + 2 = 32$ feet. Each side of the square with a border is 32 feet. Find the area.
$$A = s^2$$
$$A = 32^2$$
$$A = 1{,}024 \text{ square feet}$$
Subtract the area of the square without the border, 784 square feet, from the area of the square including the border, 1,024 square feet, to find the area of the border.
$$1{,}024 - 784 = 240$$

2. 475 square feet

Find the area of the meeting room.
$$A = s^2$$
$$A = 25^2$$
$$A = 625 \text{ square feet}$$
Find the area of the stage.
$$A = lw$$
$$A = 15 \times 10$$
$$A = 150 \text{ square feet}$$
Subtract the area of the stage, 150 square feet, from the area of the room, 625 square feet.
$$625 - 150 = 475$$

Page 170

3. yes

Find the area of each of the 3 rectangular rooms. Add to find the total area.
$$A = lw$$
$$A = 18 \times 12 = 216$$
$$A = 8 \times 14 = 112$$
$$A = 4 \times 8 = \underline{32}$$
$$\phantom{A = 4 \times 8 = }360 \text{ square feet}$$

4. 630 square feet

Find the area of the triangular area using the formula, $A = \frac{1}{2}bh$ and the area of the driveway using the formula, $A = lw$. Add the two areas.

$A = \frac{1}{2}bh$ $A = lw$

$A = \frac{1}{2} \times 10 \times 30$ $A = 16 \times 30$

$A = \frac{1}{2} \times \frac{\overset{5}{\cancel{10}}}{1} \times \frac{30}{1} = \frac{150}{1}$ $A = 480 \text{ sq.}'$

$A = 150 \text{ sq.}'$

$150 + 480 = 630 \text{ sq.}'$

5. 1,200 square feet

Find the area of the side measuring 36 feet by 10 feet. Two sides will have this area.
$$A = 36 \times 10$$
$$A = 360 \text{ square feet}$$
Find the area of the side measuring 24 feet by 10 feet. The other two sides will have this area.
$$A = 24 \times 10$$
$$A = 240 \text{ square feet}$$
Add the four sides.
$$360 + 360 + 240 + 240 = 1{,}200 \text{ square feet}$$

6. 89 square feet

Find the total area of the wall.
$$A = lw$$
$$A = 15 \times 8$$
$$A = 120 \text{ square feet}$$
Find the area of the door.
$$A = lw$$
$$A = 7 \times 3$$
$$A = 21 \text{ square feet}$$
Find the area of the window.
$$A = lw$$
$$A = 2\frac{1}{2} \times 4$$
$$A = 10 \text{ square feet}$$
Subtract the area of the window and the door from the total area of the wall.
$$120 - 21 - 10 = 89$$

Page 171

1. 13 inches

   Use the formula $a^2 + b^2 = c^2$ to find the hypotenuse. Substitute 12 inches and 5 inches for a and b in the formula.

   $$a^2 + b^2 = c^2$$
   $$12^2 + 5^2 = c^2$$
   $$144 + 25 = c^2$$
   $$169 = c^2$$
   $$\sqrt{169} = c$$
   $$13 = c$$

2. 10 yards

   $$a^2 + b^2 = c^2$$
   $$8^2 + 6^2 = c^2$$
   $$64 + 36 = c^2$$
   $$100 = c^2$$
   $$\sqrt{100} = c$$
   $$10 = c$$

Page 172

3.–4. Your drawings should be similar to these.

3.

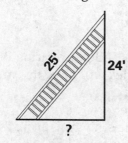

   7 feet

   Substitute the correct numbers in the formula and solve.

   $$a^2 + b^2 = c^2$$
   $$24^2 + b^2 = 25^2$$
   $$576 - 576 + b^2 = 625 - 576$$
   $$b^2 = 49$$
   $$b = \sqrt{49}$$
   $$b = 7$$

4.

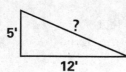

   30 feet

   $$a^2 + b^2 = c^2$$
   $$5^2 + 12^2 = c^2$$
   $$25 + 144 = c^2$$
   $$169 = c^2$$
   $$\sqrt{169} = c$$
   $$13 = c$$

   Add the lengths of the three sides to find the perimeter. $5 + 12 + 13 = 30$

5.

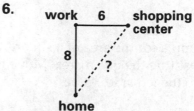

   5 miles

   $$a^2 + b^2 = c^2$$
   $$3^2 + 4^2 = c^2$$
   $$9 + 16 = c^2$$
   $$25 = c^2$$
   $$\sqrt{25} = c$$
   $$5 = c$$

6.

   10 miles

   $$a^2 + b^2 = c^2$$
   $$8^2 + 6^2 = c^2$$
   $$64 + 36 = c^2$$
   $$100 = c^2$$
   $$\sqrt{100} = c$$
   $$10 = c$$

Page 173

1. 50 feet

   Write a ratio for the proportion of the signpost to its shadow. Then write an equal ratio for the shop building to its shadow. Use n for the height of the building. Cross-multiply.

   $$\frac{4}{1\frac{1}{2}} \quad \times \quad \frac{n}{18\frac{3}{4}}$$

   $$1\frac{1}{2}n = 18\frac{3}{4} \times 4$$

   $$1\frac{1}{2}n = \frac{75}{\overset{1}{\cancel{4}}} \times \frac{\cancel{4}}{1} = \frac{75}{1}$$

   $$n = 75 \div 1\frac{1}{2} = \frac{75}{1} \div \frac{3}{2} = \frac{\overset{25}{\cancel{75}}}{1} \times \frac{2}{\underset{1}{\cancel{3}}} = \frac{50}{1}$$

   $$n = 50$$

2. 12 feet

Write a ratio for the proportion of the height of the storage shed to its shadow. Write an equal ratio for the height of the doghouse to its shadow. Cross-multiply.

$$\frac{n}{9} \times \frac{4}{3}$$

$$3n = 36$$
$$n = 36 \div 3 = 12$$
$$n = 12$$

Page 174

3. 50 feet

Add 60' to 15' to find the shadow of the taller tree. $60 + 15 = 75$

$$\frac{10}{15} \times \frac{n}{75}$$

$$15n = 75 \times 10$$
$$n = 750 \div 15$$
$$n = 50$$

The taller tree is 50 feet tall.

4. 27 feet

$$\frac{d}{45} \times \frac{36}{60}$$

$$60d = 45 \times 36$$
$$d = 1,620 \div 60$$
$$d = 27$$

The distance across the pond is 27 feet.

5. 60 yards

$$\frac{6}{8} \times \frac{45}{d}$$

$$6d = 45 \times 8$$
$$d = 360 \div 6 = 60$$
$$d = 60$$

The distance across the lake from point A to point B is 60 yards.

6. 24 feet

$$\frac{15}{12} \times \frac{30}{d}$$

$$15d = 30 \times 12$$
$$15d = 360$$
$$d = 24$$

The distance across the river is 24 feet.

Page 175

1.	36 inches	**2.**	60 min.
3.	$\frac{1}{2}$ or .5 quart	**4.**	$\frac{1}{2}$ or .5 T.
5.	120 min.	**6.**	26 weeks
7.	135 ft.	**8.**	$1\frac{1}{8}$ or 1.125 c.
9.	13 qt.	**10.**	9 miles 880 yards
11.	$2\frac{1}{2}$ or 2.5 pints	**12.**	40 inches
13.	2 min. 10 sec.	**14.**	15 days 6 hours
15.	2 yd. 1 ft. 6 in.	**16.**	3 T. 1,200 lb.
17.	1 pint	**18.**	63 lb. 2 oz.
19.	6 pints $1\frac{1}{2}$ cups	**20.**	600 cm
21.	.45 g	**22.**	30°
23.	140°	**24.**	75°
25.	65°	**26.**	120°
27.	30°		

Page 176

28.	120°	**29.**	$\overline{AB} = 2$
30.	39 '	**31.**	88 '
32.	36 square m	**33.**	28.26 square "
34.	28 cubic cm	**35.**	49
36.	27	**37.**	4
38.	5	**39.**	1
40.	45	**41.**	9
42.	3	**43.**	6
44.	768	**45.**	16
46.	4	**47.**	−16
48.	−12	**49.**	25
50.	−9	**51.**	−10

Page 177

52.	$x = 27$	**53.**	$x = -71$
54.	$x = 3$	**55.**	$x = 10$
56.	$x = -2$	**57.**	$x = 9$
58.	24	**59.**	−18
60.	5	**61.**	−3
62.	$x = 4$	**63.**	$x = -4$
64.	$x = 12$	**65.**	$x = 12$
66.	$x = 3$	**67.**	$x = 15$

MATH SYMBOLS

=	equal to
≈	approximately equal to
>	greater than
<	less than
~	similar to
°	degrees
∠	angle
△	triangle
π	pi (≈ 3.14 or $\frac{22}{7}$)
⊥	perpendicular to
‖	parallel to
√	square root

FORMULAS

Shape	Description	Formula
Perimeter		
□	square	**P = 4s**
▭	rectangle	**P = 2l + 2w**
○	circumference (C) of a circle	**C = πd** **C = 2πr**
Area		
■	square	$A = s^2$
▬	rectangle	**A = lw**
▰	parallelogram	**A = bh**
▲	triangle	$A = \frac{1}{2}bh$
●	circle	$A = \pi r^2$
Volume		
cube shape	cube	$V = s^3$
rectangular solid shape	rectangular solid	**V = lwh**
cylinder shape	cylinder	$V = \pi r^2 h$
right triangle with sides a, b, c	Pythagorean Theorem	$a^2 + b^2 = c^2$

TABLE OF MEASUREMENTS

Measures of Length

1 foot (ft. or ') = 12 inches (in. or ")

1 yard (yd.) = 36 in.

1 yd. = 3 ft.

1 mile (mi.) = 5,280 ft.

1 mi. = 1,760 yd.

Measures of Weight

1 pound (lb.) = 16 ounces (oz.)

1 ton (T.) = 2,000 lb.

Measures of Capacity

1 cup (c.) = 8 fluid ounces (fl. oz.)

1 pint (pt.) = 2 c.

1 quart (qt.) = 4 c.

1 qt. = 2 pt.

1 gallon (gal.) = 4 qt.

Measures of Time

1 minute (min.) = 60 seconds (sec.)

1 hour (hr.) = 60 minutes (min.)

1 day = 24 hr.

1 week (wk.) = 7 days

1 year (yr.) = 52 weeks

1 yr. = 12 months (mo.)

Order of Operations

1. Do operations within parentheses.

2. Do operations with powers and roots.

3. Do all multiplication and division operations from left to right.

4. Do all addition and subtraction operations from left to right.

Note: If expressions do not have parentheses or powers and roots, start with Rule 3.

Adding and Subtracting Signed Numbers

Addition Rule 1. To add two or more numbers with the same sign, add the numbers. Give the answer that sign.

Addition Rule 2. To add numbers with different signs, find the difference between the numbers. Give the answer the sign of the larger number.

Addition Rule 3. To add three or more signed numbers, add the positive numbers. Add the negative numbers. Then add the two totals. Use Rule 2 to find the sign.

Subtraction Rule: To subtract signed numbers, change the sign of the number being subtracted. Then add.

Multiplying and Dividing Signed Numbers

Multiplication Rule 1. To multiply numbers with the same sign, multiply and give the answer a positive sign.

Multiplication Rule 2. To multiply numbers with different signs, multiply and give the answer a negative sign.

Division Rule 1. To divide numbers with the same sign, divide and give the answer a positive sign.

Division Rule 2. To divide numbers with different signs, divide and give the answer a negative sign.